NARRATIVE CROSSINGS

Alexander Gelley

NARRATIVE CROSSINGS
Theory and Pragmatics of Prose Fiction

THE JOHNS HOPKINS UNIVERSITY PRESS   Baltimore and London

This book has been brought to publication with the generous assistance of the Andrew W. Mellon Foundation.

The Johns Hopkins University Press
701 West 40th Street
Baltimore, Maryland 21211
The Johns Hopkins Press Ltd., London

The paper used in this publication meets the minimum requirements of American National Standard for Information Sciences—Permanence of Paper for Printed Library Materials, ANSI Z39.48-1984.

LIBRARY OF CONGRESS CATALOGING-IN-PUBLICATION DATA

Gelley, Alexander.
  Narrative crossings.

  Bibliography: p.
  Includes index.
  1. Fiction—Technique. 2. Narration
(Rhetoric) 3. Pragmatics. I. Title.
PN3383.N35G45 1987   808.3   86-45447
ISBN 0-8018-3289-6 (alk. paper)

59, 228

Contents

Acknowledgments

A Fulbright Research Fellowship to Germany, together with a sabbatical leave from the University of California, Irvine, in 1975–76, provided the opportunity for my initial systematic study of many of the issues dealt with in this book. A summer faculty fellowship from the School of Humanities at Irvine in 1984 facilitated completion of the manuscript.

My colleagues in the Department of English and Comparative Literature and the Program in Critical Theory at Irvine have shown consistent interest and confidence in this project, and graduate students in my seminars in recent years on narrative theory and the novel have been a source of stimulation and insight. I am grateful to them all.

Of the many individuals who have provided important leads for one or another of the chapters I will name only Michael Clark, Dennis Foster, James McMichael, and John Carlos Rowe. Herman Rapaport has furthered my thinking on theoretical matters in innumerable ways. And Philip Kuberski provided an exceptionally helpful commentary on the manuscript at a late stage.

I dedicate this book to the memory of three scholars whom I would have wished to have as its readers: Peter Colaclides, Michel de Certeau, and Paul de Man, men whose intellectual curiosity and generosity remains exemplary for me.

Introduction

Il y aurait en somme deux réalismes: le premier déchiffre le "réel" (ce qui se démontre mais ne se voit pas); le second dit la "réalité" (ce qui se voit mais ne se démontre pas); le roman, qui peut mêler ces deux réalismes, ajoute à l'intelligible du "réel" la queue fantasmatique de la "réalité."[1]   ROLAND BARTHES

Recent work in the social sciences has done much to reveal the workings of narrative patterns in quotidian practices. Literary structures have proved intriguing to linguists, sociologists, and historians, and there has been a widespread tendency to identify fictive or, more generally, rhetorical practices in various experiential, life-world contexts.[2] But a leakage has taken place in the other direction, too. Fiction is in no sense governed by a comprehensive and coherent set of rules. Concepts like Bakhtin's heteroglossia or Barthes's *scriptible* or "writerly" text mark a decisive displacement of the concept of the unified, closed work. And correlatively, the neat label "fictionality," which had been used to set off a precinct and authorize a long and rich tradition of intrinsic interpretation, no longer claims unqualified acceptance.

1. *Le plaisir du texte* (Paris, 1973), p. 73f. In English: "In short, there are two realisms: the first deciphers the 'real' (what is demonstrated but not seen); the second speaks 'reality' (what is seen but not demonstrated); the novel, which can mix these two realisms, adds to the intelligible of the 'real' the hallucinatory tail of 'reality.'" *The Pleasure of the Text,* trans. Richard Miller (New York, 1975), p. 45f.

2. Cf. Hayden White, *Metahistory: The Historical Imagination in Nineteenth-Century Europe* (Baltimore, 1973); Konrad Ehlich, ed., *Erzählen im Alltag* (Frankfurt am Main, 1980); and Reinhart Koselleck, "Representation, Event, and Structure," in *Futures Past: On the Semantics of Historical Time* (Cambridge, Mass., 1985), pp. 92–104.

Michel Foucault has written of Don Quixote, "It is his task to recreate the epic, though by a reverse process: the epic recounted (or claimed to recount) real exploits, offering them to our memory; Don Quixote, on the other hand, must endow with reality the signs-without-content of the narrative."[3] The kind of reality-testing that Foucault ascribes to Cervantes's protagonist is, in my view, a preeminent function of the modern novel. But in order to demonstrate Foucault's premise, to illustrate how a text is able to "endow with reality the signs-without-content of the narrative," we must learn to discern a method of indirection, of deviancy, that has been designated by such terms as "the figural," "the dialogic," "the parasitic." Not that these notions are equivalent, but they reflect a new aesthetics of fiction or (since both terms in this phrase are themselves now suspect) a new exploration of textual practices that has emerged within the past two decades. It is an exploration that draws on a variety of disciplines—philosophy, linguistics, semiotics, psychology, anthropology, the pictorial arts—and that, as I have suggested, feeds back into them.

In the sphere of literary criticism, fictionality and its near cousin representation seem to me notions that are both inescapable and, finally, irreducible. That is to say, they are not to be further generalized or abstracted but can only be shown to function within conceptual orders that have been elsewhere elaborated. Thus, the fictive is not a quality or a generic category of texts, in spite of certain classifications that have become standardized (e.g., fiction/nonfiction). Any extended consideration of the fictive involves a series of related concepts like illusion, reality, reading, textuality—concepts that evidently touch on fundamental philosophical issues.

For the post-Renaissance tradition it has been a characteristic of fictive representation both to assume and to stipulate an object. In telling us *about* an object, fictive discourse exercises a thetic, or positional, function, endowing the object with a kind of reality. What this endowment of reality consists of, the special status of "referentiality" in a work of fiction, has been subject to the most divergent explanations. Certain approaches to the question have, on the whole, been concerned with definitions of fictionality that would be coordinate with global, extratextual concepts of truth and reality. But what is most pertinent with respect to a theory of fictionality is not whether the objects described refer to empirically verifiable, "real" models, but rather how the mode of transmission, the representational practice, is

3. *The Order of Things* (New York: Vintage, 1973), p. 47.

able to project a meaning that derives from and yet transcends phenomenal reality and sensory experience. There is, it would seem, no decisive manner of indicating in purely textual terms whether what is represented is real or fictive. Language in its own terms cannot authenticate what lies outside language, its designata. Nonetheless, readers of fiction are perfectly able to situate a fictive world in relation to their experiential life-world. How this kind of accommodation takes place—and it does, repeatedly, quite naturally—is a matter of great interest to the literary theorist. We have learned that "reality" as a criterion of truth is dependent on the kind of representational conventions that obtain in a given era, and consequently that the sense of reality that is granted a literary text cannot be separated from the institutional practices that govern it. "Realism" as a cultural-stylistic category testifies to this very condition.[4]

Although the limitations of mimetic theories have long been recognized, a parallel principle of literary reception has only recently been subjected to searching criticism. Phenomenology posits a fundamental homology between the way the mind constitutes phenomenal reality and the way it structures that other reality—the product of the imagination, the fictive—that comes into being as a result of the reading process. The "endowment of meaning" (*Sinngebung*) operative through intuition-perception was taken by phenomenologically-oriented criticism to be exemplary for the production of meaning in works of art. And the principle of "constitution," conceived in terms of a fundamental linkage of subject, perception, and world, was assumed to be applicable to the domain of literature without fundamental alteration. Unquestionably, a theory of fiction can draw much from phenomenological thought of this century (Husserl, Ingarden, Merleau-Ponty, Poulet). Yet the kind of integrative principle of consciousness and reality that it has sought to justify is no longer tenable. We have been witness to a radicalization of the phenomenological problematic (by Heidegger, Foucault, and Derrida, among others) that has moved us to another stage of speculation, one for which there is, as yet, no single name.

Marianne Moore's formula, that poetry presents "for inspection, imaginary gardens with real toads in them," conveys the sense of an uncertain crossing between the fictive and its other. Chiasmus is the trope that identifies certain semantic crossings, crossings in which the

4. Cf. Harry Levin, *The Gates of Horn: A Study of Five French Realists* (New York, 1973), esp. chaps. 1 and 2.

interchange is presumed to be equivalent and stable. But, as Paul de Man once observed, a chiastic displacement of terms can radically alter the signifying relation, so that, instead of an exchange of elements, the system itself is put under threat. A trope of this kind represents a transgressive factor incorporated into the system of language itself. Representation as a literary mode exists in the space of such crossings, although the tendency of the representational tradition has undoubtedly been to camouflage the difference, to naturalize its marginality. Yet the very multiplicity of representational techniques, their variety, their radical incompatibility with one another in many cases, tend to undermine any principle of unity, any consistent rule of fictionality. Coleridge's "willing suspension of disbelief" is not a kind of magic key. What is involved, rather, are diverse practices that, to varying degrees and in complex permutations, are both formative and reflexive.

My interest in literary representation is guided by the assumption that its devices, its constructive work, can be foregrounded without canceling out what may be termed the effects of illusion. On the contrary, in the dominant literary forms of our tradition the strategies of rendering and the modes of reception—simulation and illusion—do not cancel one another out but are essentially imbricated and reinforcing. Representation, as I understand it, testifies to an inherent reflexivity or self-explicitation in language. For language is never directly manifesting—in the sense of a self-exhibiting, a *Zurschaustellung* (Ingarden) of the referent—but is continually analytic, exposing the grounds for its work of ideation, of image formation, of re-presentation.

What I attempt in these chapters is to take certain familiar concepts of fictive representation—concepts like description, character, dialogue, setting, and scene—and probe them in terms of their *other*, of a negating or shadow side. I want to make use of strategies intrinsic to fiction in order to reveal its porous fabric. Thus, in the case of description, I begin with the ambiguity implicit in the word itself (*describere*), the contradiction of a scriptive and a pictorial rendering, and pursue it in terms of the concept and of its function within a more general structure of fiction (Chap. 1). The rendering of space, the very idea that space can be *written,* poses the issue of description in very different terms (Chap. 2). A demonstration of Flaubert's zealous pursuit of objectivity in rendering a represented world is intended to bring to light certain impasses of realist description (Chap. 7). For the concept of character, I have sought to reassess certain familiar ways of designating personality and consciousness in fiction (such as "person," "narrator," or "protagonist") in the light of postphenomenological and psychoanalytic theories of the subject (Chaps. 3, 5, and 8).

One feature of modern realist forms has occupied me in various contexts, namely, that a level of language derived from the subject matter, ostensibly on mimetic principles, may also be understood as a counterforce to representational assumptions. In one chapter I have drawn on Heidegger's concept of *Gerede* in conjunction with Serres's notion of "parasite" to explore this issue (Chap. 4); in another I develop it in terms of a pervasive "dialogic" pattern (in Bakhtin's sense) in a single novel (Chap. 6). My intent throughout has been to identify and thus to expose certain representational practices that are normally taken for granted, and thus remain invisible.

Although the essays in this volume are divided into a theoretical section and one of practical criticism (or interpretations), the distinction is by no means a sharp one. Three of the essays in Part 1 (Chaps. 2, 3, and 4) undertake fairly detailed interpretations in the course of dealing with theoretical issues, and all the essays in Part 2 seek to make their theoretical framework perfectly explicit.

This book reflects my continuing interest in the ways that theoretical reflection—whether the source be philosophy, psychoanalysis, or cultural history—might be related ("applied" is too barbarous a term in this connection) to specific issues of practical criticism. I have drawn on the contemporary thinkers who seemed most relevant for the matters treated: Heidegger, Benjamin, Bakhtin, Lotman, Lacan, Blumenberg, Trilling, de Man, Derrida, Barthes, Serres, Genette, Lyotard, and de Certeau have each provided something essential to one or another of the essays. Of earlier philosophers, Kant figures centrally in the second chapter and Husserl in the first. But my intention was never simply to summarize a thinker's position on some issue. Rather, I have drawn on specific insights or arguments and sought to extend them in my own discussion of a particular work or an aspect of literary form.

Whoever has followed the theoretical debates of the last two or three decades knows that the dominant tendencies of the fifties and sixties—let us label them the New Criticism, intrinsic interpretation, phenomenology, and *Geistesgeschichte*—have been supplanted by radically different orientations. The essays in this volume undoubtedly reflect certain tensions and inconsistencies that derive from this shift in the climate of criticism and theoretical speculation. I have not sought to eliminate them altogether. In the present context the earlier phenomenological, historical, and formalist approaches have not disappeared, though they have, in very significant ways, been challenged and modified by other tendencies, tendencies that may be identified by such rubrics as semiotics, deconstruction, and psychoanalytic theory. I have tried to profit from this fluid but highly stimulating state of affairs.

PART I

1 Premises for a Theory of Description

*Content is a glimpse of something, an encounter, like a flash. It's very tiny—
very tiny, content.* WILLEM DE KOONING[1]

A PORTRAIT

I shall begin with an example. Although it is the description of a
character in a novel, Proust's *À la recherche du temps perdu*, the issues
evoked are applicable to description more generally. The whole episode from which the passage is drawn provides Proust's narrator with
an occasion for a sustained reflection on perception, representability,
and identity. In the following exerpt, Marcel is in the church at Combray and sees the Duchesse de Guermantes for the first time.

> Tout d'un coup, pendant la messe de mariage, un mouvement que fit le
> suisse en se déplaçant me permit de voir assise dans une chapelle une
> dame blonde avec un grand nez, des yeux bleus et perçants, une cravate
> bouffante en soie mauve, lisse, neuve et brillante, et un petit bouton au
> coin du nez. Et parce que dans la surface de son visage rouge, comme si
> elle eût eu très chaud, je distinguais, diluées et à peine perceptibles, des
> parcelles d'analogie avec le portrait qu'on m'avait montré, parce que
> surtout les traits particuliers que je relevais en elle, si j'essayais de les
> énoncer, se formulaient précisément dans les mêmes termes: un grand
> nez, des yeux bleus, dont s'était servi le docteur Percepied quand il avait
> décrit devant moi la duchesse de Guermantes, je me dis: Cette dame
> ressemble à Mme. de Guermantes. (1:174)[2]

1. *The North Atlantic Light,* 1960–1983 (Amsterdam, 1983), p. 79.
2. Parenthetical references are to the Pléiade edition, *À la recherche du temps perdu,*
3 vols. (Paris, 1954). In English: "Suddenly, during the nuptial mass, the verger, by moving
to one side, enabled me to see in one of the chapels a fair-haired lady with a large nose,

This is, first of all, a determinate *action* within the novel, that is, the narrative of a specified temporal segment ("pendant la messe de mariage") oriented toward the unfolding of a connected series of events or, in Roland Barthes's sense, a "kernel action" within the global structure of the plot. At the same time, it is part of a fictive *scene*, that is, a narrative segment organized in terms of a type of illusionist effect. In a scene of this sort the devices that serve to organize the presentation in a quasi-theatrical manner—framing, foreshortening, focalization—are themselves diegetically motivated, made to seem coordinate with the referent or the primary object of the fictive representation.

In another sense, the passage offers a *portrait* of one of the characters of the novel. Or rather, we may term it an experiment in verbal delineation which deploys a convention of literary portraiture, the listing of attributes or epithets,[3] as part of a more complex signifying process in which this convention is itself radically qualified. In the whole passage the list of traits recurs no less than seven times, each time slightly modified, though always recognizable as a variant of the initial instance: "une dame blonde avec un grand nez, des yeux bleus et perçants, une cravate bouffante en soie mauve, lisse, neuve et brillante, et un petit bouton au coin du nez." This very reiteration, together with the successive displacement of the constituent elements, attenuates the representational force of the catalogue. But what is equally significant is that throughout the passage Proust introduces terms drawn from alternative representational systems, preeminently from the sphere of pictorial art (thus, in parts of the passage not quoted above: "une revue illustrée . . . une tapisserie . . . un vitrail . . . ce croquis," 1:174–77), although there are also references

piercing blue eyes, a billowy scarf of mauve silk, glossy and new and bright, and a little pimple at the corner of her nose. And because on the surface of her face, which was red, as though she had been very hot, I could discern, diluted and barely perceptible, fragments of resemblance with the portrait that had been shown to me; because, more especially, the particular features which I remarked in this lady, if I attempted to catalogue them, formulated themselves in precisely the same terms—*a large nose, blue eyes*—as Dr. Percepied had used when describing in my presence the Duchesse de Guermantes, I said to myself: 'This lady is like the Duchesse de Guermantes.'" *Remembrance of Things Past*, trans. C. K. Scott Moncrieff and Terence Kilmartin (London, 1981), 1:190.

3. As Roland Barthes makes clear, the inventory of parts should be understood as no more than one of the devices or conventions of description: "As a genre, the blazon expresses the belief that a *complete* inventory can reproduce a *total* body, as if the extremity of enumeration could devise a new category, that of totality: description is then subject to a kind of enumerative erethism: it accumulates in order to totalize, multiplies fetishes in order to obtain a total, defetishised body." *S/Z: An Essay* (New York, 1974), p. 114.

to a dream image, to a costume ball, to a theatrical simulation, and to a quality of color inherent in certain syllabic sounds. Thus the image of the Duchesse that is constructed in the course of the episode involves a complex juxtaposition of two opposed registers: the first we may call descriptive in a narrow sense, that is, an enumerative practice that draws on a semantic code appropriate to a given object and conventionally associated with it. The second, quite explicit in this passage, although often functioning only implicitly, we will call a register of visibility. This involves some alternative representational practice, such as the pictorial, as a means of making good, of "supplementing" the incapacity of language to make its referents "visible."[4]

But our passage does not merely cite or juxtapose the two registers, the semantic and the visualizing. It goes further and claims that the signifying function involves an effort, however tenuous or incomplete, of combination and interpenetration.

> Mais en même temps, sur cette image que le nez proéminent, les yeux perçants épinglaient dans ma vision . . . , sur cette image toute récente, inchangeable, j'essayais d'appliquer l'idée: "C'est Mme. de Guermantes," sans parvenir qu'à la faire manœuvrer en face de l'image, comme deux disques séparés par un intervalle. (1:175)[5]

The superposition, the near convergence of the "two discs" figures the repeated, though never fully realized, effort on the part of Proust's narrator to fuse the diverse cognitive modalities involved in an act of perception.

As with many instances of description, this one evokes an experience of recall as a way of accrediting a perception. The Duchesse de Guermantes, before she is ever seen by Marcel, is for him a name, a concept, an "idea." I need not rehearse the complex of personal and historical associations that, for this narrator, fill out the name of Guermantes.[6] Marcel is trying to make a fit between the concept

4. I draw here on Jacques Derrida's sense of *supplément* as a substitutive signifying practice, a gesture that at once marks a blind spot within a representational system and moves to overcome it. "Le concept de supplément est une sorte de tache aveugle . . . , le non-vu qui ouvre et limite la visibilité." *De la grammatologie* (Paris, 1967), p. 234.

5. In English: "But at the same time, I was endeavouring to apply to this image, which the prominent nose, the piercing eyes pinned down and fixed in my field of vision . . . , to this fresh and unchanging image, the idea: 'It's Mme. de Guermantes'; but I succeeded only in making the idea pass between me and the image, as though they were two discs moving in separate planes with a space between." *Remembrance of Things Past* 1:191f.

6. Cf. Roland Barthes, "Proust and Names," in *New Critical Essays*, trans. Richard Howard (New York, 1980), pp. 54–67, and Gérard Genette, "Proust and Indirect Language," in *Figures of Literary Discourse*, trans. Alan Sheridan (New York, 1982), esp. pp.

(signified by the name) and the immediate experience, his perception. But this intradiegetic action (Marcel's act of recognition and, beyond that, the scene as a whole) should also be understood as the vehicle of a second-order signifying operation oriented toward the reader. At this level, the binarism that was operative for the narrator, the tension already discussed between "idea" and percept, between the semantic repertoire underlying a portrait and the scenic presentation that the narrator experiences—this binarism itself collapses into a new signifier whereby the reader seeks to construct an image of the Duchesse, indeed, of the whole scene. What was an act of re-cognition, the construction of a resemblance, on the intradiegetic level, serves as the condition for an effort of ideation or visualization at the level of reception. But this effort cannot be said to yield a presentation (in the sense of *Gegenwärtigung*)[7] that would allow the reader to assume the position of a privileged viewer. He finds himself instead to be the operator of diverse representational modalities. Like Proust's narrator, though for quite different reasons, the reader can only maneuver the discs toward one another but can never altogether eliminate the gap between them.

REFERENTIAL MODELS

Description, as I conceive it, is not to be taken narrowly as a "part" or "level" of an aesthetic construct, specifically, of a work of fiction. Rather, like other functions in the analysis of fiction—plot, character, narration—description involves fundamental assumptions regarding the scriptive mode in which a writer or reader is involved. This includes, of course, the very conditions of such involvement. The tendency of formalist approaches has been to treat descriptive elements as micronarratives that need to be assimilated to a larger narrative pattern. While this may result in coherence at the level of narrative form, it tends to obscure or suppress issues that are implicit in any theory of description but that necessarily move beyond a formalist problematic. I have in mind issues like the status of the referent in fiction, visibility as a privileged mode of narrative cognition, and spatiality as the organizing principle of world in fiction.

My claim, then, is that description is not a homogeneous catego-

---

236–49. For Marcel's subsequent reflections on this name, see *À la recherche du temps perdu* 2:28f, 204f, and 209.

7. Cf. Edmund Husserl, *Ideen zu einer reinen Phänomenologie und phänomenologischen Philosophie. Erstes Buch* (The Hague, 1950), #99, p. 249f.

ry, a clearly delimited subclass within narrative. Rather, it represents a confluence of diverse representational practices. It will be convenient, at this point, to distinguish its four primary constituents.

1. A practice of denomination and classification, more generally, a cultural taxonomy. The object described must have a place in the system of language. It partakes of a nomenclature, a semantic register, that is never more than partially activated in any text. It cannot be inserted into an action, or "seen," or inscribed into a world unless it has first been spoken and named.[8]

2. An event or act. Within larger narrative structures, micronarratives serve to justify descriptive data in various ways: who needs or wants to know? for what purpose? to what extent or what degree of complexity? The global narrative structure, the plot (or *sjužet*, in the terminology of the Russian Formalists) may be understood as a means of motivating the description of the setting as a whole, while subsidiary actions, micronarratives in Philippe Hamon's sense, are oriented to specific descriptive elements.

3. A means of disclosure, in the sense of an opening or an aperture (as in a camera) or a framing device that focuses on or illumines what is described. Terms relating to sight and light have a special significance within this category. They should not be taken primarily as predicates for the contents of a description, but as facilitators of an *effect* of description. But the ambiguity implicit in representing vision, in textualizing perception (as the etymology suggests—*de-scribere*), brings into play complex and even contradictory valorizations. Thus, sight may be exalted (as "visionary," as imagination) or degraded (as illusion, as simulation). This kind of judgment will invariably affect the status of the subject involved, the agent of disclosure, the observer, reflector, or manipulator of what is "seen."

4. A world model. This implies both an order of totality and a principle of relativization and thereby serves as the basis for the discrete "worlds" characteristic of modern fiction. It operates primarily in terms of spatial modeling systems—locales, diagrams, maps, perspectival views. At the same time, it is related to a universalizing tendency that characterizes the institution of literature in the Western

---

8. Philippe Hamon calls description "the lexicographical consciousness of fiction." He goes on: "To describe is almost always to actualize a latent lexical paradigm based on an underlying system of referential knowledge about the world. . . ." "What Is a Description?" in *French Literary Theory Today: A Reader*, ed. Tzvetan Todorov, trans. R. Carter (Cambridge, 1982), p. 159. Hamon's whole discussion of the semantic field, especially with regard to readability or reader comprehension (pp. 158–67), is pertinent to my argument.

tradition, what Jurij Lotman has termed the text's mythological dimension.[9]

Let me now suggest how these four constituents may be connected. Description as inventory and taxonomy serves to delimit a cultural context. But such a taxonomy already goes beyond a mere listing of discrete objects. Rather, it situates objects in use. By differentiating and correlating the objects named it implies a structuring of experience and perception. And it articulates such a structure not only intradiegetically, in terms of how objects are perceived and used within a narrative, but also extradiegetically, at the level of reception, of cultural context. (Barthes's semic code overlaps here with his cultural or referential code.)[10] Lotman's concept of narrative as a second-order modeling system, or, as he puts it, a "secondary structural semantic field," is relevant at this point.[11] Lotman hypothesizes, as a condition of all narratives, a "plotless text," a system of classification capable of accounting for the aggregate of customs and conventions in a given society. Such a semantic field provides the basis for qualitative, valorized discriminations, but it does not yet indicate how these come into being. What is requisite is the intervention of a personal will, an act of choosing (thus Barthes's use of the Greek word for choice, *proairesis,* to designate the code of action in narrative).

For Lotman narrative action, the basic constituent of plot, involves the transgression of boundaries within a cultural context as just defined. And this transgressive path, the violation of conventions or boundaries, is what constitutes the hero or protagonist in Lotman's sense. What I find especially valuable in this analysis is that it structures the fictive world in terms of a fundamental interconnection of context and action. I would develop it in the following way: In most novels there are two or more agents who mark out a transgressive path; in a sense, any kernel action, any determinate act of choice, represents an infraction in a system of norms and thus constitutes such a transgression. The plot as a whole, conceived in terms of such a field structure, brings about the tracing of multiple interwoven paths. The *world* of a novel, in the sense in which I wish to develop it, projects the level of agents and action onto its appropriate backdrop of cultural norms. It accounts for the imbrication of personal choice and

9. See *The Structure of the Artistic Text,* trans. Ronald Vroon (Ann Arbor, 1977), pp. 209–12.

10. Barthes's definitions of the codes can best be traced through the summary of contents in *S/Z: An Essay,* p. 261f.

11. See *The Structure of the Artistic Text,* p. 233.

contextual determinants that is basic to our representational tradition.

The issues of denomination and classification (number one in the list above) have, in recent years, been treated in both a linguistic and a sociological context. The level of plot and action (number two above) represents the principal focus of structuralist criticism of the novel. While I acknowledge its importance, it needs to be integrated into a more comprehensive framework. Here I will deal primarily with the third and fourth of the constituents I have outlined, visibility as a representional register and the spatial form of world models in the novel.

A MARGINAL PRACTICE

The word *description* itself suggests some of the paradoxes inherent in the concept. *Hypographe*, the Greek equivalent of *descriptio*, is, in Aristotle, a subordinate form of *definitio*, that is, a definition in terms of accidents rather than of essences.[12] Further, the Greek word, like its modern equivalents, is derived from a scriptive term (*grapho, scribere*), although it serves primarily to signify visual and pictorial values. (Some modern synonyms will foreground this latter sense, e.g., G *schildern*, F *dépeindre*, E *sketch* or *delineate*. But the dominant term, at least during the past four centuries, has been "description.") Thus, at a conceptual level, the word suggests a subordinate form of cognition, one not of truth but of circumstantial features, "accidents." And in its semiotic form it reflects a contradiction between scriptive and pictorial modes of transmission. Yet this very contradiction, or "crossing" of signifying registers, shall prove to be a valuable clue in this analysis.

Traditionally, description has been taken as an ancillary or ornamental feature of narrative form, an hors d'oeuvre.[13] Thematic criticism often treated it as an instance of a topos, and this in a double sense: first, as a recurrent literary device associated with certain genres (e.g., the idyll, the Gothic) and, second, as a typical locale or spot (e.g., *locus amoenus*) that derives more from cultural and mythological

---

12. Cf. Hans Christoph Buch, *Ut Pictura Poesis: Die Beschreibungsliteratur und ihre Kritiker von Lessing bis Lukács* (Munich, 1972).

13. Gérard Genette writes, "Description is naturally *ancilla narrationis* [the handmaiden of the narration], the slave always necessary, always submissive, never emancipated. Narrative genres like the epic, the short story, the novella, the novel, do exist where description can occupy a very large place, indeed the largest, without ceasing to be, as if by choice, a simple auxiliary of narrative." "Boundaries of Narrative," *New Literary History* 8(1976–77): 1–13. This passage is on p. 6 (translation slightly modified).

sources than from strictly literary exigencies.[14] Another kind of thematic approach seeks to crystallize the imaginary world of a single writer through certain exemplary realizations, landscapes of the mind, that organize and infuse the whole of an *œuvre*.[15] For thematic criticism in general, the marginal, extranarrative nature of description is in a sense made absolute. The descriptive is granted autonomous status, either in terms of a principle of genre or as the extension of a form of consciousness.

A very different focus on description has been that of recent French formalist critics, who seek to separate it from any integrative concept of author or work and to determine its elements primarily by semiological means. While these critics recognize that description is a constituent of any moderately extensive narrative, they tend to restrict its function to the "surface" of a work, to its texture or style. As such, description does not figure in a work's *armature,* or structural form. In this respect the structuralist critics continue a traditional view, which is conveniently summarized in Marmontel's article "Description" in the *Encyclopédie:*

> A description is the enumeration of the attributes of a thing, of which several are accidental, as when one describes a person by his actions, his words, his writings, etc. . . . It does not make it known in depth, because it does not enclose it or does not expose the essential attributes.[16]

From this point of view we can understand why the structuralists initially avoided treating description and then came to see a tension, even a pronounced incompatibility, between the aims of narrative (*récit*) and those of description. Thus Jean Ricardou writes:

> Far from harmonizing, the two categories seem caught, paradoxically enough, in a net of absolute contradiction. If narrative cannot do without description in order to gain validation from it, description comes into being only by troubling the course of narrative. In other words, the text of fiction is a site of continuous belligerence.[17]

14. Ernst Robert Curtius's study of the ideal landscape in *European Literature and the Latin Middle Ages* (New York, 1953) illustrates both aspects of such a topos concept. Leo Spitzer's "Milieu and Ambiance" in *Essays in Historical Semantics* (New York, 1948), pp. 179–225, although apparently based on linguistic evidence, is another thematic study tracing the persistence of certain types of locale and atmosphere in Western literature.

15. Cf. Jean-Pierre Richard, *Littérature et sensation* (Paris, 1954), and *Paysage de Chateaubriand* (Paris, 1967).

16. Cited in Edward S. Casey, "Literary Description and Phenomenological Method," *Yale French Studies (Towards a Theory of Description)*, no. 61 (1981), p. 187.

17. "Belligérance du texte," in *La Production du sens chez Flaubert*, ed. C. Gothot-Mersch (Paris: Edition 10/18, 1975), p. 85. Here and throughout this book the English

This antinomy is particularly evident, he argues, at the level of the temporal structure, the sequential organization of a story: "The encounter of narrative and description reveals itself as a chronicity [or, a chronicle] undone by an achronicity."[18]

We find ourselves, not surprisingly, thrown back to an aspect of Lessing's argument in the *Laocoön*, "that succession of time is the province of the poet just as space is that of the painter."[19] And the solution that the structuralists offer also echoes Lessing, at least in part, namely, that description can best be accommodated to the needs of narrative by being "narrativized," that is, by assimilating its essentially static, atemporal mode (in Lessing, its "spatial form") into a sequential pattern.[20] Thus, we recall that Lessing had praised Homer's manner of attaching a description to the account of a process or an action. Agamemnon's royal garb is delineated not by means of an enumeration, a catalogue, but through an account of the act of dressing and a history of the royal scepter. Similarly, Ricardou argues, even a set piece like the account of Charles Bovary's cap is presented in terms of a "diegetization," that is, through the use of deictic or temporal terms that serve to organize the order of presentation of the segments and their attributes and whose effect is to suggest a second-order narrative, what Ricardou terms "a specious narrative" ("un récit fallacieux").[21] Such conclusions are not particularly original, but they are symptomatic, I think, of the difficulty that the structuralists have with the phenomenon of description and of their consequent efforts to bend it to their own uses.

Now with the notion of diegesis Ricardou alludes to an influential essay by Gérard Genette, "Boundaries of Narrative." Genette's

---

translations are mine unless otherwise indicated. Cf. also Ricardou's *Problèmes du nouveau roman* (Paris, 1967).

18. Ibid., p. 87. In French: "la rencontre du récit et de la description se présente comme une chronique rompue par une achronie."

19. *Laocoön*, trans. Edward Allen McCormick (Baltimore, 1984), p. 91.

20. David Wellbery's recent study *Lessing's Laocoön: Semiotics and Aesthetics in the Age of Reason* (Cambridge, 1984) restates Lessing's position with the greatest clarity. "According to Lessing," he writes, "the principle common to all forms of aesthetic signification is the motivation of signs, the reduction of arbitrariness and therewith the achievement of an optimal degree of naturalness (similarity) in the relation between expression and content" (p. 201). Since description, operating in terms of a successivity of signs, tends to foreground the parts of an object at the cost of its unity, its integral wholeness, the poet must find ways of restoring an illusion of unity. Here is where the narrative element becomes decisive. Wellbery continues, "Narrative alleviates the problem of dissolution that confronts us in description. . . . *Narrative fulfills the aesthetic function because it maintains the structure of perception, the totalizing regard within the present instant*" (p. 212f.).

21. "Belligérance du texte," p. 92.

point is a more fundamental one, namely, to challenge the traditional association of narrative with mimesis. Genette takes up Plato's distinction in *The Republic,* bk. 3, between mimesis and diegesis and argues that we must go even further than Plato did in separating these two aspects of a narrative. Plato had divided the act of narration (*lexis*) into simple narrative (*diegesis*) and imitation proper (*mimesis*). The former involved whatever information the narrator recounted in his own name (action, description, indirect discourse), whereas the latter was restricted to directly quoted dialogue. He considered the genre of epic a mixed form, and for that reason inferior to drama. The effect of Plato's distinction was to establish diegesis—which is to say, narrative in general—as a deficient mode of mimesis, though still allied to it. Genette proposes that we radicalize the Platonic distinction and in effect purge narrative of its alliance to mimesis. Insofar as there is mimesis proper within narration, it can only be dialogue or direct quotation. But to call it "mimesis" would, in his view, be tautological, for "language can imitate perfectly only language itself."[22] What remains as the only fruitful field of analysis is what language can say about non-linguistic phenomena—mental representations, states of affairs, actions, objects. And this, Genette argues, is diegesis. Thus, virtually all forms of representation are to be incorporated within the category of diegesis, the telling or discourse function of narrative.

One critic who has assiduously occupied himself with the "diegetization" of description is Philippe Hamon.[23] He begins with the basic denotative units and their qualifiers—essentially, nouns and adjectives, the signifiers of "content" in a description. This is the level of the "achronic" units, in Ricardou's formulation, which impede the flow of narrative. In order that these may be accommodated to the narrative syntagma, something else is required: an enabling function, a principle of linkage. Hamon calls this *thématiques vides* (empty thematics), blanks insofar as the principal action is concerned but essential for motivating descriptive data. For example, the narrative will produce a character (an expert, a native of a place) capable of conveying specialized data or simply of offering information unfamiliar to the other characters. Conversely, it may introduce a neophyte or a stranger, figures whose ignorance provides a motive for descriptive data.

22. "Boundaries of Narrative," p. 4 (translation modified).
23. I draw primarily on "What Is a Description?" Hamon has developed his theory in *Introduction à l'analyse du descriptif* (Paris, 1981). A section of this book is translated in *Yale French Studies,* no. 61 (see n. 16 above), pp. 1–26.

For Hamon, as for Ricardou, there is an unbridgeable gap between the ends of description and those of narrative. Realist fiction is required to manufacture innumerable *récits,* second-order narratives or "specious narratives," in Ricardou's sense, to support a proliferating mass of descriptive data. Hamon writes:

> We defined a description . . . as a unit which triggered a proliferation of themes introduced to enhance plausibility . . . , which constitute what we called an *empty* or *pseudo*-thematics. We then saw that the description is the point where the narrative comes to a temporary halt, while continuing to organize itself. . . . it can thus be seen that the fundamental characteristic of realist discourse is to deny, to make impossible, the narrative, any narrative. This is because the more it becomes saturated with descriptions, the more it is concomitantly forced to multiply its empty thematics and its redundancies, and the more it becomes organized and repetitious, thus becoming increasingly a closed system: instead of being referential, it becomes purely anaphoric; instead of evoking the real ("things" and "events") it constantly evokes itself.[24]

Hamon gets around this impasse by claiming that the goal of realist fiction is to turn "the *empty* thematics into a *full* one, to bring it about that those figures or incidents that serve as the *occasion* for a description actually have a role to play in the story and do not simply remain filler material."

To view the issue in this way, however, to argue that the plausibility of a description should not be constructed ad hoc but should be integrated into the principal action of a narrative, does not really resolve the theoretical problem but only displaces it. The inherent incompatibility of the two modes, the descriptive and the narrative, still remains. Or rather, the structuralist solution is to define narrative as a certain kind of discourse about action ("diegesis" in Genette's sense) and then to subordinate description to this definition, so that description can only be analyzed as realizing the goals of narrative, e.g, motivation of characters, progress of the action, and so on. What is lacking in this explanation is any discrimination of what may be called a distinctive mode of descriptive cognition. Narrative, in the sense of storytelling, may well be the more inclusive class. But that does not exclude the possibility that various kinds of cognitive involvement, of *interest,* are aroused and sustained within narrative forms. And description isolates one such register, a register that cannot simply be subsumed by the form of narrative.

24. "What Is a Description?" p. 170. The following passage is also on p. 170.

THE DIMENSION OF RECEPTION

We have seen that in formalist terms, description constitutes a suspension of the narrative flow, a stasis. The temporal dimension of the diegesis, the plot proper, is slowed down while the temporal dimension of the act of reading is stretched. In the terminology of Eberhardt Lämmert, we can say that description pushes to the maximum the gap between *Erzählzeit* and *Erzähltezeit*, or reading time and narrative time.[25] Of course, a typical manifestation of this phenomenon is that a reader may simply become bored with a description and hurry it along or else skip it altogether. ("[J]'abhorre la description matérielle," Stendhal wrote in the *Souvenirs d'égotisme*. "L'ennui de la faire m'empêche de faire des romans."[26] Nonetheless, this kind of stillness in the narrative may be likened to islands of repose for the reader, moments of collection. The hold that the level of plot, speech, and action exercises on him is loosened. His attention may wander, but it may also adjust to a changed mode of apprehension. I am suggesting that the more circumstantial the description and the more separate from the narrative in which it is embedded, the greater will be the reader's part, and the more he will be forced to assume a stance for which the narrative proper offers little support. This kind of displacement of the reader's interest (and Stendhal's boredom with description signifies nothing else) should not be passed over too lightly. When the familiar codes of narrative are blocked or diverted, reading/writing becomes problematic, and the subject of/in the narrative shifts from the characters or the author to the reader (or to the writer as reader). We might also say that, like other forms of marginal discourse, description tends to exhibit what is otherwise implicit or suppressed. It provides more immediate access to elements of ideology, of epistemology, of the unconscious.

What I have in mind is illustrated, though perhaps to the point of parody, by a passage in the "Reading" chapter of *Madame Bovary*. Emma is viewing illustrations in the keepsake albums passed around by her comrades in the convent. A series of sentences delineate some of the pictured scenes. Then the discourse suddenly switches to second person:

25. *Bauformen des Erzählens* (Stuttgart, 1967), pp. 23 and 73–94.
26. *Souvenirs d'égotisme*, in *Œuvres intimes*, ed. Henri Martineau (Paris: Pléiade, 1955), p. 1420. In English: "I abhor concrete description. The boredom of writing this prevents me from writing novels."

Et vous y étiez aussi, sultans à longues pipes, pâmés sous des tonnelles aux bras des bayadères, djiaours, sabres turcs, bonnets grecs, et vous surtout, paysages blafards des contrées dithyrambiques, qui souvent nous montrez à la fois des palmiers, des sapins, des tigres à droite, un lion à gauche, des minarets tartares à l'horizon, au premier plan des ruines romaines, puis des chameaux accroupis;—le tout encadré d'une forêt vierge bien nettoyée, et avec un grand rayon de soleil perpendiculaire tremblotant dans l'eau, où se détachent en écorchures blanches, sur un fond d'acier gris, de loin en loin, des cygnes qui nagent.[27]

The exclamatory vocative "Et vous y étiez aussi" breaks through the third-person narration, destabilizing the reader's position. Is he the one being addressed? Evidently not, but he cannot help being swept along in this invocation to scenes drawn from a repertoire of commonplaces that is as much his property as it is Emma's or Flaubert's. One might answer that it is precisely because the scenes evoked here are drawn from a debased register that Flaubert can allow himself this kind of rhetorical gesture accentuating the vividness and the immediacy of the image. The trope here is prosopopeia, since it is the pictures that are being called to life. Of course, in this episode Emma is the viewer. For her, the illustrated scenes represent not commonplaces but vivid, enticing wish images. We readers are once removed from what she views; we see through her eyes. But we are removed in yet another sense. She sees pictures, we read words. And the exclamation "Et vous y étiez aussi" is at the level of words, of tropes. What is it that chiefly strikes us in it? Is it the appeal to participate, *to see* as vividly as Emma sees, or is it the narrator's mocking extravagance of tone? In a sense Flaubert has it both ways, since, in the realist aesthetic, such tropes of presencing (*enargeia*) are necessarily transgressive. They may be resolved only through a movement outside the text, to what I would term a habitus of reception. The reader is entangled in a form of participation he cannot help but question.

27. *Madame Bovary*, ed. E. Maynial (Paris, 1961), p. 36. In English: "And you, too, were there, Sultans with long pipes reclining beneath arbours in the arms of Bayadères; Giaours, curved swords, fezzes; and you especially, pale landscape of dithyrambic lands, that often show us at once palm-trees and firs, tigers on the right, a lion to the left, Tartar minarets on the horizon, Roman ruins in the foreground with some kneeling camels besides; the whole framed by a very neat virgin forest, and with a great perpendicular sunbeam trembling in the water, where, sharply edged on a steel-grey background, white swans are swimming here and there." *Madame Bovary*, trans. Paul de Man (New York: Norton Critical Edition, 1965), p. 27.

What kind of reader is being posited here? This cannot be answered simply. Some critics have attempted to reconstruct the standpoint of a historical readership. But, although much historical data could be assembled to characterize certain classes of the population who were also readers of literature, there is no general agreement as to just which factors in the act of reception—the reading process—should be identified with preexistent cultural attitudes.

Genette touches on this general issue when he considers how historical factors could affect the operation of mimetic illusion:

> It goes without saying, for example, that the same text can be received by one reader as intensely mimetic and by another as an only slight "expressive" account. Historical evolution plays a critical role here, and it is likely that the audience for the classics, which was so sensitive to Racinean "figuration," found more mimesis than we do in the narrative style of a d'Urfé or a Fénelon, but would undoubtedly have found the so richly and minutely described accounts in the naturalistic novel to be only chaotic proliferation and "murky mess," and would thus have missed the mimetic function of those accounts.[28]

Clearly, in order to proceed along the lines suggested by Genette we would need to gather evidence from a given period regarding the quality and intensity of the reception of works of art. Such evidence is not easy to come by, and it is not likely that, lacking a clear theoretical basis, there will be agreement as to what would count as evidence for such an investigation.

We are dealing here with a prospective factor, or, more generally, with an aspect of the hermeneutics of interpretation. The present-day critic or scholar can never be assured of possessing a neutral or comprehensive standpoint from which to assess earlier readings. Literature constructs its readership. The historical audience for a given work (and, in a more general sense, for literary forms or genres) is not simply there as a passive element before the appearance of the work. It is the work itself that incites a certain development and creates an audience that, without its appearance, might not have come into being. When we attempt to determine retrospectively how the readership of a work is to be defined and what constitutes the work's climate of reception, we come up against something like a temporal lag. The interpretive *choice* that a past readership must have made is not recoverable since this choice as a determinate, discrete element has

28. *Narrative Discourse: An Essay in Method*, trans. Jane E. Lewin (Ithaca, N.Y., 1980), pp. 165f.

now become part of a new readership, one fashioned in part by the work in question.[29] Thus, while any historical reconstruction of a climate of reception is blocked, the historical nature of reception itself remains a valid sphere of reflection and investigation. What I termed a reader's "entanglement" at the formal level of the text is continuous with reading as a cultural practice, one that is interrelated with a complex network of correlative practices. Description is a particularly revealing category for this type of investigation, since it involves, as we have seen, not only established technical features of literary form but, in equal measure, the much less explored issues of concretization and reception as well.

In a chapter entitled "Passive Syntheses in the Reading Process" in *The Act of Reading,* Wolfgang Iser stresses "the peculiar hybrid character that our images possess during the course of our reading: at one moment they are pictorial, and at another they are semantic."[30] Iser's is one of the most lucid and systematic accounts we have of "the process of image-building." One of the virtues of his analysis lies in its awareness of a break between a perceptual and a textual model of image formation. What he calls "impeded ideation" involves a type of reception in which the reader is "forced out of first-degree images" (those fashioned on a perceptual model) so as to become capable of a more complex, dialectic form of image formation. At this level, "we can watch what we are producing, and we can watch ourselves while we are producing it." In a subsequent essay Iser argues for a deep structure of "the imaginary,"which he conceives of as a primordial impulse of the mind and the very condition for fiction making.[31] The imaginary, for Iser, is resistant to any definitive semantic articulation and thus to the kind of normalization that interpretation strives for, but this also puts it beyond the reach of historical discriminations. In effect, he ascribes to it a universal, anthropological status. Admittedly, Iser allows for the fact that social norms and contemporary allusions

29. Cf. Hans Robert Jauss, "Literary History as a Challenge to Literary Theory," in *New Directions in Literary History,* ed. Ralph Cohen (Baltimore, 1974), pp. 11–41, esp. p. 30, and the discussion of G. Buck's idea of "negative experience," p. 37. The idea is already adumbrated in Proust: "Il faut que l'œuvre (en ne tenant pas compte, pour simplifier, des génies qui à la même époque peuvent parallèlement préparer pour l'avenir un public meilleur dont d'autres génies que lui bénéficieront) crée elle-même sa postérité." *À la recherche du temps perdu* 1:531f.

30. (Baltimore, 1978), p. 147. The following citations are on pp. 142 and 189.

31. "The Current Situation of Literary Theory: Key Concepts and the Imaginary," *New Literary History* 11(1979–80): 1–20. Iser does not specify the filiations of this concept, but it seems to derive more from Sartre's *L'Imaginaire* than from Lacan's work.

(what he terms "the repertoire" in *The Act of Reading*) play a significant part in the process of image building, but he does not provide a framework for dealing with the differential between the sensory and the linguistic registers as itself determinant of the context of reception. Iser's analysis needs to be supplemented by a theory that is attentive to the inescapable warping or displacement that takes place between a linguistic and a perceptual model. In my view, the *systematic* disjunction between pictorial and semantic modes in the apprehension of texts is fundamental to the system of realist representation and serves to reveal its historical condition. Visibility, as one element of the referentiality of this system, derives from this kind of disjunction.

It should not be overlooked that we ourselves, as readers of fiction, have to a considerable extent been fashioned by a mimetic representational system, a system that is bound up with an ocular model of reception. We touch here on a level of submerged assumptions, elements of an episteme, in Foucault's sense, that require the most alert self-reflection and hermeneutical awareness. French structuralist criticism, in its pronounced antiphenomenological bias, has, as I have argued, almost totally ignored the perceptual component of the act of reading, the corporality that impinges on the image (Barthes is a notable exception).[32] Many of the essays in this volume attempt to account for the "seen" (and "scene") in fiction in ways that draw on the discursive strategies of structuralist criticism as well as on the kind of psychic investigations of the act of reading that phenomenological and psychoanalytic approaches have made available.

TROPES AND VISIBILITY

We know now, on the basis of work by numerous scholars, that vision has its own history, a history marked by many shifts in its dignity and

---

32. In a very different spirit from that of Barthes, recent German historians of ideas have begun to chart a tradition of *aesthesis*. For Joachim Ritter the pre-Romantic sense of landscape represents a compensatory realization of what in antiquity had been the mind's orientation toward the whole of the natural order, in a stance both participatory and cognitive, notably in Aristotle's *theoria tou kosmou*. "Landscape as an aesthetic experience," Ritter writes, "is in essence the appearance [*das Scheinen*] of the lost totality of Nature." *Landschaft: Zur Funktion des Ästhetischen in der modernen Gesellschaft* (Munster, 1963), p. 47. Hans Robert Jauss, developing Ritter's argument, sees in the Romantic interiorization of landscape the transformation of the negativity of the aesthetic into a positive accomplishment, as most fully realized in the Romantic and post-Romantic category of memory. See "Sketch of a Theory and History of Aesthetic Experience," *Aesthetic Experience and Literary Hermeneutics* (Minneapolis, 1982), pp. 3–151. In spite of the Hegelian orientation implicit in the work of Ritter and Jauss, their analysis of *aesthēsis* as

by varying assessments of its relation to cognition and truth values.[33] What Hans Blumenberg developed as the criterion of reality based on "instantaneous evidence," with its source in the Platonic doctrine of ideas, has persisted even in world views far removed from the Platonic. Geoffrey Hartman has reminded us that "the assumption that aesthetic experience is related to perception (or perceptibility, *Anschauung,* the sighting of insight)"[34] is itself a philosophical presupposition that should not be left unexamined. We are the heirs of what Hartman terms the "now historical liaison between image and formal values in art or between image and any model poetics—despite the counterthrust of semiotic theory and deconstructionist mediation. Perceptibility—that all things can be made as perceptible as the eye suggests—may itself be the great *classic* phantasm, the mediterranean fantasy." Hartman himself has traced an epistemological shift from the eighteenth century's confidence in the physical eye, in the adequacy of perception to its objects, to a resistance to sight in many of the Romantics, a sense that vision must be rescued from its dependence on the earthly, on the sensible.[35]

---

an accreditation and institutionalization of sensuous apprehension is most relevant to present-day discussions of textuality and reception.

33. Cf. Bruno Snell, *The Discovery of Mind* (Cambridge, Mass., 1953); Hans Blumenberg, "Licht als Metapher der Wahrheit," *Studium Generale* 10, no. 7 (1957): 432–47; Hans Jonas, "The Nobility of Sight: A Study in the Phenomenology of the Senses," in *The Phenomenon of Life* (Chicago, 1982), pp. 135–52; and E. H. Gombrich, "Icones Symbolicae," in *Symbolic Images* (London, 1972). See also n. 32 above.

34. *Criticism in the Wilderness: The Study of Literature Today* (New Haven, 1980), p. 25.

35. See *The Unmediated Vision* (New Haven, 1954), and *Wordsworth's Poetry, 1787–1814* (New Haven, 1964). Wordsworth's lines in *The Prelude* on first viewing Mont Blanc,

> . . . and grieved
> To have a soulless image on the eye
> That had usurped upon a living thought
> That never more could be.   (6:525ff.)

exemplify this awareness of the ineffectuality, the occulting force of sight. Goethe, we should recall, termed sight "der gefährliche Sinn." As E. M. Wilkinson and L. A. Willoughby have demonstrated, Goethe was led, under the impact of Herder's thought, to challenge the preeminence of vision that had been dominant in philosophy through the seventeenth century. Goethe became strongly aware of the punctuality of mere vision, its limitation to the surface of objects (what Herder had called "Vogelansicht" or seeing "wie ein Specht"), and thus of the need to correct and supplement sight. In "Der Blinde und der Dichter," *Goethe Jahrbuch* 91[1974]: 33–57. In this connection an entry in Goethe's *Briefe aus der Schweiz* (a preeminently descriptive work that deals with his second journey through Switzerland of 1779–80) is revealing: "Meine Beschreibung fängt an unordentlich und ängstlich zu werden; auch brauchte es eigentlich zwei Menschen, einen der's sähe und einen der's beschriebe." Cited in N. Haas, "Sehen und Beschreiben: Zu Goethes zweiter Schweizerreise," in *Reise und soziale Realität am Ende des 18. Jahrhunderts,* eds. W. Griep

One cannot, at the present stage of theoretical development, simply append a visual phenomenology (in the sense of Mikel Dufrenne)[36] to a theory of representation. To do this would assume a thoroughgoing homology between experiential structures, on the one hand, and signifying structures, on the other. Nevertheless, a phenomenological approach in a narrower sense, one that is attentive to the semiosis of perceptual data, could be fruitful. In this section I want to explore a number of ways in which vision enters into the signifying work of narrative. In a sense, to do this is to recover certain traditional functions of tropes, functions that have been neglected by recent, primarily structurally oriented, treatments of figuration.

At an initial level—the "natural attitude" in a phenomenological sense—the reader's ability to imagine or visualize something by means of language implies a conception of language as a wholly transparent medium through which the reader "sees." On the one side there is the reader who "looks through" language; on the other, there is a represented (depicted, *dargestellt*) reality, what Roman Ingarden calls the stratum of represented objects.[37] The imagined scene or represented world is activated by means of language but then seems to become independent of it and achieve a status that is subject not to the rules of langauge but to the workings of intuition and perception. Yet this explanation is subject to all sorts of qualifications. Neither the transparency of language nor a model of the imagination based on perception can be maintained to any degree of complexity. The medium of language repeatedly draws attention to its own distinctive formation. And the mind's image-forming power, the "imagination," proves to be only partially congruent to the workings of perception. Or, as Merleau-Ponty might argue, we would require a far more differentiated conception of perception than is normally assumed in order to draw any useful inferences about the ways we apprehend aesthetic phenomena.[38]

---

and H.-W. Jäger (Heidelberg, 1983), p. 9. What is "ängstlich" (fearsome, uncanny) is that the work of description manifests a fundamental schism in the subject, a division between the instance of vision and the agent of writing. This kind of recognition is often implicit in Goethe's descriptive practice in his fiction.

36. See *Phénoménologie de l'expérience esthétique*, 2 vols. (Paris, 1953).

37. *The Literary Work of Art*, trans. George G. Grabowicz (Evanston, Ill., 1973), pp. 217ff.

38. Some of Merleau-Ponty's speculations on the interplay of linguistic and pictorial elements are found in the first two essays of *Signs*, trans. R. C. McCleary (Evanston, Ill., 1964). On the issue of the pictorial component in image formation see Edward S. Casey, *Imagining: A Pheomenological Approach* (Bloomington, Ind., 1976). The most trenchant

Sartre's remarks on the thetic or positional component of image formation are relevant to this issue: "What we ordinarily designate as *thinking* is a consciousness which affirms this or that quality of its object but without realizing the qualities on the object. The *image*, on the contrary, is a consciousness that aims to produce its object: it is therefore constituted by a certain way of judging and feeling of which we do not become conscious as such but which we apprehend *on* the intentional object as this or that of its qualities."[39] When Sartre speaks of projecting a type of judgment and perception onto the intended object, of making it, through its qualities or attributes, the index of the intending operation, he touches on the fundamental Husserlian issue of the noetic-noematic correlation.

In the context of Husserl's later work this involves an attempt to isolate the noematic level (the cogitatum or object pole) and use it as an index in determining the constituting intentionalities, that is, the noetic acts of a cogito. In the second of the *Cartesian Meditations* Husserl delineates the movement back from the dimension of the cogitatum to the constitutive acts of the cogito in the following manner:

> When the phenomenologist explores everything objective, and whatever can be found in it, exclusively as a "correlate of consciousness," . . . he penetrates the anonymous "cogitative" life, he uncovers the *definite* synthetic courses of the manifold modes of consciousness and, further back, the modes of Ego-comportment, which make understandable the objective affair's simple meantness for the Ego, its intuitive or non-intuitive meantness. Or, stated more precisely, they make it understandable how, in itself and by virtue of its current intentional structure, consciousness makes possible and necessary the fact that such an "existing" and "thus determined" Object is intended in it, occurs in it as such a sense.[40]

If we take this as an abstract model for a task, we still need to determine just what constitutes the noemata of a literary form, and specifically of the novel, before we can proceed in the manner indicated by

recent critiques of the perceptual model in relation to language are Jacques Derrida, *Speech and Phenomena*, trans. D. B. Allison (Evanston, Ill., 1973), and Richard Rorty, *Philosophy and the Mirror of Nature* (Princeton, 1979).

39. *The Psychology of Imagination* (New York, 1961), p. 138. The original version is *L'Imaginaire: Psychologie phénoménologique de l'imagination* (Paris, 1940).

40. *Cartesian Meditations: An Introduction to Phenomenology*, trans. Dorion Cairns (The Hague, 1977), p. 50. The *Meditations* were first delivered by Husserl as lectures in Paris in 1929.

Husserl to disclose the sources in consciousness ("the anonymous 'cogitative' life") of "the objective affair's simple meantness for the Ego." The specific manner in which such a correlation comes about in a given field—the constitution of the fictive world, in our case—represents a basic task for interpretation and analysis. But there is no ready-made formula, no generally recognized method for this task.

One way we might circumscribe the noematic field in a manner appropriate to our subject would be to deal with description in terms of certain tropes that stress vividness and visual presence—*ekphrasis, enargeia, hypotyposis* (Barthes has spoken in this connection of a "radiance of desire" [*éclat du désir*]).[41] It is true that rhetoric by definition concentrates on the linguistic sphere and that rhetorical figures have generally been conceived as a means of accommodating perceptual and intentional impulses to a system of language. It is possible, however, to view tropes in a different light, that is, as a use of language that marks a transgression of the logic of discourse. Thus a study of tropes, of rhetorical traditions, may help to determine how, within given conventions, linguistic forms are understood to relay and transform non-linguistic data, to function as an intermediary between perception at one end and fantasy and illusion at the other. The tropes mentioned above serve as directives for response, incitements to feel and envision in a manner that moves beyond what is articulated in the text, beyond what any *text* can articulate. Paul de Man has turned our attention to this intermediary status of tropes in the economy of a text. "Tropes," he writes, "are transformational systems rather than grids."[42] De Man would make us attentive to what takes place between a textual strategy as a rule-governed procedure (literature as a

41. Barthes, in discussing the trope of hypotyposis, argues that its function within the tradition of classical rhetoric was to institutionalize the production of fantasy. It served "to 'place things before the hearer's eyes', not in a neutral manner, merely reporting, but by giving to the scene all the radiance of desire." "The Reality Effect," in *French Literary Theory Today*, p. 14. It is worth noting that Barthes, in contradistinction to other structuralist critics, drew significantly on phenomenological ideas transmitted through Merleau-Ponty and Sartre and combined them with his own formalist and semiotic concerns.

42. *Allegories of Reading* (New Haven, 1980), p. 63. De Man has also written: "My main point stresses the futility of trying to repress the rhetorical structure of texts in the name of uncritically preconceived text models such as transcendental teleologies or, at the other end of the spectrum, mere codes. The existence of literary codes is not in question, only their claim to represent a general and exhaustive textual model. Literary codes are subcodes of a system, rhetoric, that is not itself a code. For rhetoric cannot be isolated from its epistemological function however negative this function may be. It is absurd to ask whether a code is true or false but impossible to bracket this question when tropes are involved—and this always seems to be the case." "The Epistemology of Metaphor," *Critical Inquiry* 5(Autumn 1978): 13–30. This passage is on p. 29.

set of codes) and its effects at the level of reading and reception. In this sense he can argue that tropes necessarily involve the deflection or warping of a message. It follows that the visualizing capacity ingrained in description is to be conceived neither as a code attached to a literary category (narrative) nor as the direct rendering of perceptual experience, but rather as a tropological medium in de Man's sense.

In nineteenth-century fiction one of the primary goals of representation was to endow objects, locales, and figures with what may be called ocular value, that is, not merely to designate them but to motivate their appearance, to justify "visibility" by means of a code of verisimilitude. The thematics of vision (including, of course, forms of occlusion) thus became a fundamental element in the representation of reality. One of the principal functions of character in the novel was to serve as an agency for vision, and, in this way, to authenticate the represented objectivities of the text. In tracing such objectivities, understood as noemata, back to the noetic processes specifically correlative to them, we come upon a conception of character in fiction that stresses not so much motives for behavior and the general traits of personality as those latent yet habitual responses of perception and sensation that betray a figure's interaction with the environment.

While the function of vision as a key to the constitution of a fictive world has been noted in many individual studies, it has seldom been pursued at a theoretical level. F. O. Matthiessen, in his study of Henry James, noted that "an interesting chapter of cultural history could be written about the nineteenth century's stress on sight. . . . The distance that [Henry James] had travelled from Emerson may be measured by the fact that though both knew their chief subject matter to be consciousness, the mind's awareness of its processes, for Emerson that awareness reaffirmed primarily the moral laws. James was also a moralist, but aesthetic experience was primary for him, since *aesthētikos* meant perceptive. He had turned the double-edged word 'seer' back to this world."[43] This link between a visionary tradition (American Transcendentalism) with one of its latter-day heirs reminds us that James's recurrent preoccupation with seeing may be understood as an effort to test consciousness as a source of both experiential and moral truth.

Dorothy Van Ghent, in her study of *The Portrait of a Lady*, offers an excellent formulation of how the mutually implicated structure of object and perceiver gives rise to the represented world of a novel. "In

43. *Henry James: The Major Phase* (New York, 1944), p. 32.

James's handling of the richly qualitative setting, it is characteristically significant that he suggests visual or scenic traits almost always in such a way that the emphasis is on *modulations of perception in the observer.* The 'look' of things has thus the double duty of representing external stimuli, by indirection in their passage through consciousness, and of representing the observer himself."[44] Traditional criticism of the novel is generally attentive to the second of Van Ghent's proposals, that the rendering of objects and locales serves to represent "the observer himself" in the sense of a character of the work of fiction. But it is less sensitive to the first, that the representation of external stimuli takes place "by indirection in their passage through consciousness."

Consciousness is for James in no sense a stable entity but rather the arena for innumerable accommodations among diverse, often mutually incommensurable, signs. While perception, in its endless filling and emptying operation, provides the mind's preeminent access to reality, the mind cannot help but acknowledge what James termed "that spectre of impotence which dogs the footsteps of perception and whose presence is like some poison-drop in the silver cup."[45] The Jamesian reflector, at its most complex, enacts this struggle for meaning and serves, in the process, as a model for the reader's own engagement with the text. James was well aware of the anomaly of fictive representation, that acts of vision incorporated into the narrative can also become markers of visualization. They function not only in the diegesis, the level of the narrative, but also as facilitators of "imaging," of the imaginary in Sartre's sense.

This mutually implicated process of perceiving and construing, what may be termed the aesthetization (in both senses, *aesthēsis* and aesthetics) of consciousness in James, can be illustrated by means of a well-known episode in *The Ambassadors*.[46] Strether, in search of a model for that "certain small Lambinet that had charmed him long years before," sees drifting toward him, on the current of a rural stream near Paris, two individuals whom he recognizes quickly enough as the couple that had concealed their intimacy (their very status as a couple) up to this moment. There is something emblematic in the way that this unexpected sight of Chad and Madame de Vionnet

44. *The English Novel: Form and Function* (New York, 1953), reprint 1964, p. 216.

45. *The American Scene* (Bloomington, Ind., 1968), p. 307, cited in John Carlos Rowe, "James's Rhetoric of the Eye: Re-Marking the Impression," *Criticism* 24(1982): 247.

46. Citations are from the Norton Critical Edition (New York, 1964), pp. 301 and 307f. (bk. 11, chaps. 3–4).

violates the genteel pastoralism which Strether, that day, had been at pains to recapture. He had gone in search, we recall, of "that French ruralism, with its cool special green, into which he had hitherto looked only through the little oblong window of the picture-frame. It had been as yet for the most part but a land of fancy for him—the background of fiction, the medium of art, the nursery of letters; practically as distant as Greece, but practically also well-nigh as consecrated." When the couple in the boat, instead of blending into the scene and thus becoming part of an aesthetic image ("It was suddenly as if these figures, or something like them, had been wanted in the picture"), are revealed to Strether as his friends, they stand exposed, veritably *in delicto* in terms of the moral sensibilities that he cannot but apply, and the beauty of the rural scene is destroyed, even more, desecrated (as earlier it had been "consecrated").

James brings together here the props of fictive setting with an almost Flaubertian insistence on their stereotypical status ("a land of fancy . . . the background of fiction, the medium of art, the nursery of letters"). Strether's effort to recover in "reality" an aesthetic experience modeled on a work of art, a painting, is disappointed, but not by any insufficiency in his aesthetic sensibility. His effort to focus on the still indeterminate figures in the boat and integrate them into the scene dissolves into a shocked recognition. The perceptual act is displaced. Its availability for an aesthetic effect is withdrawn as it is put in the service of a moral judgment. But what comes between the two, the aesthetic and the moral, is a destabilization of vision. Strether's "impression" is caught by the "drift," the wavering of the approaching boat. It is in such scenes that James was able to trace the "indirection" of external stimuli operative in consciousness.

For James, of course, pictorial and plastic forms served as a constant point of reference for that testing of consciousness which was his principal subject matter. Such a foregrounding of the aesthetic may have multiple functions. For one thing, the novel's own construction of reality is validated by setting it off against a more palpable, exposed instance of simulation. More specifically, a pictorial aesthetic cannot help but affect the representational effects of a text. There have been a number of studies in recent years along such lines.[47] Thus Raymonde Debray-Genette has shown the persistence in novels of the Baroque period of a "plastic mimesis" in which painting and the other plastic

---

47. One of the most searching, though still unpublished, is Neil M. Flax's *Written Pictures: The Visual Arts in Goethe's Literary Works* (Ph.D. diss., Yale University, 1978).

arts serve as a model of reference for literary description. "To describe is not necessarily an answer to a need to know or inform," she writes, "but also—or first of all—an answer to an imaginative need. In fact, all poetics of description are based on an ideology of description which is not to be confused with the ideological discourse emanating from the text."[48] Debray-Genette argues that in the post-Renaissance novel realistic verisimilitude, the referentiality of what is represented, is repeatedly justified in terms of some form of pictorial modeling. This explains the importance of the "plasticizing" or image-inducing objects that have been so common a feature of novels since the Baroque period, objects like rings, buckles, cups, precious stones, mirrors, gardens. Such objects, it should be noted, are usually treated as ornamental elements, but Debray-Genette underscores a significant complication of an ornamental mimesis. "In this redoubling—or rather this sophisticated simplification—of plastic mimesis," she writes, "I see the beginning of that appeal to referentiation which will mark so-called realist description."

What Debray-Genette refers to as the "ornamentality" of objects and materials in a description is coordinate with a "self-representational" characteristic, a tendency to "show forth" or "stand out" that is by no means exceptional but is in fact ingrained in "an ideology of description" in the novel. (The trope of *ekphrasis,* the ostensive delineation of an object or scene *as if* it were a pictorial representation, is identified precisely by this quality of self-display.) Her analysis thus supports my argument that description operates at a level of innate aesthetization, at the threshold of perceptibility and textuality.

Geoffrey Hartman has asked, "Is there anything comparable to the mirror stage on the level of language?" And though he added that this question "may seem unanswerable in terms of Lacanian psychiatry,"[49] he touched thereby on one of the most productive elements of Lacan's thought, one in which Lacan avowedly pursued a phenomenological impulse. Merleau-Ponty had begun to question the validity of conceiving language as a speech authored by a normative, stable self, and posed it rather as a thinking from without. Man does not simply constitute language or invent it; rather, he is a product of language. In his earlier work Merleau-Ponty challenged the traditional metaphysical distinction between man and world, between

    48. "Some Functions of Figures in Novelistic Description," *Poetics Today* 5, no. 4 (1984): 677–88. This quotation is on p. 681, the following is on p. 679.
    49. "Psychoanalysis: The French Connection," in *Psychology and the Question of the Text,* ed. Geoffrey Hartman (Baltimore, 1978), p. 93.

what is inner and what is outer, through an analysis of the status of language. Later, in *The Visible and the Invisible*,[50] he stressed a conception of vision as a radically reflexive capacity.

Lacan argues that Merleau-Ponty transcended an earlier, intuitionist philosophy where the subject's "constitutive presence," his "total intentionality," was taken as the basis of "the regulatory function of form"[51] and moved toward a position where perception is treated as a discontinuous, oblique mediation, no longer the prop of a stable subject. According to Lacan, Merleau-Ponty "set out to rediscover . . . the dependence of the visible on that which places us under the eye of the seer. . . . What we have to circumscribe, by means of the path he indicates for us, is the preexistence of a gaze—I see only from one point, but in my existence I am looked at from all sides." This exposed status of the subject is the basis, in Lacan's argument, not only for its irredeemable *méconnaissance* (both mistaking and being misapprehended) but also for the genesis of that "spectacle of the world" which both dazzles and shrinks the subject. "I mean," Lacan writes, "and Maurice Merleau-Ponty points this out, that we are beings who are looked at, in the spectacle of the world. That which makes us consciousness institutes us by the same token as *speculum mundi*." Man as mirror or image of the universe—this might be taken as the humanist sense of the phrase. But Lacan underscores the disabling ambiguity implicit in derivatives of the Latin root *species:* (1) that which is seen, the view; (2) the spectacle in the sense of theatrical illusion, mere effect; and (3) the mirroring or reflecting back on itself of the viewing instance.

Lacan's concept of the gaze (*le regard*) builds on Merleau-Ponty's argument that vision can never serve as a reliable avenue to the world or to the self, to truth or to identity.[52] There is an inaccessibility of the visible that is constitutive of man's commerce with the world and not simply the consequence of contingent factors. But the recognition of a "flaw" in ocular knowledge (or, better, of its occulting potential) should not lead to a neglect of the thematics of vision and cognition in fictional texts. We may now, perhaps, more properly approach the issue in terms of an "effet de visibilité" (on the analogy of Barthes's

50. (Evanston, Ill., 1968).

51. Jacques Lacan, *The Four Fundamental Concepts of Psycho-Analysis*, trans. Alan Sheridan (New York, 1981), p. 71. The following passages are on pp. 72 and 74f.

52. See "Sighting the Scene" in this volume for a more detailed discussion of the Lacanian gaze.

"effet de réel"),[53] that is, of vision or visibility as a troping that necessarily enters into the production of meaning of a text.

TEXTUAL WORLDS

In the previous section I attempted to isolate for analysis certain representational mediations or formalizations for perception. I want now to consider that a sense of world is, like perception, a fundamental cognitive schematism within the form of the novel since the Renaissance. The novel, in spite of its difference from earlier narrative forms, assumed one of the primary functions of traditional epic, which was to project a world model. As Hans Blumenberg has written, "Fixing (or causing) a world [*Welthaftigkeit*] as a formal, overriding structure is what constitutes the novel."[54] What Blumenberg stresses is that the modern novel has itself assumed control over the formal elements of a world structure, although never altogether losing sight of the older goal of epic narrative, which was to grasp the cosmos as the totality of the natural order. As his analysis makes clear, the criterion of reality at work in the modern novel is validated neither on transcendental nor on intersubjective grounds. It is a new concept, which he characterizes as "the *reality of the possible,* whose unreality had to be the premise for the relevance of its actualization." And regarding the mode of manifestation and transmission of this type of reality, he writes, "Reality can no longer be considered an inherent quality of an object, but is the embodiment of a consistently applied *syntax of elements.* Reality presents itself now as never before as a sort of text which takes on its particular form by obeying certain rules of internal consistency." Blumenberg has provided a basis for converting the concept of world from an ontological to a textual premise. His argument finds support in the work of other contemporary thinkers.

To begin with, Michel de Certeau's discussion of narrative form as a "foundational" cultural practice based on juridic principles is relevant.[55] In a study on spatiality in narrative he recalls Dumézil's analysis of an Indo-European root *dhē,* and its Latin derivative *fās,* etymons that denote the stipulation of a framework, the establish-

53. Cf. "The Reality Effect."
54. "The Concept of Reality and the Possibility of the Novel," in *New Perspectives in German Literary Criticism,* ed. R. E. Amacher and V. Lange (Princeton, 1979), pp. 29–48. This passage is on p. 48, the following ones are on pp. 40 and 42. Blumenberg draws on Georg Lukács's argument in *The Theory of the Novel* (originally published in 1916) regarding the "world shaping" function of epic form.
55. "Récits d'espaces," in *L'Invention du quotidien,* vol. 1, *Arts de faire* (Paris: Edition 10/18, 1980), pp. 205–27. The following passage is on p. 219.

ment of a foundation in order to "make space," to provide a "base," a "field," a "theater" for those acts that a cultural system authorizes. "This precisely is the original role of narrative," de Certeau writes, "to establish a *theater* of legitimacy for effective *action*. It creates a field which authorizes social practices that are subject to risk and contingency." Narrative practices follow this type of juridic model. They are conceived as establishing boundaries, creating an accredited "theater" of action, a "scene." World projection in this sense implies a dual function: to totalize but at the same time to relativize. Put in other terms, we have here a model of relative totalities, analogous to the discrete "worlds" of modern fiction.

What is pertinent to our analysis is that the language of world models operates preeminently in terms of a spatial schematism, a "metaphorizing" (or transposition) of categories of placement, relation, orientation, distance, and magnitude into terms of space.[56] The spatial metaphor is so pervasive that we cannot easily disentangle it from fundamental patterns of thought, from the ways that we conceive of the self, of human action, of the world. This practice has been analyzed in various ways: as "chora" by Julia Kristeva, the "imprint of an archaic moment, the threshold of space" in the infant;[57] as "milieu" and "ambiance" by Spitzer, modern variants of the Greek concept of *to periechon*—a "warm" abstraction, in Spitzer's view, "which is visualized and which has not severed its ties with life, but remains organic and close to the bodily";[58] and as "topocosm" by Northrop Frye, a mapping of the universe that draws on the religious, philosophical, and scientific beliefs of an age and adapts them as the setting for its mythical narratives.[59]

The Frye topocosm is a highly simplified construct that works in terms of equivalences between a language of orientation, direction, and distance and one of ethical values. The Classical-Medieval topocosm, whose prototype is found in Dante's *Commedia,* provided the pattern of a cosmological system in which a perfect congruence obtained between a spiritual dimension and a geographic one, a congruence that later variants of topocosm cannot match, though they will, in one way or another, refer to it. Frye's notion can be useful for

56. Cf. "Metonymy, Schematism, and the Space of Literature" in this volume.
57. "Place Names," in *Desire in Language: A Semiotic Approach to Literature and Art* (New York, 1980), p. 283.
58. "Milieu and Ambiance," p. 187f.
59. "New Directions from Old," in *Fables of Identity: Studies in Poetic Mythology* (New York, 1963), pp. 52–66.

articulating a valorized thematics peculiar to a given historical era, but we should not overlook the fact that it remains bound to a history of ideas framework, operating in terms of synchronic, self-contained units of meaning. Thus, while the concept of topocosm may be helpful in ordering certain dominant spatial themes of an age (topological) in terms of an ideal of totality (cosmological), it cannot tell us much regarding the nature of this linkage. In the post-Romantic realist tradition the problem is not so much to assign a worldly value to allegorical settings as to assess the adaptation of figurative forms to modern representational practices.

One way of constructing a model of narrative space is to conceive it as a sequence of transformations operating between two poles. At the one extreme, there is the map or atlas, a diagrammatic, isomorphic model of spatial relations; at the other, a set of directions that moves a subject through successive points and thus marks out a path. Quotidian narrative practices tend to oscillate between these poles, as de Certeau comments: "Either *to see* (this is to gain knowledge of a system of places) or else *to go* (this involves spatializing acts). Either it offers a *tableau* ('there is') or it organizes certain *moves* ('you enter, you cross, you turn')."[60] But the more complex structure characteristic of the novel must be conceived in terms of a third alternative, one capable of mediating the totalizing prospect that takes in the whole of a territory in a glance and the order of instructions that chart a traversal. Let us attempt to identify this vectorized space of narrative structures more clearly. To begin with, Michel Butor's notion of *periplum* (encircling journey, circumnavigation) is suggestive: "Thus the fundamental measure of distance in the realist novel is not only voyage but periplum; this proximity of the place described contracts in itself a whole voyage around the world."[61] The dreams of circumnavigation that spawned an immense travel literature in the sixteenth and seventeenth centuries become the model for didactic allegories and burlesque voyages in the eighteenth, and then, in the nineteenth, for internalized fantasy journeys.

Michel Serres's analyses of the mythological components of nineteenth-century literature (in Verne, in Zola)[62] have gone far in revealing the interplay of spatial and conceptual categories within a determinate historical context. History, in fact, is for Serres known

60. *L'Invention du quotidien*, vol. 1, p. 211.

61. "L'Espace du roman," in *Essais sur le roman* (Paris, 1969), p. 51.

62. See especially *Jouvences: Sur Jules Verne* (Paris, 1974), and *Feux et signaux de brume: Zola* (Paris, 1975).

essentially through the displacements negotiated through mythical narratives, "negotiated" in the sense both of traversing and of bridging. The journeys and junctures recorded in myths stake out the fundamental scientific and philosophic concerns of an age: "The fact is that in general a culture constructs in and by its history an original intersection between such spatial varieties, a node of very precise and particular connections. This construction, I believe, is that culture's very history."[63] Narratives produce a discourse that is also a *cursus*, a pathway, which serves to link discrete locales, elements of a primal chaos. Nature provides no unified map to account for the manifold of spaces, no conceptual system that can reduce the manifold to a unitary space. Euclidian space is itself a myth of unification, only one of many ways of realizing certain connections. The following passage, although dealing with *The Odyssey*, applies in principle to Serres's revisionist epistemology for the nineteenth century:

> Ulysses' journey, like that of Oedipus, is an itinerary. And it is a discourse, the prefix of which I can now understand. It is not at all the discourse (*discours*) of an itinerary (*parcours*), but, radically, the itinerary (*parcours*) of a discourse (*discours*), the course, *cursus*, route, path that passes through the original disjunction, the bridge laid down across crevices. . . . Original spaces proliferate on the map of the journey, perfectly disseminated, or literally sporadic, each one rigorously determined. The global wandering, the mythical adventure, is, in the end, only the general joining of these spaces, as if the object or target of discourse were only to connect, or as if the junction, the relation, constituted the route by which the first discourse passes. *Mythos*, first *logos*; transport, first relation; junction, condition of transport.[64]

With this model of mythic narrative as not simply the story of a journey ("discours du parcours") but a journeying by way of narrating ("le parcours d'un discours") we encounter an ambiguity in the formulation that points to an undecidability at a theoretical level, a resistance to any clear-cut division between theme and form, between journey as geography and journey as narrative.[65]

63. Michel Serres, *Hermes: Literature, Science, Philosophy*, ed. Josué V. Harari and David F. Bell (Baltimore, 1982), p. 45.

64. Ibid., p. 48f.

65. These pages do no more than suggest the possibility of tracing spatial displacements to arrive at basic models of action in the novel. Derrida, in a reference to Joyce ("the most Hegelian of modern novelists"), reminds us of the totalizing implications of the Odyssean *nostos*, the returning, homeward journey, and refers to an alternative model proposed by Levinas ("Violence and Metaphysics," in *Writing and Difference*, trans. Alan Bass

The "action" or plot underlying many nineteenth-century novels turns on the construction of an appropriate setting, a setting that then comes to serve not only as a function of the characters' acts or behavior but, more fundamentally, as index of a worldly reality. In this sense descriptive data in realist fiction may be analyzed in terms of an underlying constructive principle, a principle that accounts both for the spatial coordinates that frame the action and the shape of the action itself. Shape becomes a *shaping*. The topographic exceeds its delineating function and becomes an agency of action, a coordinate of human destiny. This is not to say, however, that we should expect to find a perfect congruence between a topographic model and the representation of action and consciousness. The topographic itself is not to be taken as a single, consistent theme but rather as the source for a variety of representational modalities. It is predicated not on a homogeneous, Newtonian conception of space but on a polyvalent topology, a topology deriving from instances of partial vision, of a distinctively *human* and self-consciously historical mode of cognition. The aesthetic form related to this kind of radical perspectivism has been suggestively formulated by a nineteenth-century theorist of art, Charles Blanc:

> Undoubtedly, it is only the eye of God that is capable of viewing the universe geometrically ["en géométral"]; man in his infirmity has only a curtailed purview ["que des raccourcis"]. Nonetheless, he allows his intelligent gaze to wander as if nature in its entirety were subject to him, and since each of his movements alters his point of view, the lines, vying with each other, come together of themselves and fashion a spectacle which is always changing, always new. . . . Man carries in himself a mobile poetry obedient to the will of his movements, a poetry that seems to have been given to us to veil the nudity of truth, to correct the rigors of the absolute, and to soften in our eyes the inexorable laws of a divine geometry.[66]

Although Blanc betrays some nostalgia for a transcendent viewpoint, "l'univers en géometral," his sense of a universe accessible to man only in "raccourcis," as a function of man's "poésie mobile," is consistent with the perspectival epistemology that had been evolving in the novel.

[Chicago, 1978], pp. 153 and 320n. I am indebted to Philip Kuberski for this reference). The relevance of such patterning for major novelists remains to be explored.

66. *Grammaire des arts du dessin,* 6th ed. (Paris, 1886). Cited in Pierre Kaufmann, *L'Experience émotionelle de l'espace* (Paris, 1969), p. 319.

Mikhail Bakhtin's concept of chronotope brings together a thematics of action and a typology of settings that is capable of doing justice to the concept of fictive world that I have been developing. Both the plot forms and the spatial models that are combined in the chronotope derive from an identifiable cultural repertoire. What the chronotopic analysis of a work could achieve is to fuse them in a figure, a mobile spatial imprint or trace. Thus Bakhtin writes:

> An event can be communicated, it becomes information. But the event does not become a figure [*obraz*]. It is precisely the chronotope that provides the ground essential for the showing-forth, the representability of events. And this is so thanks precisely to the special increase in density and concreteness of time markers—the time of human life, of historical time—that occurs within well-delineated spatial areas. . . . Thus the chronotope, functioning as the primary means for materializing time in space, emerges as a center for concretizing representation, as a force giving body to the entire novel.[67]

What is noteworthy about Bakhtin's concept is not simply that it implies a thematics of plot or action types but that it identifies a world-modeling function that is fundamental to the novel. Its function is to articulate certain constants of human experience (e.g., birth, death, journeying, laughter) in terms of specific, culturally determinate semantic registers. This yields a type of narrative matrix that can be understood as both epistemological and thematic. Thus in developing the chronotope of the road, Bakhtin suggests the following components: the road as context for the multiple habitats embedded in a larger cultural entity, "the *sociohistorical heterogeneity* of one's own country";[68] the road as metaphor for the career of the protagonist in his struggle to transcend the sphere of quotidian reality; the road as site of formative moments or acts in a personal destiny.

Bakhtin wanted to demonstrate that literary classifications, such as the genres, may be traced back to the formative work of a material imagination operative at the level of language and concept formations, an imagination that produces what he calls a "realistic emblematic."[69] When he speaks of a "folkloric base" for the "realist image" he is referring not to specific sources in folklore material but to a preliterary, pragmatic level of conceptualization which is presupposed in the formalizations of literature. Bakhtin's own work was in great

67. "Forms of Time and Chronotope in the Novel," in *The Dialogic Imagination: Four Essays*, ed. M. Holquist (Austin, Tx., 1981), p. 250.
68. Ibid., p. 245.
69. Ibid., p. 223. The following quotation is also on p. 223.

measure dedicated to working out the kind of historical epistemology—historical semiology, we might say today—that he en-
visaged in the essay under discussion. He credits Lessing with a semi-
nal role in posing the problem of time in literature, but then continues,
articulating his own goal in the process, "The problem of assimilating
real time, that is, the problem of assimilating historical reality into the
poetic image, was not posed by him, although the question is touched
upon in his work."[70] And when he writes, "Language, as a treasure-
house of images, is fundamentally chronotopic," it is important to
realize that he means not a ready-made thematic repertoire but something like a structure of cultural memory traces.

Merleau-Ponty has argued that description is continuous with
man's access to the world, to a sense of the real. "The real is to be
described and not constructed or constituted."[71] I take this to be an
expression of a fundamental imbrication of language and perception.
Description is not to be conceived as only a recording of perception,
following in its wake. Man needs to name the world in order to see it.
If Adam's naming of the animals be taken as emblematic—no perceptual knowledge without a name—then the name serves to point to an
anterior moment, a hypothetical origin that makes every act of cognition into one of re-cognition, and this marks perception, too, as inescapably derivative. Description may be understood as a formalization
adapted to a specific institutional practice ("fiction," "narrative") of a
more fundamental cognitive orientation. Such a formalization involves, of course, specific textual practices as determined by considerations of genre, of representational techniques, of modes of reception. It is at the level of such practices that we can best discern
underlying historical-epistemological assumptions, however much
the "devices" of literary art tend to camouflage or naturalize them. A
preeminent function of the modern novel, as I conceive it, has been to
evolve the concept of world as a relativized totality. In offering alternative world models, exercises in reality construction, the novel enables us to perceive the worlds that we name.

70. Ibid., p. 251. The following quotation is also on p. 251.
71. *Phénoménologie de la perception* (Paris, 1945), p. iv.

2 Metonymy, Schematism, and the Space of Literature

Comment savoir ce que veut dire temporalisation et spatialisation d'un sens, d'un objet idéal, d'une teneur intelligible si l'on n'a pas élucidé ce que "espace" et "temps" veulent dire? Mais comment le faire avant de savoir ce que c'est qu'un logos ou un vouloir-dire qui spatio-temporalise, de lui-même, tout ce qu'il énonce? ce que c'est que le logos comme métaphore? JACQUES DERRIDA[1]

I

The elements of description discussed in Chapter 1 conclude with a global model of action as it may be represented through a topographic circuit or journey, a model that, as Serres notes, links narrative (*mythos*) and topography in an irreducible manner. Now, however, I want to proceed in an inverse manner, beginning not with a notion like plot—which is in its nature highly articulated, referentially full—but with one that is more latent and indeterminate, like image or impression. One recent theorist of the novel has said that "the metaphor for the novel, more than for any other genre, is spatial, because its action unfolds literally in places, i.e., in a world where selves move and experience one another. Moreover, its illusion depends on the suggestion that the places be real, even if they be symbolic or fantastic."[2]

---

1. "La Mythologie blanche," in *Marges de la philosophie* (Paris, 1972), p. 271. In English: "How are we to know what the temporalization and spatialization of a meaning, of an ideal object, of an intelligible tenor, are, if we have not clarified what 'space' and 'time' mean? But how are we to do this before knowing what might be a logos or a meaning that in and of themselves spatio-temporalize everything they state? What logos as metaphor might be?" "White Mythology: Metaphor in the Text of Philosophy," in *Margins of Philosophy*, trans. Alan Bass (Chicago, 1982), p. 227f.
2. Ralph Freedman, "The Possibility of a Theory of the Novel," in *The Disciplines of*

Whereas Chapter 1 dealt with the illusion of real places, here I will develop the other premise expressed in this quotation, that the metaphor for the novel is spatial. Such an approach, however, must concern itself not only with the metaphoric bases of representation but also with the theoretical discourse that deals with representation. We cannot know what kind of space we are talking about unless we inquire first why we talk about space at all. Thus I begin with some considerations on the terminology of criticism insofar as it relates to the notion of fictive space.

Gérard Genette's diagnosis offers a convenient point of departure:

> All of our language is woven of space. Thus it is difficult to specify to what degree and in what manner our vocabulary today is more spatialized than that of yesterday, and what the meaning of this surplus spatialization might be. One thing appears certain at a general ideological level: the discreditation of space which was so fully expressed in Bergson's philosophy has given way to an inverse valorization which says, in its fashion, that man "prefers" space to time. . . . At present, literature—and thought in general—speaks only in terms of distance, horizon, universe, landscape, locale, site, paths, and habitations: naive figures but characteristic ones; figures par excellence where language is *spaced* so that space in it, now become language, is spoken and written.[3]

What is particularly interesting in the present context is the way in which the use of spatial concepts tends to expose a kind of impasse in the metadiscourse. In pointing to the spatiality at work at various levels of the literary text, much contemporary criticism tends to mime rather than to analyze the spatial metaphors. Here is an issue that offers exceptional insight into the way criticism will avoid, as if by incapacity, any systematic consideration of its own language. We will find, for example, the same spatial metaphors at work at different levels of a critical discourse, but without any particular note being taken of this divergence. Joseph Frank's discussion of spatial form applies the same terms both to the phenomenal space or locales depicted in a fiction and to the way the linearity of a text is projected onto a mental space.[4] Similarly, Roman Jakobson's discussions of

---

Criticism, ed. Peter Demetz et al. (New Haven, 1968), pp. 57–77. The quotation is on p. 72f.

3. *Figures* (Paris, 1966), p. 107f.

4. My argument is not to be taken as supporting Frank's renewed claim for a priority of space over time in modern literature. Cf. Joseph Frank, "Spatial Form: An Answer to Critics," *Critical Inquiry* 4(Winter 1977); related articles in the same issue by Eric S. Rabkin

metonymy involve both the contiguity of objects and places delineated in a fiction and the contiguity of semantic elements that need to be accounted for by syntax and other formal principles.[5] What I would stress in citing these instances is that we are dealing not with some accidental and egregious logical blunder but with a feature that is bound up with the underlying structure of the field itself, with the incapacity of literary criticism to mediate between its tropological and its referential language.

At the most general level we face here the problem explored by Jacques Derrida in "White Mythology": how to account for a structure of metaphor within a philosophical tradition that is itself constituted by (in the double sense of "has its origins in" and "is immanently organized in terms of") that same structure. His succinct formulation is, "philosophy is deprived of what it provides itself. Its instruments belonging to its field, philosophy is incapable of dominating its general tropology and metaphorics."[6] But if philosophy (and, by extension, literary criticism) is condemned to renounce the instruments it has itself fashioned, this deprivation can not be maintained absolutely. It seems to me that Derrida's injunction, in "White My-

---

and William Holtz; and Frank Kermode, "A Reply to Joseph Frank," *Critical Inquiry* 4(Spring 1978): 579–88. As Kant and others have shown, the representation of time through language involves an inescapable utilization of spatial concepts and terms. A position like Frank's, which differentiates so sharply between the temporal and the spatial and tends to play off one mode against the other, is beset with difficulties. Let me give one instance. Frank argues that the "synchronic relations" within the text can be suspended while "the time-act of reading" runs its course and brings the reader to that concluding point where the totality of these relations is fulfilled and the full meaning of a text is revealed in a spatial mode (p. 235). In this argument the diachronic level of a text appears to be reduced to nothing but "the time-act of reading," which, Frank continues, "is no longer coordinated with the dominant structural elements of the text." And he concludes, "Temporality becomes, as it were, a purely physical limit of apprehension, which conditions but does not determine the work and whose expectations are thwarted and superseded by the space-logic of synchronicity" (p. 235). One consequence of such a position is that the reading process is relegated to the level of a merely mechanical, automatic adjunct in the production of meaning in a text. This appears to block any significant integration of the reading process with textual structure—surely one of the leading aims of a great variety of theorists working at present. Roland Barthes's "hermeneutic code" in *S/Z*, for example, explores one way in which "the time-act of reading" is essentially implicated in the process of exposition and disclosure in a narrative text.

5. The most relevant items are "Two Aspects of Language and Two Types of Aphasic Disturbances," *Selected Writings II: Word and Language* (The Hague, 1971), pp. 239–59; "Randbemerkungen zur Prosa des Dichters Pasternak," *Slavische Rundschau* 6(1935): 357–74; and "Linguistics and Poetics," in *Style in Language*, ed. T. A. Sebeok (Cambridge, Mass., 1960).

6. "White Mythology," p. 228.

thology" and elsewhere, that the metaphoricity of a system constitutes a barrier to its self-understanding, is to be taken as a strategic move. Paul Ricoeur has challenged this tenet directly. In his view the predicative force, the productivity of the language of philosophy, cannot be disqualified because of the decay or attrition (*usure*) of the metaphors embedded in conceptual language. Such metaphors, Ricoeur argues, are not automatically subject to entropy but are susceptible to lexicalization and transformation so as to make them available for changing conceptual systems.[7] I myself believe that Derrida's actual practice has by no means blocked or short-circuited the movement of the "philosophemes," or key concepts, of the metaphysical tradition. His persistent focus on "a blind spot or central deafness" ("tache aveugle, foyer de surdité"),[8] the foundation concepts that a system cannot explicate to itself, has helped to make evident the reflexivity of the system under consideration and thus to bring these concepts into circulation once again.

To return to our initial questions: What allows the notion of space to be used as a constituent both of the physical world and of linguistic structures? What is the relation between space as the condition of phenomenal reality and space as a formal category? Is this relation only a loose analogy or is it a true homology which, if better understood, could illuminate both dimensions?

Kant's thought is relevant to this issue since he marks a point where the epistemological concerns characteristic of eighteenth-century aesthetics are developed in ways that expose certain underlying signifying operations. While his analysis does not, on the whole, directly address the issue of language in relation to intuition and aesthetic experience, it does, at certain crucial junctures, expose a problematic that has since been recognized as linguistic and rhetorical.

In general terms Kant's aesthetic theory marked a decisive turning from an eighteenth-century position (typified, for example, by Baumgarten) that classified aesthetics as a subordinate discipline within a larger systematic order of philosophy. Kant, by contrast, assigned to the aesthetic judgment a new, more central (and, as it proved, more problematic) function: namely, to underwrite the moral nature of man, to establish morality as an innate disposition whose

7. *La Métaphore vive* (Paris, 1975), pp. 362–74.
8. "White Mythology," p. 228.

preeminent model is man's sense of beauty in nature.⁹ As Joachim
Ritter writes of Kant's aesthetics, "Natural beauty becomes integral to
the sphere of subjective sentiment as well as to man's moral being. Just
as in the case of a 'schema' a corresponding appearance is provided for
the understanding, so also with Beauty as 'symbol of the morally
good,' an intuition is 'supplied' [eine sinnliche Anschauung (wird)
'unterlegt'] for 'a concept thinkable only by the reason.' "¹⁰ Ritter's
reference to the schema touches precisely on one of those concepts in
Kant where we can discern a crossing between a categorical analysis
focused on faculties of the mind and a tropological or proto-semiotic
one that is primarily oriented toward forms of linguistic combination.

The first *Critique* establishes that space and time represent the
necessary condition in the subject for all sensible experience, for intuition (*Anschauung*) in general, time being the form for inner sense and
space for outer sense or the apprehension of external reality. But the
argument of the Transcendental Aesthetic, like that of the subsequent
Analytic, which deals with the pure concepts of understanding or the
categories, remains all too abstract, unsuitable for application to experience and perception, until Kant introduces the Schematism. This
is the mediating principle, the "third thing," which allows the mind to
make connections between sensible experience, on the one hand, and
general sensible concepts or the a priori categories of the understanding, on the other. The function of the schemata appears to be to
safeguard the dimension of the conceptual as a generalizing and ordering function and yet also to make it accessible to specification, to
sense determination.

Kant distinguishes the schema of "sensible concepts" (a posteri-
ori concepts, such as general class names, e.g., dog) or mathematical
concepts from that of the "pure concepts of understanding" (the categories, such as reality and causality). In the first case, what is important is to set off the sensible concept from the image: "An *image* is a
product of the empirical faculty of reproductive imagination; the *schema* of sensible concepts, such as of figures in space, is a product and, as

9. Cf. *Critique of Judgment*, trans. J. H. Bernard (New York, 1951), # 42, p. 143. See
also Odo Marquard, "Kant und die Wende zur Ästhetik," *Zeitschrift für philosophische
Forschung* 16(1962): 231–43 and 363–74, and Paul de Man, "Phenomenality and Mate-
riality in Kant," in *Hermeneutics, Questions and Prospects*, ed. Gary Shapiro and Alan Sica
(Amherst, Mass., 1984), p. 137f.
10. *Historisches Wörterbuch der Philosophie*, vol. 1, ed. Joachim Ritter (Basel,
1971), s.v. "Ästhetik," col. 566, citing *The Critique of Judgment*, #59.

it were, a monogram, of pure a priori imagination, through which, and in accordance with which, images themselves first become possible. These images can be connected with the concept only by means of the schema to which they belong. In themselves they are never completely congruent with the concept" (B 181).[11] But in the second case (that involving the schema of the pure concepts of understanding) the image cannot apply at all, and another link to sensible experience is required. This is inner sense or time. "On the other hand, the schema of a pure concept of understanding can never be brought into any images whatsoever. It is simply the pure synthesis, determined by a rule of that unity, in accordance with concepts, to which the category gives expression. It is a transcendental product of imagination, a product which concerns the determination of inner sense in general according to conditions of its form (time)" (B 181).

This passage raises a host of questions. The first, perhaps, is in what sense can the operation of schemata be similar in the two cases, since it is not at all clear what the analogy between the image (which is related to sensible concepts) and inner sense or time (which is related to pure concepts of the understanding) consists of. Let us defer this point and turn first to the separation of image and schema that Kant underlines. The schemata are not to be thought of as a kind of adumbration or ghost of objects, for this notion, with its suggestion of a double or copy, would erode the concept by identifying it with a single instance. Kant defines the schema as an enabling agent, a "method" or "rule" or, as above, a "monogram." But this last term should not suggest a static element, akin to sign, for what is distinctive to the schema is its constructive and dynamic potential.[12] The image is necessarily fixed and singular. The schema is capable of generating a multitude of images. Taking our clue from a Greek sense of *schēmata* as gesture (in dance), we may think of it as a characteristic gestic practice of the mind which does not so much fix or stamp an image as delineate and articulate it. Kant writes, "We cannot think a line without drawing it in thought, or a circle without describing it" (B 154).[13]

11. A and B refer to the standard pagination of the first and second editions, respectively, of the *Critique of Pure Reason*. Quotations are from the Norman Kemp Smith translation (London, 1956).

12. As Cassirer remarks, "The schemata are indicative of the fact that our pure concepts are derived not from a principle of abstraction but from one of construction; they are not images or copies of things but representations of a fundamental synthetic operation." *Das Erkenntnisproblem in der Philosophie und Wissenschaft der neuern Zeit,* 2d ed. (1923; rpt. New Haven, 1971), 2:714.

13. Friedrich Kaulbach's commentary is pertinent to this point: "The schema is an

The mind's access to reality, to the sphere of outer sense, or space, involves a consecutive discriminating operation. Thus, we may say that the schema allows an exfoliation of the concept into possible instances.

This consideration, by indicating a temporal component in all schematization, reveals one kind of connection between the two cases, that is, between the sensible concepts and the pure concepts of understanding. For the latter there is no question but that Kant stressed the preeminence of time with respect to schematization: "We thus find that the schema of each category contains and makes capable of representation only a determination of time" (A 145). We may ask why this is so inasmuch as both space and time possess coordinate status as a priori forms of intuition. One type of answer stresses a kind of logical relation between the nature of time and the categories of the understanding. The directed, irreversible orientation of time represents a principle of order at the level of intuition which is akin to the order manifested in the categorical forms (e.g., magnitude, causality). Such an answer emphasizes the affinity of time with the principle of reason, and in some respects it is supported by Kant's derivation of schemata from each of the categories in the later part of the Schematism chapter (B 182–85).[14]

But a different kind of answer stresses instead the centrality of the imagination for the schematism, and within the imagination, the complex and pervasive operation of time.[15] This type of answer also finds support in the *Critique of Pure Reason,* notably in what Kant calls "the figurative synthesis of imagination" (B 151). All sense impressions must be reenacted in inner sense, by means of the productive imagination, in order to endow them with continuity. When Kant

---

enabling factor in the movement of description, which has the character of 'energeia' (Aristotle), or realization. Kant conceives it as a 'procedure' [Verfahren]. . . . The 'procedure' of the imagination, the 'schema,' is a self-generating and a self-shaping activity; it is by means of the schema that the delineating understanding, in the form of 'imagination,' etches its traces [durch das Schema schreibt die beschreibende Vernunft als 'Einbildungskraft' ihre Schriftzüge hin]: these are the product of the imagination working through the procedures and tracings of schematization [diese sind das Produkt der nach der schematischen Form ver-fahrenden und verzeichnenden Handlung der Einbildungskraft]." "Schema, Bild und Modell nach der Voraussetzungen des Kantischen Denkens," *Studium Generale* 8(1965): 465.

14. Cf. Nathan Rotenstreich, "Schematism and Freedom," *Revue internationale de philosophie* 28(1974): 464–74, esp. p. 470.

15. Heidegger's *Kant and the Problem of Metaphysics* (Bloomington, Ind., 1962; originally published in 1929), represents a major source for this direction. See esp. secs. 19–23.

writes, "*Imagination* is the faculty of representing in intuition an object that is *not itself present*" (B 151), he does not in the first instance refer to images based on memory or fantasy, but to the ordinary operation of perception which, in order to avoid an atomistic punctuality, must bring into play a temporal synthesis.

Our ability to perceive objects as determinate figures in space is, according to Kant, not only the result of a passive apprehension (the capacity of the intuition to be affected by an object); it also requires a coordinate, active participation of the mind's inner sense, time. One commentator has called this capacity one of "spontaneous geometrization."[16] It is the basis for every determination of objecthood. Perception, as has been noted, cannot hold onto or grasp an object unless the mind "draws" or "describes" it in a successive operation.

Now the priority that Kant accords to time in the Schematism is not to be taken as implying a devaluation or neglect of the function of space. For in the synthesis of imagination, neither can be properly conceived independently of the other. In fact, the very argument that has been made regarding the priority of time reveals a decisive limitation on it, namely, that it cannot be immediately *perceived*, that it is not accessible to outer sense except through the agency of space. Thus Kant writes:

> Time . . . cannot be a determination of outer appearances; it has to do neither with shape nor position, but with the relation of representations in our inner state. And just because this inner intuition yields no shape, we endeavour to make up for this want by analogies. We represent the time-sequence by a line progressing to infinity, in which the manifold constitutes a series of one dimension only; and we reason from the properties of this line to all the properties of time, with this one exception, that while the parts of the line are simultaneous the parts of time are always successive. (A33)

The exception that Kant refers to is, of course, decisive, and in this disparity—that a figure accessible to perception in a simultaneous act can never be adequate to the experience of succession—lies one of the thorniest but at the same time most fertile insights of the first *Critique*.

One recent commentator summarizes the issue as follows: "In the pure intuition of outer sense, exteriority presents itself as the equivalent of space; it is not the same for inner sense; succession is not

16. Joseph Moreau, "Le temps, la succession et le sens interne," *Kant-Studien*, Akten des 4. Internationalen Kant-Kongresses, Mainz, 1974, Special Issue 1974 (Berlin, 1974–75), 1:184–200; see pp. 193, 189.

perceived intuitively, it is only *apprehended* by inner sense in conjunction with the imagination. . . . In the time that is represented to the imagination by means of a line made up of points which correspond to instants, all the instants *conceived* as sucessive are *given* simultaneously; succession is symbolically represented."[17] Pure time, being equivalent to inner sense, can only be experienced and is not susceptible to representation in a pictorial sense. Insofar as time is to be manifested in outer sense, it must be represented "symbolically" (Kant wrote, "by analogies").

It is not easy to conceive a figure or model for the mediating function of the schematism as Kant develops it here. And this difficulty, it should be noted, is symptomatic of the point at issue, of what the schematism itself designates, namely, the possibility of constructing a figurative model for concepts to which no intuitive apprehension corresponds. Where there is no "correspondent" or natural model, one must be found, drawn from elsewhere, introduced by way of transposition or metaphorization (in its etymological sense). This consequence becomes explicit in that endlessly fascinating and problematic #59 of the *Critique of Judgment*. Here schematization is developed in relation to a modeling or figurative dimension inherent in language, a representational force (and the key term Kant uses, *hypotyposis*, is rendered by him as *Darstellung*, "sensible illustration") requisite for the articulation of certain concepts.

> Our language is full of indirect presentations of this sort, in which the expression does not contain the proper schema for the concept, but merely a symbol for reflection. Thus the words *ground* (support, basis), *to depend* (to be held up from above), to *flow* from something (instead of, to follow), *substance* (as Locke expresses it, the support of accidents), and countless others are not schematical but symbolical hypotyposes and expressions for concepts, not by means of a direct intuition, but only by analogy with it, i.e., by the transference of reflection upon an object of intuition to a quite different concept to which perhaps an intuition can never directly correspond.[18]

Kant refers here to a distinction made earlier in that section between schematical and symbolical hypotyposes or modes of presentation, but in doing so he uses "schematical" more narrowly than he had in the *Critique of Pure Reason*, where the schema applied also to what here, in the *Critique of Judgment*, is designated as symbolical. The

17. Ibid., p. 187.
18. *Critique of Judgment*, p. 198.

very distinction between schemata and symbols represents, as Paul de
Man has shown, an effort at "controlling the tropes," at distinguish-
ing between those that are rational and appropriate (*angemessen*),
such as geometrical figures, and those that "are not reliable from an
epistemological point of view," such as those indirect presentations in
language that Kant cites. De Man's underlying argument is that any
such effort to suppress an epistemological problematic by means of
tropological categorization is bound to fail.[19]

If we revert now to the argument of the *Critique of Pure Reason*
we can better appreciate the problematic status of the schematism,
what led Kant himself to call it "an art concealed in the depths of the
human soul, whose real modes of activity nature is hardly likely ever
to allow us to discover, and to have open to our gaze" (B 180). For
what the schematism is required to elucidate is nothing less than the
sensible mainfestation of what, by definition, is inaccessible to sensible intuition, namely, time taken together with space as "the pure
forms of all sensible intuition" (A 39). As I sought to demonstrate
above, the schematism is called upon to account for the imbrication of
time and space, for their correlative (though by no means symmetrical) function in enabling the dimension of intuitive presentations. But it can do so only by virtue of its association with the
imagination, thus with a constructive principle that necessarily com-
promises the primacy and immediacy of intuitive experience. As John
Carlos Rowe writes,

> Kant's schematism is the "origin" of representation, and as such it ar-
> gues against the possibility of any pure "presentation" of an object; the
> only pure objects in this sense of originary presence would have to be
> time and space themselves, which are defined by their nonempirical
> characters. Kant's medium of representation, this schematism that is the
> imaginative capability of the mind itself (and thus the basis for "aesthet-
> ics" as both perception and artistic theory), is precisely that crossing of
> time and space that is the mark of language, the defining characteristic of
> a differential system of signs.[20]

In summary, Kant sought, by means of the schematism, to justify
an analogical or metaphorical function (what he terms symbolical in
the *Critique of Judgment*) in terms of a necessary (or transcendental)

19. "The Epistemology of Metaphor, " pp. 26–29.
20. "James's Rhetoric of the Eye: Re-Marking the Impression," p. 250. In revising
this chapter from an earlier version I have profited from Professor Rowe's discussion of Kant
in this article.

condition of the mind. But in doing so he slighted a contingent and adaptive dimension of the schema, what marks it as "a reflective modulation of an act of self-transcendence."[21]

II

We are in a position now to appreciate why Ernst Cassirer, while fully cognizant of the priority of time in schematism, was led to investigate spatial determination in language as the primary and most immediate type of schematic representation available to human expression. "In designating temporal determinations and relations," he writes, "language is at first wholly dependent on the mediation of space; and from this involvement with the spatial world there results also a bond with the world of things, which are conceived as existing in space. Thus the form of time is here expressed only insofar as it can in some way be based on spatial and objective determinations" (3, 163).[22]

Cassirer took Kant's remark that the human intellect is an intellect "in need of images" ("ein der Bilder bedürftiger Verstand") and added, "we should rather say that it is in need of symbols."[23] We see here that Cassirer seeks to push the Kantian clue from an epistemological to a cultural level. In investigating language as the preeminent mode of man's symbolizing activity, Cassirer saw that the pervasiveness of spatial terms in language is not to be explained by analogy to empirical space but represents a highly differentiated and multilayered modus of apprehension and projection, an insight that derives from the Kantian analysis of the disparity between time and space with regard to perception and representation. "What we call 'space,' " Cassirer writes, "is not an independent object that is mediately represented to us, that presents itself and is to be recognized by certain signs; rather, it is a particular mode, a peculiar schematism of representation itself. And through this schematism, consciousness gains the possibility of a new orientation—it gains a specific direction of spiritual sight which transforms all the configurations of objective, objectivized reality" (3, 149).

In stressing the spatiality of the schematism, Cassirer recognized that the spatiality of language is not an ultimate but a derivative

21. Angel Medina, "Discussion: On Narrative and Narratives," *New Literary History* 11(1979–80): 574.

22. References to *The Philosophy of Symbolic Forms*, 3 vols. (New Haven, 1955) are given in the text.

23. *An Essay on Man* (New Haven, 1944), p. 57. Kant's phrase is in the *Critique of Judgment*, # 77.

feature, one that refers back to a nonpictorial function of the mind. The schemata are not to be identified with a spatial ground or a reservoir of Platonic forms. Rather, schematization is an activity of the imagination that forms and dissolves images endlessly, endowing concepts and abstract relations with a kind of corporeality, "figuring" them in relation to the perceived world.[24] In *The Philosophy of Symbolic Forms*, Cassirer attempted to work out mediating structures for the fundamental expressive forms in culture. Whereas for Heidegger Kant's synthesis through imagination represents a preeminent instance of the temporal and finite constitution of human existence, for Cassirer it provides the means for tracing the expressive and representational faculties to their sources in human institutions. Kant did not go much beyond locating the schemata as mediating elements logically required by the heterogeneity of the sensible and the intelligible; Cassirer sought to specify and systematize their role within cultural, and particularly linguistic, forms.

Cassirer's linguistically oriented revision of the Kantian schematism represents a link to more recent views regarding the issue of the spatiality of language, notably Roman Jakobson's influential proposals on the metaphoric and metonymic poles in language. This opposition is, of course, part of a more comprehensive theory of the binary axes in langauge. While the theory in itself is not original with Jakobson, his merit lies in his applying it to a great variety of language uses, for example, to literature and to aphasia.[25] The two axes are identified as the syntagmatic and the paradigmatic and can be characterized through oppositions like the following:

Paradigmatic	Syntagmatic
selection	combination
substitution	contextual integration
similarity	contiguity
encoding	decoding
metaphor	metonymy

24. In the recent work of Jurij Lotman we find a confirmation of this approach on a purely formalist level: "The special character of visual perception inherent to man is such that in the majority of cases visible spatial objects serve as the denotata of verbal signs; as a result verbal models are perceived in a particular way. . . . Thus the structure of the space of a text becomes a model of the structure of the space of the universe, and the internal syntagmatics of the elements within a text becomes the language of spatial modeling." *The Structure of the Artistic Text*, p. 217.

25. Elmar Holenstein has shown some of its sources—in the works of the Polish linguist Kruszewski, of Saussure, and others. See *Jakobson ou le structuralisme phénoménologique* (Paris, 1974), pp. 164ff.

Many of us are familiar with the axiom that Jakobson proposed in "Linguistics and Poetics": "The poetic function projects the principle of equivalence from the axis of selection into the axis of combination." Equivalence is normally understood as a paradigmatic feature exemplified by similarity/dissimilarity or synonymity/antonymity, and it operates primarily along the axis of selection, that aspect of the poetic process that connects a concept with an image, a tenor with a vehicle, and so forth. On the axis of combination the principle normally at work is not equivalence but contiguity, as exemplified by syntactic rules that predetermine the association and sequence of terms. Now the poetic function, Jakobson argues, requires that this axis of combination cannot be preeminently organized according to principles of syntax, logic, or temporal sequence, but must also be constituted by the other—the paradigmatic or selective—axis.

This definition of the poetic function may be taken as an illustration, though not as a rule, for the operation of the biaxial theory. More relevant to the subject of this discussion is the application that Jakobson offered in an earlier essay which contrasts the style of Pasternak with that of Mayakovsky.[26] Pasternak's imagination, he argues, is characterized by a penchant for metonymy in place of metaphor, a feature that can be illustrated even in his lyric poems, where one would normally expect metaphor to be predominant. In these poems the subjective hero is hard to locate, Jakobson argues: "Instead of the hero we are shown a series of objectified situations together with a selection of objects, animate as well as inanimate, that surround him. . . . What is typically heroic, the hero's deeds, eludes our gaze; in place of action we are shown a topography."

In a later essay, "Two Aspects of Language and Two Types of Aphasic Disturbances," Jakobson utilizes the metaphoric-metonymic opposition to specify a stylistic feature of nineteenth-century realism:

> The primacy of the metaphoric process in the literary schools of romanticism and symbolism has been repeatedly acknowledged, but it is still insufficiently realized that it is the predominance of metonymy which underlies and actually predetermines the so-called 'realistic' trend, which belongs to an intermediary stage between the decline of romanticism and the rise of symbolism and is opposed to both. Following the path of contiguous relationships, the realist author metonymically digresses from the plot to the atmosphere and from the characters to the setting in space and time.[27]

26. "Randbemerkungen," see n. 5 above. The following quotation is on p. 369.
27. *Selected Writings II*, p. 255.

Jakobson will use such stylistic contrasts (between writers, between periods) to illustrate certain possibilities inherent in the biaxial model. "A competition between both devices, metonymic and metaphoric, is manifest in any symbolic process, be it intrapersonal or social," Jakobson writes near the end of "Two Aspects of Language." Jakobson's work does not provide any systematic analysis of literary devices within the structure of language. Yet he has refined our understanding of representation and figurative language in literature by providing a more variable semiotic basis for the concept of spatiality as derived from Kant and Cassirer.

One interpreter of Jakobson, Elmar Holenstein, maintains that while oppositions along the two axes can be fruitful in clarifying certain issues, the axes themselves are not to be taken as ultimate contrastive principles.[28] Thus, for example, the syntagmatic and paradigmatic opposition will function differently when understood in a formalist as opposed to a phenomenological sense. Whereas similarity can be understood as constitutive for paradigmatic selection in both senses, contiguity is a primary feature of syntagmatic combination only when taken formally or descriptively, but not in motivational or phenomenological terms. Here other principles of association than proximity or sequence are at work. One consequence of this discrepancy is to put into question the symmetrical status of metaphor and metonymy that the biaxial model suggests. The kind of interpenetration of the figures that will be developed in the following section derives, as we shall see, from a more fundamental signifying principle than the structure of the tropes themselves can reveal.

III

I should like now to undertake an application of the Kantian model to a literary text, and for this another essay by Gérard Genette offers a useful point of departure. In "Métonymie chez Proust" Genette offers a detailed and original application of Jakobson's theory.[29] This study

28. In *Linguistik Semiotik Hermeneutik* (Frankfurt am Main, 1976), pp. 76–113. See esp. pp. 88f. and 100f.
29. In *Figures III* (Paris, 1972), pp. 41–63. Subsequent citations are given in the text. This volume also contains a lengthy theoretical study of narrative form, *Discours du récit*, based primarily on *À la recherche du temps perdu* (in English: *Narrative Discourse: An Essay in Method*, trans. Jane E. Lewin [Ithaca, N.Y., 1980]). What is noteworthy is that this systematic analysis of narrative functions finds no place for the issue of description, surely one of the principal components of Proust's narrative art. It is symptomatic of the structuralist enterprise, which Genette so well represents, that this issue—which could hardly be omitted altogether in a study of Proust—is dealt with in the context of the essay on metonymy but is not incorporated into the more general theory of narrative.

does not merely illustrate a type of reciprocal interplay between metaphor and metonymy but argues for a fundamental revaluation of the nature of metaphor in Proust's novel. In it, Genette argues, the authentification of metaphor occurs by means not primarily of analogy or resemblance (the basis of metaphoric relations in the traditional sense) but rather of spatio-temporal—but particularly spatial—contiguity. Thus, in an instance where the image of two tapered fish is applied to church steeples that Marcel thinks of, the narrator takes pains to justify the figure by reference to the season, the place, the mood in which Marcel finds himself at that point in the narrative. Genette remarks that "it is the idea of bathing, the proximity (spatial, temporal, psychological) of the ocean which orients the metaphoric imagination toward an aquatic interpretation" (p. 43). What is central to Proust's figurative language, in this view, is not so much the occasion that initially releases a metaphor (what Genette calls "le *détonateur* analogique" [p. 56]), but the manner in which the image is elaborated and extended through association with the speaker's context or locale (what Proust would term "l'irradiation" of the image [p. 56]).

Genette illustrates how prevalent in Proust is "la contagion du site" (p. 51) or what he calls (adapting a cinematic term) "métaphores diégétiques" (p. 48), that is, metaphors that derive from the situation of the narrator (thus diegetic) or, more generally, from the spatio-temporal context of the narrative. Thus, various steeples or church spires are likened now to ears of wheat, then to a large loaf of "holy bread," then again to two ancient, tapered fish. This is to be explained, according to Genette, not so much according to a principle of selection based upon the observable features of the object, but rather according to one of combination and contiguity that aligns the vehicle to the context of the tenor or of the observer.

Genette has undoubtedly isolated a significant characteristic of Proust's descriptive technique, namely, its tendency to "suppress all demarcation" (p. 52) between a setting and the images to which it gives rise or, to echo Jakobson's definition of the poetic function, its tendency to project patterns of analogy onto relations of contiguity (p. 53). But Genette weakens or abandons a number of distinctions basic to Jakobson's position. First of all, Genette's idea of metonymy screens out a large range of its functions as a trope and narrows it to the operation of spatial contiguity at the semantic level. Then, metonymy as he understands it is meant to naturalize metaphor, to tame its potential alterity. The differential between the tenor and the vehicle is minimized by referring the vehicle back to a stratum anterior to the tenor, and this shift has the effect of normalizing any disjunction or tension between tenor and vehicle. Genette's analysis stresses a unifying principle in the novel, a principle realized through the labor of memory. But in the process it minimizes what Georges Poulet has called the "qualitative" dimension, a principle of singularity and heterogeneity that is no less significant for Proust's representational practice.[30]

Before attempting a more specific critique of Genette's argument I want to outline the conception of Proust's work that serves as context for my discussion. The *Recherche* is a work whose narrative subject matter converges with the enabling act for the work itself. As has long been recognized, it is a work essentially about its own formation. But here an important distinction needs to be made. The narrative subject matter, the sequence of actions and episodes oriented toward a determinate goal, is, in the most general sense, the emergence of the writer's vocation. However, there is another, underlying thematic, which may be considered the condition of the former. It is paradigmatic rather than syntagmatic, that is, its elaboration involves a logical or formal ordering rather than a progressive, sequential disclosure. At this level the novel testifies to the formation of consciousness and personal identity. This formation is twofold: it is based, first of all, on perceptual experience (impressions) and its sedimentation in consciousness (memory) and then on the function of language, notably proper names, as a source of cultural consciousness.

The *Recherche,* then, traces a double genesis, an empirical one of the subject as writer, and an ontological one of consciousness as the seat of perception and language. But while the former genesis, the narrative or plot level, can only emerge gradually in consequence of determinate acts, the latter represents the condition of the writing from the start. It cannot await the realization of the narrator's vocation. At the same time the narrator's place cannot be supplied by means of an omniscient consciousness, by "Proust" as distinct from "Marcel." Thus, the structure of the work will be not simply cumulative but proleptic and progressive. Consciousness must be shown as fully operative from the start, even while the narrative re-

30. "[T]he world of Proust . . . affirms the qualitative and the heterogeneous. As soon as a thing manifests itself in its own quality, in its 'essence,' it reveals itself as different from all other things (and their essences). From it to the others there is no passage." Georges Poulet, *Proustian Space,* trans. Elliott Coleman (Baltimore, 1977), p. 40.

counts the awakening and progressive formation of the subject as writer.

This sketch alerts us to the centrality of the impression in the *Recherche,* the impression not as a punctual, evanescent fragment of experience but as the key to the kind of investigation (*recherche*) that is at the heart of Proust's method. Proust himself stressed the significance of this notion more than once:

> Seule l'impression, si chétive qu'en semble la matière, si insaisissable la trace, est un critérium de vérité, et à cause de cela mérite seule d'être appréhendée par l'esprit, car elle est seule capable, s'il sait en dégager cette vérité, de l'amener à une plus grande perfection et de lui donner une pure joie. L'impression est pour l'écrivain ce qu'est l'expérimentation pour le savant, avec cette différence que chez le savant le travail de l'intelligence précède et chez l'écrivain vient après. (3, 880)[31]

Only recently has criticism demonstrated how consistently Proust was able to effect a conversion of the impression into such a medium of "experimentation," into, in effect, the primary constructive instrument of his fictive world.

Raymonde Debray-Genette has argued that the category of description in a restricted sense is inapplicable to the *Recherche.* Narrative and descriptive functions, she writes, "engender each other; it is as if they were metabolic in relation to one another."[32] Whereas description in the realist tradition puts into play certain semantic classes as determined by requirements of the narrative, thus making a paradigmatic structure subject to constraints of the syntagmatic, in Proust the underlying subject matter may be conceived as a discovery of the appropriate paradigmatic classes. The narrative strand then becomes "nothing but an efflorescence, a ramification" of the paradigmatic order. Thus a given image or impression (such as that of the hawthorns that Debray-Genette analyzes in detail) is the nexus of a series of transformations which generate the primary narrative elements. Debray-Genette is able to demonstrate, for example, how the

---

31. In English: "Only the impression, however trivial its material may seem to be, however faint its traces, is a criterion of truth and deserves for that reason to be apprehended by the mind, for the mind, if it succeeds in extracting this truth, can by the impression and by nothing else be brought to a state of greater perfection and given a pure joy. The impression is for the writer what experiment is for the scientist, with the difference that in the scientist the work of the intelligence precedes the experiment and in the writer it comes after the impression." *Remembrance of Things Past,* 3:914.

32. "Thème, figure, épisode: genèse des aubépines," in *Recherche de Proust* (Paris, 1980), pp. 105–41. This quotation is on p. 118, the following one is on p. 107.

inversion of tenor and vehicle and the corresponding shift of metaphor into metonymy assume a proleptic function and determine basic
elements of the narrative. It is in this sense that the image in Proust
takes on an instrumental or schematizing function. The tropological,
we may say, is repeatedly deflected from a principle of classification to
an instrumentality of representation.

We may now look more closely at a passage that Genette singles
out and in which he notes (but without elaborating the point) a
significant "proximity" between the literal and the figurative. It is
found in *Combray*. The narrator, seeking to extract from the landscape in the vicinity of Roussainville an intense, sensuous realization,
envisions a peasant girl as the focal point of his desire: "Mais errer
ainsi dans les bois de Roussainville sans une paysanne à embrasser,
c'était ne pas connaître de ces bois le trésor caché, la beauté profonde"
(1, 157). The girl is imagined, "criblée de feuillages, . . . comme une
plante locale d'une espèce plus élevée seulement que les autres et dont
la structure permet d'approcher de plus près qu'en elles la saveur
profonde du pays" (1, 157).[33] For Genette the passage is significant
because the evocation of this girl is to be understood as a kind of
intratextual narrative of the formation of an image. "One surprises
here, in a certain manner," he writes, "the analogy at its nascence, at
the moment when it has yet barely disengaged itself from the proximity to the physical which gives it life" (p. 46). Genette wants us to
understand the fictive narrator's explicit wish to evoke a girl in the
forest as homogeneous with the formation of an image for the forest.
The association of the girl with the locale would thus serve as another
illustration of the link between images and a continuous ground or
context in the recollections of the narrator. "Certainly no other text,"
Genette concludes, "better illustrates *that fetishism of place* which the
narrator will subsequently denounce as a youthful error and an 'illusion to be purged,' but which is still, without doubt, a fundamental
condition of the Proustian sensibility" (p. 46).

In speaking of a "fetishism of place" Genette accepts at face value
a kind of mystification that is put into question later in the *Temps
retrouvé* (as he himself notes) and in this very passage. This episode

33. In English: "But to wander thus among the woods of Roussainville without a
peasant-girl to embrace was to see those woods and yet know nothing of their secret
treasure, their deep-hidden beauty. That girl whom I invariably saw dappled with the
shadows of their leaves was to me herself a plant of local growth, merely of a higher species
than the rest, and one whose structure would enable me to get closer than through them to
the intimate savour of the country." *Remembrance of Things Past*, 1:171f.

represents not so much a formative moment in the metaphoric process as a more tenuous characteristic that might be called, in Paul de Man's phrase, a "figure of the unreadability of figures."[34] Such "unreadability" may be glossed in two ways, one intertextual or historical, the other structural.

First, the passage may be viewed in the context of a Romantic topos of the *genius loci*. In its Romantic version, spirit of place—as studied most suggestively by Geoffrey Hartman[35]—represents an indissoluble component, a source both genetic and authoritative, of the poet's vision, of his capacity to envisage a scene and to communicate the specific potency of the place depicted. Hartman reminds us that the relation of eighteenth-century descriptive poetry to the lyric forms of Romanticism can be viewed as a shift from indication or conventional invocation to a new type of participating evocation. The relation of speaker or poet to the object of description changes radically, and this leads to the high Romantic ideal of "the union of poetical genius with English spirit of place." Embedded in this Romantic mode are a number of ambiguities which will prove richly suggestive subsequently for both poetry and prose. One of the most significant involves the nature of the *genius loci*. Is it a spirit immanent in the spot or a divine spirit manifesting itself through the spot? This alternative will give rise both to ambiguities of valorization (the spirit as benign or demonic agent) and to an indeterminancy regarding the tropes that are put into play, e.g., personification, prosopopeia. In certain Romantic works the locale is singled out not because of its supernatural associations (which would be characteristic of earlier symbolic systems) but as itself the source of a preternatural potency, resistant to further elucidation. The spot, relic of some decisive but eternally shrouded event, persists as pure memorial or sign. *What* it might say has ceased to be available, and the curiosity aroused serves only to inaugurate a potentially endless process of decipherment or interpretation. But *that* it is somehow empowered to speak, *that* it preserves a kind of message or truth, remains as the preeminent characteristic of such a spot.

In the Roussainville passage what we find in not so much an effort to restore a spirit to the place as a testing of the very mechanism of

---

34. A term Paul de Man applies to another Proustian image in *Allegories of Reading* (New Haven, 1980), p. 61.
35. "Wordsworth, Inscriptions, and Romantic Nature Poetry" and "Romantic Poetry and the Genius Loci," both in *Beyond Formalism* (New Haven, 1970). The following quotation is on p. 329.

personification and image formation. As topos it could be termed an instance of *genius loci absconditus*. Near the end of the passage the narrator parodies the tone of a Petrarchan lover whose devotion is both interminable and futile:

> En vain, tenant l'étendue dans le champ de ma vision, je la drainais de mes regards qui eussent voulu en ramener une femme. . . . Je fixais indéfiniment le tronc d'un arbre lointain, de derrière lequel elle allait surgir et venir à moi; l'horizon scruté restait désert, la nuit tombait, c'était sans espoir que mon attention s'attachait, comme pour aspirer les créatures qu'ils pouvaient recéler, à ce sol stérile, à cette terre épuisée."
> (1, 158)[36]

This is not merely an instance of a negative evocation (which might still be the case with the passage cited above: "Mais errer ainsi dans les bois de Roussainville sans une paysanne à embrasser"). The presence-absence of the girl could in no sense point to a restoration of the spirit of place through the agency of memory and imagination. Rather, the passage renders the nonappearance of the Roussainville girl in a manner that stresses an undecidability between personification and image.

In addition to this kind of intertextual approach a more strictly formal consideration is in order. If we follow Genette, the Roussainville girl would serve essentially to endow the locale with a more intense sensuous presence; she would be understood as an image that is both metaphoric (the narrator's attraction to the locale being likened to his desire for such a girl) and metonymic (the girl herself being a natural product of that soil). But it is not a similarity or identity between the locale and the girl that is established here. Rather, the passage poses the possibility of two mutually exclusive readings, one oriented toward the immediate, sensuous apprehension of a specific reality (a place, a girl), the other toward the abstracting, de-realizing effects that are being employed.[37] What is at work, then, is not so much an alternation between metaphoric and metonymic figures as between different signifying systems. Neither the girl nor the woods is accorded precedence, but together they refer to an unfigured other

---

36. In English: "In vain I compressed the whole landscape into my field of vision, draining it with an exhaustive gaze which sought to extract from it a female creature. . . . I would stare interminably at the trunk of a distant tree, from behind which she would emerge and come to me; I scanned the horizon, which remained as deserted as before; night was falling; it was without hope now that I concentrated my attention, as though to draw up from it the creatures which it must conceal, upon that sterile soil, that stale, exhausted earth." *Remembrance of Things Past*, 1:172f.

37. Cf. Paul de Man, *Allegories of Reading*, p. 72.

that impinges on the narrator's consciousness and cannot be made to appear. Personification is pushed to a limit here that cannot be accounted for either in terms of mimetic representation or of a system of tropes.

That the narrator is perfectly cognizant of this sort of aporia is borne out throughout the section. In the very passage where he most directly affirms a faith in the inimitable specificity of a locale he also exposes the inescapable junction of desire and trope:

> C'est qu'aussi—comme il arrive dans ces moments de rêverie au milieu de la nature où, l'action de l'habitude étant suspendue, nos notions abstraites des choses mises de côté, nous croyons d'une foi profonde à l'originalité, à la vie individuelle du lieu où nous nous trouvons—la passante qu'appelait mon désir me semblait être non un exemplaire quelconque de ce type général: la femme, mais un produit nécessaire et naturel de ce sol. (1, 156f.)[38]

The conclusion of the section, with its reference to the stereotypes of popular fiction, is still more explicit:

> Ils [the narrator's desires] n'avaient plus de lien avec la nature, avec la réalité qui dès lors perdait tout charme et toute signification et n'était plus à ma vie qu'un cadre conventionnel, comme l'est à la fiction d'un roman le wagon sur la banquette duquel le voyageur le lit pour tuer le temps. (1, 159)[39]

Thus the text itself, in articulating the interplay of the phenomenal and the linguistic, the unavoidable substitutability of a topos as a figure of speech for a topos as an imagined place, provides the basis for a deconstructive reading.

IV

Let me return to the original problem: how to account for a spatial terminology in which a phenomenal and a linguistic sense are mixed,

---

38. In English: "Moreover—just as in moments of musing contemplation of nature, the normal actions of the mind being suspended, and our abstract ideas of things set aside, we believe with the profoundest faith in the originality, in the individual existence of the place in which we may happen to be—the passing figure which my desire evoked seemed to be not any specimen of the genus 'woman,' but a necessary and natural product of this particular soil." *Remembrance of Things Past*, 1:171.

39. In English: "They [the narrator's desires] no longer had any connection with nature, with the world of real things, which from then onwards lost all its charm and significance, and meant no more to my life than a purely conventional framework, what the railway carriage on the bench of which a traveller is reading to pass the time is to the fictional events of his novel." Ibid., 173.

perhaps confused. I have already referred to Derrida's idea of a blind spot embedded in the Western philosophical (or "metaphysical") tradition, an element that cannot be mastered by way of a purer, non-metaphoric discourse and yet must not be evaded or suppressed either. Kant's notion of schematism in the *Critique of Pure Reason,* when taken in conjunction with his discussion of hypotyposis in the *Critique of Judgment,* addresses this issue in a provocative, if inconclusive, way. Schematization is not itself either spatial or temporal but identifies a capacity of the mind in which logical and categorical relations can be specified in terms of the intuition or sensible faculties. Kant referred to it as a process of sense endowment, or *Versinnlichung,*[40] a term that suggests both the richness and the insufficiency of the mind's imaging capacity. The presence of this issue in both the first and the third *Critiques* is, in a sense, emblematic of the problematic status of aesthetics in modern philosophy, namely, as a theory based on an act of the reflective judgment (in Kant's sense) that is at the same time called upon to provide an epistemological foundation for phenomenal experience.

Jakobson's biaxial theory, with multiple operators that allow for analogies and conversions along different signifying chains, might be seen as the basis for a semiotic version of the schematism. While Genette's demonstration of metonymy as a pervasive mode of metaphorization in Proust could appear to be a confirmation of Jakobson's theory, it takes the diverse features that Jakobson ranked on the syntagmatic axis and reduces them to a principle of spatial contiguity. Genette thus drastically alters Jakobson's sense of the metaphoric-metonymic poles as flexible operators that function at phenomenal and linguistic levels. By subsuming metaphor into metonymy in Proust, Genette reduces the apparently luxuriant and involuted structure of Proustian imagery to certain "effets de contagion" (p. 58). His concentration on diegesis, on the narrative process as the focus for all the effects of figuration, is certainly a simplifying explanation but possibly also a reductive one.[41]

40. *Critique of Judgment,* # 59. Here the term is used appositively for hypotyposis, but what is being discussed is a species of schematization.

41. Paul de Man has raised similar objections to the ultraformalism of some recent French critics, including Genette: "One of the most striking chracteristics of literary semiology as it is practiced today, in France and elsewhere, is the use of grammatical (especially syntactical) structures conjointly with rhetorical structures, without apparent awareness of a possible discrepancy between them. In their literary analyses, Barthes, Genette, Todorov, Greimas, and their disciples all simplify and regress from Jakobson in letting grammar and rhetoric function in perfect continuity, and in passing from grammatical to rhetorical

As I have tried to demonstrate, the issue that Genette addresses in Proust's text forces us to look beyond a rhetorical dimension to one in which language is poised between a latent model and an emergent image. It is here that the notion of schematism operates. To expose this type of reflexivity in the text does not necessarily mean that the figurative language is made inoperative. But, once disclosed, this feature directs us to a new level of analysis. Genette is correct to see that Proust is involved, as, in another sense, the reader will be, in a "contagion du site." But this site can no more be reduced to a rhetorical space than to a phenomenal one. The "spatiality" in question needs to be analyzed, as I have argued, in terms of an "imaging" or schematizing function that is distinct from the system of figures. I have tried to explore it in terms of the Kantian "third thing," the schema. At the same time I have tried to move that notion beyond its place among the faculties of the mind that Kant assigned to it, to de-ontologize and in a sense semioticize it, and thus make it available for a clarification of the singular status of spatiality in the novel.

---

structures without difficulty or interruption." "Semiology and Rhetoric," in *Allegories of Reading*, p. 6.

3 Character and Person: On the Presentation of Self in the Novel

I

While my discussion in Chapters 1 and 2 dealt with the concept of the world of the novel largely in terms of setting, the diegetic context of the action and the characterization, I want now to investigate world in relation to the idea of character. I will be exploring forms of consciousness within a specific tradition of the novel, that of the later eighteenth and early nineteenth centuries, as instances of a commerce or interchange between self and world. Also it seems to me that the representation of character in this period undergoes an important change that is bound up with a new kind of participation by readers in the affective and moral sensibilities of the characters. My approach here will be essentially phenomenological, but it also has sociological implications since it attempts to define features of a life-world to which this new form of the novel has itself contributed.

My intention may be clarified by a principle that Maurice Natanson called "methodological solipsism." Natanson distinguishes between "metaphysical solipsism," "the traditional claim that the individual is the sole reality," and "methodological solipsism," "the less familiar message that the proper method of philosophy calls for the examination of all experience from an egological perspective." He elaborates as follows:

> Methodological solipsism may be understood as a way of providing an account of the history of consciousness in the formation of sociality. . . . It is not free to invent the world; it is responsible for reflecting what the constitutive history of the world demands if there is to be a coherent, let alone cohesive, order to sociality. If metaphysical solipsism concerns

itself with the reality of the self, its methodological counterpart investi-
gates the essential (eidetic) character of the mundane. Sociality becomes
a problem of the *Lebenswelt*. . . . The novel of character may perhaps be
reconsidered in terms of an intentional theory of consciousness. . . . The
everyday world made possible by the typifying activity of consciousness
may be the matrix within which character is generated.[1]

What Natanson suggests is that character be considered not as an
isolated, substantial entity (its "substance" justified in psychological
or ideological terms), nor as a mere function of the action of narrative
(as pure agent or actant), but as the enabling condition for the order of
sociality. By "sociality" I believe he means the kind of world structure
that has been operative in the novel since at least the eighteenth century, that is to say, *world* understood not as an aggregate of objects,
places, and circumstances, but as the correlate of a structure of consciousness; Husserl's notion of *Lebenswelt* is germane here. Such a
structure can never be reduced to the viewpoint of one or more of the
characters or of the narrative voice or persona of a novel. How it may
be thematized is precisely the issue I am exploring. To seek "the
typifying activity of consciousness" at the level of character means that
we must look for a centrifugal tendency in character—an exploratory,
percipient impulse oriented toward, and thus constitutive of, its appropriate world.

The attack upon the concept of character so vigorously pursued
by structuralist criticism had already been articulated in its main
outlines by Natalie Sarraute as early as 1956. "As regards the character," she wrote in *The Age of Suspicion,*

> [the reader] realizes it is nothing other than a crude label which he
> himself makes use of, without real conviction and by way of conve-
> nience, for the purpose of orienting, very approximately, his own behav-
> ior. . . . He has watched the watertight partitions that used to separate
> the characters from one another give way, and the hero become an
> arbitrary limitation, a conventional figure cut from the common woof
> that each of us contains in its entirety, and which captures and holds
> within its meshes the entire universe. . . . [T]he psychological ele-
> ment . . . is beginning to free itself imperceptibly from the object of
> which it was an integral part. It is tending to become self-sufficient and,
> in so far as possible, to do without exterior support.[2]

1. "Solipsism and Sociality," in *New Literary History* 5(1973–1974): 237–44. This
passage is on p. 241; the following one is on pp. 243ff.
2. Trans. Maria Jolas (New York, 1963), pp. 61, 62, 68.

The exposure of the seductive power of character has been, of course, a theme not only of Sarraute's critical writings but also of her fiction, and of the work of the *nouveaux romanciers* subsequently.

The structuralists, taking their lead from Vladimir Propp's *Morphology of the Folktale,* focused their work initially on the more schematic forms of narrative (thus fairy tales for Propp, Boccaccio's novellas for Todorov, the American detective story for Barthes)[3] and sought to limit the concept of character strictly to that of an agent or participant with respect to the action. The aim of structuralist analysis, according to Barthes, is to define "character [*le personnage*] not as a 'being' [*un 'être'*], but as a 'participant.' . . . The point is to define character through its participation in spheres of action, these spheres being few in number, typical, classable."

There is some truth in Barthes's view that the concept of character, in the sense of a unique, individualized personality, represents "a purely historical form, one that is restricted to certain genres (which, to be sure, are the best known to us)." And certainly the structuralists' efforts to demystify the concept have proved salutary in exposing some of the stereotypes with which traditional criticism of the novel has operated. But if the notion of the existential autonomy and psychological fullness of characters in the novel represents an illusion, it is one that has not been simply manufactured by critics but that has been inextricably bound up with the evolution of the genre since the eighteenth century. In the realist-psychological novel the function of character cannot be restricted to denoting certain types of agents for certain typical acts. Such a limitation ignores, for one thing, how character has served within this tradition to elicit the interest and participation of the reader in ways that mark a departure in narrative art. As Ian Watt and others have shown, the novel of the earlier eighteenth century is both an indicator of and a stimulus for a new form of consciousness, and one of its principal effects has been to awaken and sustain an identification by the reader with the figures and the world of the novel. The eighteenth-century novelists fashioned a readership capable of entering imaginatively into another personality, the fictive character, in ways not available in earlier narrative forms. This dimension may well represent an ideological component of literature, as many of the structuralists claim, but it is nonetheless

3. Propp's work appeared originally in Russian in 1928 and in English in 1958 (Bloomington, Ind.); Todorov, *Grammaire du "Decameron"* (The Hague, 1969); Barthes, "Introduction à l'analyse structurale des récits," *Communications* 8(1966): 1–27; the following quote is on p. 16.

an operative function that needs to be accounted for as part of the strategy of the text.

In the chapter "Private Experience and the Novel" in *The Rise of the Novel*, Ian Watt has drawn a convincing picture of the social conditions that nurtured Samuel Richardson's type of fiction, which focused on personal relations with unprecedented intensity, both assuming and reinforcing the new sense of privacy. Surveying the social history of the seventeenth century, Watt relates the Puritan habit of self-examination to the growth of individualism. He notes certain consequences of the process of urbanization, such as the facilitation of correspondence and the increased possibilities for privacy and seclusion in one's home. The practice of reading seems to enter a new phase. The easy availability and unquestioned authority of print "is complemented by its capacity for securing a complete penetration of the reader's subjective life."[4] This form of solitary and prolonged reading brings with it a different kind of involvement with the subject matter of fiction, one that calls on the reader's sensibility, emotions, and powers of intellect in a manner quite new to narrative literature. Richardson's fiction, Watt comments, "brought about a much deeper and unqualified identification between the reader and [the] characters." This line of investigation helps us to assess the irreversible impact of Richardson's work, and it can well serve as a point of departure for the issue I have in view. The evidence that Watt offers comes from an essentially sociological perspective. I turn now to an instance where a similar point is made as part of the emergent aesthetics of the novel in the period.

In Rousseau's lengthy second preface to *La Nouvelle Héloïse* subtitled "Entretien sur les romans," we find a far-reaching argument for the attitude toward fiction that Richardson had inaugurated. This preface is cast in the form of a dialogue between N., a sympathetic though not uncritical reader of the work, and R., the author. At first sight the dialogue appears to revolve around the issues familiar in the contemporary debate regarding the novel, notably, the alleged authenticity of the collection of letters and the moral consequences of reading novels. But Rousseau orients both topics toward an analysis of the type of involvement required of a reader, and from this he draws more general conclusions regarding the form of the novel.

This work, he argues, is directed toward a new community of "âmes sensibles," sensitive souls, a community that attempts to find

---

4. *The Rise of the Novel* (Berkeley, 1957), p. 198. The following quote is on p. 201.

its model in the work itself. What was implicit, and to a great extent unconscious, in Richardson now becomes a specific goal for fiction. In justifying the authenticity of the lovers' letters, R. introduces standards of persuasion and involvement that are meant to apply not only to the fictive lovers but also to the prospective readers: "On se sent l'âme attendrie; on se sent ému sans savoir pourquoi . . . [N]e trouvant nulle part ce qu'ils sentent, ils se replient sur eux-mêmes; ils se détachent du reste de l'univers, et, créant entre eux un petit monde différent du nôtre, ils y forment un spectacle véritablement nouveau."5 Such passages refer to the lovers, but they provide the basis for a new defense of fiction. It is hardly surprising that in the preface a pair of ideal readers is evoked: "J'aime à me figurer deux époux lisant ce receuil ensemble."6 Upon finishing the novel, we are told, they would return to their familiar world, but effectively transformed by the experience: "Ils rempliront les mêmes fonctions; mais ils les rempliront avec une autre âme, et feront en vrais patriarches ce qu'ils faisaient en paysans."7

The standard of sensibility and feeling that governs the relations of the characters within the novel, becomes the model for an aesthetic process, the apprehension of the world of the novel by the reader. N., at the conclusion of the dialogue, comments on the benign but compelling power of sympathy at work in the collection of letters: "J'observe que dans une société très intime les styles se rapprochent ainsi que les caractères et que les amis, confondant leurs âmes, confondent aussi leurs manières de penser, de sentir et de dire. Cette Julie, telle qu'elle est, doit être une créature enchanteresse; tout ce qui l'approche doit lui ressembler; tout doit devenir Julie autour d'elle; tous ses amis ne doivent avoir qu'un ton; mais ces choses se sentent et ne s'imaginent pas."8 The consequence of this principle of sympathy for the

5. *Julie, ou La Nouvelle Héloïse* (Paris, 1960), pp. 741, 743. In English: "One feels deeply affected, one is moved without knowing why. . . . [N]ot finding anywhere a model of what they feel, they turn to one another; they detach themselves from the rest of the universe and, creating between themselves a small world different from ours, they fashion a truly new spectacle."

6. Ibid., p. 749. In English: "I like to imagine a married couple reading this collection together."

7. Ibid. In English: "They will fulfill the same functions, but they will do so with a different spirit and achieve as true patriarchs what they had been doing as peasants."

8. Ibid., p. 755. In English: "I notice that in a very intimate society styles approach one another as do characters, and that friends, mingling their souls, mingle also their ways of thinking, of feeling, and of speaking. That Julie, as she is shown, must be an enchanting creature; everything that approaches her must resemble her; everything must become Julie

reading process is that the reader's interest is directed less toward the singularity of the several characters than toward a spirit that unites them, a spirit concentrated, in this case, in the figure of Julie. And, correspondingly, this figure relinquishes some of its distinctive identity as she comes to embody the atmosphere of the world of the novel.[9]

My aim with this example was to single out a historically determinate model of reading that implies a certain mode of presentation of the self. For the notion of character can only be clarified by relating a formal function within the literary structure with an extraliterary (societal or historical) impulse. We can pursue this kind of methodological discussion along different lines. The concept of fictional character derives from and, correlatively, helps to shape a variety of other concepts outside the province of fiction. "Person," "self," "individual," and "soul" should be considered, and they bring into play sociological, ethical, legal, and theological dimensions that cannot readily be accommodated to one another or, what is more, oriented toward the formal problems of fiction. Thus, it is useful to consider an essay by the philosopher Amelie O. Rorty which attempts to provide a logical underpinning for a historical typology of character and allied concepts. As Rorty makes clear, the notion of character, in contradistinction to soul or self, for example, is strongly oriented toward a social context and is, furthermore, marked by a high degree of self-display or exteriorization:

> The qualities of character are the predictable and reliable manifestations of their dispositions: and it is by these dispositions that they are identified. . . . Dispositional traits form an interlocking pattern, at best mutually supportive but sometimes tensed and conflicted. There is no presumption of a core that owns these dispositions. . . . To know what sort of character a person is, is to know what sort of life is best suited to bring out his potentialities and functions. Theories of the moral education of characters have strong political consequences.[10]

Thus character, understood as a structure of dispositions and traits, implies a thoroughgoing principle of manifestation or exteriorization. What is stipulated as the essence of a figure must be revealed, or at

---

around her; all her friends will have only one tone; but these things are felt and cannot be imagined."

9. For a fuller discussion of the status of Julie, see Chap. 5 below.

10. "A Literary Postscript: Characters, Persons, Selves, Individuals," in *The Identities of Persons*, ed. A. O. Rorty (Berkeley, 1976), p. 304f.

least be capable of revelation, through speech, behavior, or act. The outward is presumed to serve as a reliable and sufficient index for the inward. This kind of definition, preliminary and schematic though it is, already helps us to look for some of the sources of the notion of character in the ideal of *Bildung* of German Idealism and in the ethos of "worldliness" of seventeenth- and eighteenth-century French culture.

We find in Goethe's *Die Wahlverwandtschaften* (1809) a maxim specifically derived from the code of eighteenth-century aristocratic society which also articulates the principle of character outlined above: "Man nimmt in der Welt jeden, wofür er sich gibt; aber er muß sich auch für etwas geben."[11] Heinz Otto Burger, although he is writing here on Wilhelm Meister's sense of a public stance, indicates the background for this kind of social norm:

> [The] cultivated individual cuts a figure in good society and in public and becomes thereby a "person." Goethe here follows the language and the image of man of the seventeenth century; one thinks of the *Arte de ser Persona* in the works of the Spanish Jesuit Baltasar Gracian. These strongly recommend that the individual in society represent something and thus be someone, a person . . . Not that seeming is incompatible with being; rather, the latter is assumed so that what in reality is will also "appear in its full splendor."[12]

"Person," as understood in many seventeenth- and eighteenth-century codifications of manners, denotes the single bearer of a variety of traits, but the emphasis is all on the interplay and display of the traits.

As Rorty's typology suggests, however, there is a significant shift in emphasis in moving from the notion of character to that of person. "Character" reflects the requirement of a restricted, worldly society that an individual should exhibit his qualities and cut a figure;[13]

---

11. In *Goethes Werke* (Hamburg, 1958), 6:396. In English: "In society we accept everyone as he presents himself, but he must appear to be something."

12. "Europäisches Adelsideal und deutsche Klassik," in *"Dasein heißt eine Rolle spielen": Studien zur deutschen Literaturgeschichte* (Munich, 1963), p. 219.

13. Roland Barthes's discussion of La Bruyère is particularly instructive in this connection: "*Les Caractères* is in a sense a book of total knowledge; on the one hand, La Bruyère approaches social man from every angle, he constitutes a kind of indirect *summa* . . . of the various kinds of the *socius* available at the end of the seventeenth century (it will be noted that this man is indeed much more social than psychological): . . . [T]he 'characters' were almost all drawn from a personalized society: nomination here is a strict function of enclosure, the worldly type (and it is here that it probably differs from the typical roles of comedy) is not born of abstraction, quintessence of countless individuals: the wordly type is an immediate unit, defined by his place among adjacent units whose 'differen-

"person" moves toward a sense of self that represents a locus of responsibility in public terms but may well conceal the motives that actuate behavior. Thus, Rorty writes of the sphere of person as "the idea of a unified center of choice and action, the unit of legal and theological responsibility."[14] Then, at a further remove from character, we come to the notion of soul as the pure expression of will: "The shadow of disembodiment that was implicit in the idea of a legal person moves forward, stands stage center; we have a person who is a pure *res cogitans* (or, in the religious versions, one that can survive death). . . . From character as structured dispositions, we come to soul as pure agency, unfathomable, inexpressible." At this level the stress is on the uniqueness of the individual, on the freedom and autonomy of the agent. Correspondingly, defining traits or specifications, especially in relation to social categories or forms, will be played down, for these now appear as qualifications of the freedom of action and choice.

My discussion has thus far suggested a filiation between a public or socially accredited stance of the individual and the status of character in fiction, but I did not mean to imply that the other tendency, the relatively hidden and autonomous element expressed in the concepts of person and soul, is not involved in the structure of fictive character. This is an issue to which I shall turn later. At this point, however, I wish to focus briefly on the polarity itself, on the opposing tendencies of display and concealment in the presentation of self.

Georges Gusdorf, in *La Découverte du soi,* taking his point of departure from Sartre's analysis of the conflict between self-understanding and self-revelation, undertakes a historical conspectus of the concept of the self in terms of a "continually present displacement between person and character [*personne et personnage*]."[15] The common etymon for these two terms is not available in English, of course, where they are rendered as *person* and *character*. And although *character* can be translated *personnage,* the word contains a number of other meanings that complicate the issue.[16] Gusdorf argues that all efforts to know oneself, to become aware of one's essential nature (*personne*), are undermined by an interference from one's roles, the

---

tial' contiguity forms the inland of worldliness." "La Bruyère," in *Critical Essays,* trans. R. Howard (Evanston, Ill., 1972), pp. 224, 229.

14. "A Literary Postscript," p. 309; the following quotation is on p. 312.

15. (Paris, 1948), p. 234.

16. Cf. Joel Weinsheimer's survey of fifteen usages of the term "character" and its cognates in "Theory of Character: *Emma,*" *Poetics Today* 1(1979): 189ff.

reified versions of personality that serve to represent the self to others (*personnage*). Although the thrust of Gusdorf's argument is largely ethical, his distinction helps us to understand that different historical epochs gave a very different value to certain roles or patterns of public behavior. It thus provides materials for, as Gusdorf puts it, "a history of social roles [*du personnage social*] which would at the same time be a contribution to a history of self-consciousness."[17] Further, it draws attention to the historicity of the very notion of person, a notion that can arise, in Gusdorf's model, only in consequence of an awareness of a split between *personne* and *personnage*: "A knowledge of the self can appear only when the role [*personnage*] is revealed to be nothing but a role. The discovery of the role is a discovery that the role is other than myself. This deep-seated discrepancy gives rise to an unrest, an anguish which opens the way to a more demanding sincerity."[18]

Lionel Trilling, in *Sincerity and Authenticity*,[19] shares Gusdorf's awareness that any notion of integral selfhood can only arise dialectically from a state of alienation or a moment of self-reflexivity. But his analysis is less concerned with pointing to possible resolutions of the dilemma in contemporary thought than in trying to determine what, in the formative stages of modernity, produced it. For Trilling, the breach in consciousness serves both to awaken a need for reintegration and for placing it definitively out of reach. He argues that the fabric of post-Enlightenment society came to provide the principal means of individuation and self-definition for the individual, but only at the cost of an irreversible movement toward alienation (see particularly chap. 2 on *Le Neveu de Rameau* and on Hegel's reading of it). In an earlier essay on *Mansfield Park,* which anticipates some of the ideas of *Sincerity and Authenticity,* Trilling wrote:

> Hegel speaks of the "secularization of spirituality" as a prime characteristic of the modern epoch, and Jane Austen is the first to tell us what this involves. She is the first novelist to represent society, the general culture, as playing a part in the moral life, generating the concepts of "sincerity" and "vulgarity" which no earlier time would have understood the meaning of, and which for us are so subtle that they defy definition, and so powerful that no one can escape their sovereignty.[20]

17. *La Découverte du soi*, p. 220.
18. Ibid., p. 233.
19. (Cambridge, Mass., 1971).
20. In *The Opposing Self* (New York, 1959), p. 228.

Trilling demonstrates how those very qualities that appear to testify to what is most personal and inalienable in the individual are elevated to the status of ethical values by means of a social system designed to pervert or suppress them. Insofar as "society is understood to be the field on which man runs his spiritual course"[21]—as Trilling, paraphrasing Pascal, writes of *Le Neveu de Rameau*—man's spiritual nature has become capable of expression only in reaction to society or, what is the same, in an alienated identification with it. Trilling thus provides a valuable confirmation of my thesis that the presentation of self in the novel is to be sought not in terms of an a priori notion of the ego but by way of what I have termed the structures of sociality that operate in literary works.

II

La Vie de Marianne is in an important sense exemplary for the eighteenth-century novel, because in it the heroine's active interest in the social world, her desire to understand and penetrate it, serves as the very basis of her emergent self-consciousness. As Peter Brooks writes, in this novel Marivaux is primarily interested "only in a moment of his character's life, the moment of confrontation with worldliness. This confrontation provokes Marianne's 'explicitation' of self, and it is her movement into a state of lucid social consciousness and self-consciousness that forms the true subject of the novel."[22] Diverging from earlier interpretations of the work, Brooks sees Marianne's character not as a pure exemplification of *tendresse* and *sensibilité* but as the end product of an already highly self-conscious social code. "The World is Marianne's vocation," he writes further, "her natural field of exploration, new to her but not at all foreign." Her "natural aristocracy" enables her "not only to behave with perfect propriety, but also to detect in others behavior which is in violation of social norms."

What interests me particularly in the novel is the way that its

---

21. *Sincerity and Authenticity,* p. 30. Trilling's condensed history of the concept of personality since the eighteenth century may be supplemented by Jean Starobinski's suggestive essay "Truth in Masquerade," which was originally titled "Stendhal pseudonyme" (In *Issues in Contemporary Literary Criticism,* ed. Gregory T. Polletta [Boston, 1973], pp. 233–46. The French version is in *L'Œil vivant* [Paris, 1961]). Stendhal's "systematic 'polynymity,' " in Starobinski's words, may be viewed as a belated Enlightenment effort to escape the rigid constraints of a determinate identity, a fixed "character" in the nineteenth-century sense.

22. *The Novel of Worldliness* (Princeton, 1969), p. 135; the following quotation is on p. 99.

heroine's impulse for social acceptance is consubstantial with her capacity for perception and understanding. Marianne writes of her first impression of Paris: "Il y avait une douce sympathie entre mon imagination et les objets que je voyais, et je devinais qu'on pouvait tirer de cette multitude de choses différentes je ne sais combien d'agréments que je ne connaissais pas encore."[23] Marianne's "douce sympathie" is not only the token of an instinctive knowledge, an intimacy between her and the world she aspires to;[24] it also serves to mark the interconnection of need and vision, of affect and perception. Few novels of the period expose so clearly the mechanism whereby need and desire activate cognition: self-interest and interest in the world fuse in a single intentional arc. This conjunction is particularly well illustrated in Marianne's remarks on *coquetterie:*

> Nous avons deux sortes d'esprit, nous autres femmes. Nous avons d'abord le nôtre, qui est celui que nous recevons de la nature, celui qui nous sert à raisonner, suivant le degré qu'il a, qui devient ce qu'il peut, et qui ne sait rien qu'avec le temps.
>
> Et puis nous en avons encore un autre, qui est à part du nôtre, et qui peut se trouver dans les femmes les plus sottes. C'est l'esprit que la vanité de plaire nous donne, et qu'on appelle, autrement dit, la coquetterie.[25]

These reflections occur in the scene in church where Marianne first shows off her charms to an assemblage of good society, eliciting strong, though opposing, responses from members of both sexes. Surveying the crowd, Marianne remarks on the transparency of what she sees: "Et moi, je devinais la pensée de toutes ces personnes-là sans aucun effort; mon instinct ne voyait rien là qui ne fût de sa connaissance."[26] She calls the cause of this power of divination *coquetterie*. It is capable of revealing to her "les façons de ces femmes," and it also

23. *La Vie de Marianne* (Paris, 1947), p. 33f. In English: "There was gentle sympathy between my imagination and the objects that I saw, and I sensed that I would be capable of obtaining from this multitude of things innumerable pleasures of which I had no conception at the time."

24. Following Brooks's view that here it "is not a question of isolated objects only, but of a whole world, the one World that counts," *The Novel of Worldliness,* p. 98.

25. *La Vie de Marianne,* p. 71. In English: "We have two sorts of spirit, we women. There is first our own, which we receive from nature and which enables us to reason according to its powers; it becomes what it can and knows nothing except through the passage of time. And then we also have another, which is separate from our personal one and which may be found in the most stupid of women. It is a spirit which the vanity to please gives to us, and it is called, in a word, coquetry."

26. Ibid. In English: "and I, I guessed the thought of every one of those individuals; nothing there escaped my instinct."

allows her to enter into the minds of the men because, she continues, "avec une extrême envie d'être de leur goût, on a la clef de tout ce qu'ils font pour être du nôtre."[27]

In contrast to many later instances of such self-analysis, Marianne's mixture of reflection and feeling, of self-knowledge and self-interest, does not tend to inhibit her affective or egotistical impulses. The "douce sympathie" of her outgoing glance reflects a preexistent affinity between her spirit and the world into which she moves, and it is itself an active agent of exploration and cognition. Marianne, then, is an early but striking instance of the way a fictive figure is made to serve as a means of access to a world structure. Her reflexive posture is to be taken not as proof of her sincerity or as the exposure of essential character traits, but as the exercise of the kind of out-reaching consciousness that represents a new function of character in this period.

In *Wilhelm Meisters Lehrjahre* we find a comparable, though more ambiguous, instance of self-revelation, and again I hope to illustrate thereby how a figure's self-understanding serves at the same time to disclose the constitution of the world of the novel. Nearly at the midpoint of the book we find a letter in which Wilhelm justifies his decision to join a theatrical troupe. He is writing to his friend Werner, who had tried to convince him to undertake a commercial career and thus return to the bourgeois sphere from which their families had come. Wilhelm's response begins with a ringing declaration that typifies the whole tradition of the *Bildungsroman*: "Daß ich Dir's mit *einem* Worte sage: mich selbst, ganz wie ich da bin, auszubilden, das war dunkel von Jugend auf mein Wunsch und meine Absicht."[28] The same sentiment is echoed at the end of the letter: "Ich habe nun einmal gerade zu jener harmonischen Ausbildung meiner Natur, die mir meine Geburt versagt, eine unwiderstehliche Neigung."[29] Wilhelm seems to be appealing to an irreducible core of the self as the preeminent goal of growth and development. But lest we identify this goal with present-day notions of existential freedom or personal authenticity, we had better examine the context of these statements. For this

27. Ibid. In English: "For, with a powerful desire to appeal to their taste, one possesses the key to everything they do to appeal to ours."

28. *Goethes Werke*, 7:290. In English: "To speak it in a word: the cultivation of my individual self, wholly as I am, has from my youth upwards been constantly though dimly my wish and purpose." *Wilhelm Meister's Apprenticeship*, trans. T. Carlyle (New York, 1962), p. 274.

29. Ibid., p. 291. In English: "Now this harmonious cultivation of my nature, which has been denied me by birth, is exactly what I most long for." *Wilhelm Meister's Apprenticeship*, p. 275.

makes it apparent that Wilhelm derives his model of self-fulfillment from the social code of the aristocracy.[30]

The body of the letter offers an extended contrast between the possibilities open to a bourgeois individual (*Bürger*) and to a nobleman (*Edelmann*). The mediating term, which allows us to chart the fluidity of the concepts involved, is "public person" (*öffentliche Person*):

> Ein Bürger kann sich Verdienst erwerben und zur höchsten Not seinen Geist ausbilden; seine Persönlichkeit geht aber verloren, er mag sich stellen, wie er will. Indem es dem Edelmann, der mit den Vornehmsten umgeht, zur Pflicht wird, sich selbst einen vornehmen Anstand zu geben, indem dieser Anstand . . . zu einem freien Anstand wird, da er mit seiner Figur, mit seiner Person, es sei bei Hofe oder bei der Armee, bezahlen muß, so hat er Ursache, etwas auf sie zu halten und zu zeigen, daß er etwas auf sie hält. Eine gewisse feierliche Grazie bei gewöhnlichen Dingen, eine Art von leichtsinniger Zierlichkeit bei ernsthaften und wichtigen kleidet ihn wohl, weil er sehen läßt, daß er überall im Gleichgewicht steht. Er ist eine öffentliche Person. . . . Wenn der Edelmann durch die Darstellung seiner Person alles gibt, so gibt der Bürger durch seine Persönlichkeit nichts und soll nichts geben. Jener darf und soll scheinen; dieser soll nur sein, und was er scheinen will, ist lächerlich oder abgeschmackt.[31]

If we had expected to find in this letter a justification for authentic, autonomous self-realization, then Wilhelm's longing for a conventionally accredited role, for the ceremonial manners of aristocratic society, must strike us as very strange.

Jürgen Habermas, commenting on this letter, has stressed that Wilhelm's concept of individuality should be understood as an inter-

---

30. On this point see Hans Rudolf Vaget, "Liebe und Grundeigentum in *Wilhelm Meisters Lehrjahren*: Zur Physiognomie des Adels bei Geothe," in *Legitimationskrisen des deutschen Adels 1200–1900*, ed. P. U. Hohendahl and P. M. Lützeler (Stuttgart, 1979), pp. 137–57.

31. *Goethes Werke*, 7:290f. In English: "A burgher may acquire merit; by excessive efforts he may even educate his mind; but his personal qualities are lost, or worse than lost, let him struggle as he will. Since the nobleman, frequenting the most polished society, is compelled to give himself a polished manner; since this manner . . . grows at last an unconstrained one; since . . . his figure, his person, are a part of his possessions, and it may be, the most necessary part, he has reason enough to put some value on them, and to show that he puts some. A certain stately grace in common things, a sort of gay elegance in earnest and important ones, becomes him well; for it shows him to be everywhere in equilibrium. He is a public person. . . . If the nobleman, merely by his personal carriage, offers all that can be asked of him, the burgher by his personal carriage offers nothing, and can offer nothing. The former has a right to seem; the latter is compelled to be, and what he aims at seeming becomes ludicrous and tasteless." *Wilhelm Meister's Apprenticeship*, p. 274f.

mediate stage between a premodern sense of "representing" a public role or function and the emergent bourgeois sense of an autonomous, self-determining personality.[32] As Habermas points out, the designation of the nobleman as "a public person" derives from the public sphere within a feudal structure, where certain individuals were called upon to represent the sovereign through their rank or office. Representation in this sense clearly imposes a certain kind of appearance and demeanor on the individual without introducing any inconsistency or conflict between a private and a public sphere. The private, in fact, in the sense of an inner and self-determining modus of individuality, is not yet available as a category;[33] it is not yet either a refuge for the individual or a motive for alienation from his social context. In Wilhelm's admiration for the grace, the self-confidence, the public manners of the nobleman, we see a vestige of the "representative" function available to the individual within a feudal order, a function that automatically integrates him into a hierarchy and endows his demeanor with the sanctions of the natural.

In Wilhelm's letter there is, of course, an impulse that moves beyond the dimension of this "representative" or public individuality, and this is, in Habermas's words, "the altogether bourgeois notion, already conceived within the neohumanism of the German Classical period, of an autonomously evolving personality."[34] The incompatibility between this ideal of *Bildung* and the principles of the feudal tradition is never brought to the surface and directly thematized in the novel, but its consequences are evident in the equivocal solution Wilhelm proposes for the kind of self-realization that the nobleman possesses by virtue of his class but that the burgher can obtain only by the exercise of his talents and capacities. We do not even have to look to the later parts of the novel to become aware of the insufficiency of Wilhelm's theatrical ambitions; at the end of the very chapter we are considering (bk. 5, chap. 3), his enigmatic vision of Natalie (as yet known only as the Amazon) suggests that, in spite of his conscious intention to pursue a theatrical career, another sphere of self-realization stands ready to displace it.

We recall Wilhelm's confident, ringing declaration, "mich selbst,

32. *Strukturwandel der Öffentlichkeit* (Neuwied, 1974), pp. 19ff. In his discussion of "representation" Habermas is indebted, as he acknowledges, to Hans Georg Gadamer, *Truth and Method* (New York, 1975), pp. 125ff. and pp. 513ff., nn. 53 and 54.

33. Cf. Raymond Williams, *Keywords: A Vocabulary of Culture and Society* (New York, 1976), esp. the entry on *private*.

34. *Strukturwandel der Öffentlichkeit*, p. 26.

ganz wie ich da bin, auszubilden," and see now that this moment, when the hero might have been expected to disclose the deepest, most essential core of his personality, represents only a provisional stage, and, to a certain extent, a delusive one. In any case, he shows himself to be surprisingly dependent upon a public, conventionally accredited image; what originality might be claimed for Wilhelm lies not in any revelation of inward resources but rather in his ambition, in his drive to transcend the social class to which his origins have assigned him.

In the novel as a whole we may say that all stages of *Bildung,* of growth and maturation, involve role-playing, an effort to adapt oneself to the codes of a new social milieu. Wilhelm, as an individual who is forced to seek his personality in the world and through the world, cannot help but embrace the pretensions and affectations of the various circles through which he moves, though the narrator may signal by means of irony that each of the stages is provisional. Even the last in the *Lehrjahre,* Wilhelm's initiation into the Society of the Tower ("Die Gesellschaft vom Turm") can hardly be viewed as the final goal of his quest. Werner's remark when he meets him at this point, "so bist du doch indessen ein Persönchen geworden,"[35] can be taken as an ironic echo of Wilhelm's earlier resolve to fashion his own personality (*Persönlichkeit*). The Society of the Tower itself is quickly exposed by its leading members, Jarno and Lothario, as a youthful project, a kind of mystical brotherhood, which had once engaged their adherence but is now viewed as little more than mystifying mummery.

Yet the sphere of wordly ambition and conventions is not, in this novel, to be taken as only an illusory facade behind which some greater truth lies hidden. Goethe does adumbrate another dimension, transcending the social, embodied in certain floating, unrooted figures such as Mariane, old Barbara, Philine, the Harp Player, Wilhelm's son Felix and, most important, Mignon. But this dimension makes itself felt only intermittently in the *Lehrjahre* (although Goethe attempted to realize it more fully in the *Wanderjahre*), and it offers, in any case, no decisive challenge to the other. The doctrine of the novel seems to be that every individual must master the codes of the social world, must achieve integration with its standards before he is ready to seek inner harmony and self-sufficiency. Lothario, Theresa, and a host of other "worldly" figures testify to this, and so does the aunt, or "schöne Seele," who has chosen a religious vocation. Thus, in an important sense the novel stands within that tradition Peter Brooks

---

35. *Goethes Werke,* 7:499. In English: "well, you've turned into quite a figure."

has designated "novels of worldliness," and its lesson is that accommodation to the social sphere is at least a necessary, if not a sufficient, condition for the achievement of personal integrity and authenticity. To return to Wilhelm's letter, we can see now that his effort to name and fix an essence of personality serves to expose an instability of identity that is elaborated, though not resolved, in the subsequent action. Wilhelm's effort to know himself leads him not to some recess of inwardness but toward those roles that a new and alluring social context makes available to him. The themes of ceremony, masquerade, and dissimulation, so prominent in this novel, as in much eighteenth-century fiction, are shown to be integral to the determination of character as moral essence and to the formation of fictive character or *personnage*.

For both Wilhelm and Marianne, the quest for self-definition has served to further the articulation of a social sphere. What each figure is in itself, as essence or substance, has been shown to be indissolubly bound up with an order of possible realization available to it in society, and until such possibilities come to be articulated in one way or another, its substance remains indeterminate.

III

I turn now to the other principle of the presentation of self mentioned earlier, namely, that which is directed to an essential but veiled core of personality, a singular and unique individual substance. In contrast to character as a socially adaptive persona, this kind of selfhood is private, and thus resistant to exteriorization or self-exhibition, and self-determining, and thus shielded from the models imposed upon it by the social context.

One source for this version of character presentation can be traced, as Holger Jergius has argued, to Leibniz's notion of individuality. Leibniz drew on a Scholastic concept of *forma substantialis,* where each individual is at the same time a single and unique exemplar, the sole instance of a species. In medieval thought this could apply only to angels. But Leibniz, adapting it to the human individual, claimed "that everything a person might encounter is already contained in a virtual state in his nature or concept, like the characteristic of a circle in its definition."[36] For Leibniz, the acts and circumstances

36. Cited in Holger Jergius, "Versuch über den Charakter: Ein Beitrag zur Begriffsgeschichte der Poetik des 18. Jahrhunderts," *Jean-Paul-Gesellschaft Jahrbuch* 6(1971): 7–45; this quote is on p. 25.

that befall an individual are not causally linked to his nature or substance. Rather, both individual and context are accounted for in relationship to each other through the theory of pre-established harmony. This is a form of "modified occasionalism," as Jergius puts it, and he summarizes it as follows: "In conceiving a certain individual, God at the same time fashions all the circumstances that are required so that that individual can, in his historical existence, bring to full expression that concept of himself that is implanted in a priori fashion in his existence."[37]

If we apply this to the delineation of character in fiction, the narrative is to be understood primarily as the occasion for revealing the essential nature of the principal participants, their a priori essence. Thus Jergius writes:

> The hero is here revealed through his deeds, not for the sake of a given deed and its consequences but in order to make visible by means of the action the ideal essence of the individual. Thus only such deeds and situations should be chosen as would allow the character to be revealed as sharply and distinctly as possible. Everything regarding the person who is delineated must in a sense be exemplary for his nature.[38]

The consequences of such a theory for the poetics of the novel are complex and can only be touched on here. Undoubtedly, we can draw on it to help explicate the intimate connection between figure and context, between character and its world, that is so typical a feature of the novel from the eighteenth century on. We may be in a better position now to understand the paradox that, although the notion of character in fiction has served to support the ideology of unique, autonomous selfhood, this support derives not so much from the worldly, self-dramatizing type analyzed earlier but rather from a contrasting type, a type revealed only through the nexus of converging circumstances, tending in extreme cases toward a fusion with the context.

We touch here on the decisive function of atmosphere and milieu in the modern novel, as an element both determinant and expressive of the individual, both context and emanation. Consider in this connection the narrator's reflections near the end of *Die Wahlverwandtschaften:* "Was einem jeden Menschen gewöhnlich begegnet, wiederholt sich mehr, als man glaubt, weil seine Natur hiezu die

37. Ibid., p. 27.
38. Ibid., p. 26.

nächste Bestimmung gibt. Charakter, Individualität, Neigung, Richtung, Örtlichkeit, Umgebungen und Gewohnheiten bilden zusammen ein Ganzes, in welchem jeder Mensch wie in einem Elemente, in einer Atmosphäre schwimmt, worin es ihm allein bequem und behaglich ist."[39] Such a fusion of character and context does not, however, necessarily signify a weakening of the sense of individuality in a novel but may be taken as evidence of a different form of character delineation, one that diverges from the self-exhibiting procedures of some eighteenth-century fiction, as discussed earlier, and also from the psychological methods that gained ascendance in the nineteenth century.

I have already cited the maxim from *Die Wahlverwandtschaften,* "Man nimmt in der Welt jeden, wofür er sich gibt; aber er muß sich auch für etwas geben," as an illustration of the code of eighteenth-century aristocratic society. But I did not note that the passage appears, paradoxically, as an entry in the diary and commonplace book of Ottilie, a figure who collects such rules of social decorum as an outsider, as someone whose nature is not attuned to the worldly sphere. At once caught up in a social circle and distanced from it, she serves to expose and undermine its codes and values. The aristocratic group depicted in the novel does not appear, at first sight, particularly blameworthy. We find in it the kind of self-complaisance that in the *Lehrjahre* suffered at most a mild ridicule. The principal figures of *Die Wahlverwandtschaften* appear hardly deserving of the catastrophic events that lie in store for them. Ottilie enters this circle early in the novel as a novice who seeks to adapt herself to the prevailing norms. The artless manner with which she collects and occasionally comments on maxims of worldly wisdom serves both to crystallize the social code and to put it into question. For, in spite of her interest in the rules of this society, she is herself unable to "cut a figure" ("sich für etwas geben"). When, during a private Christmas celebration, her former tutor enters unexpectedly and sees her taking the part of the Virgin Mary in a tableau of the Nativity, Ottilie thinks to herself: "Wie seltsam muß es ihm vorkommen, dich, die er nur natürlich

---

39. *Goethes Werke,* 6:478. In English: "Much that ordinarily happens to a person repeats itself more often than we think, because a person's nature is the immediate determinant of this. Character, individuality, inclination, disposition, environment and habits form together a whole, in which every human being floats, as it were, in an element, an atmosphere, in which alone he feels comfortable and at ease." *Elective Affinities,* trans. E. Mayer and L. Bogan (Chicago, 1966), p. 290.

gesehen, als Maske zu erblicken?"[40] Ottilie's unwillingness to be perceived "als Maske" characterizes a being who resists specification through self-presentation. Her outward nature, her appearance, is repeatedly revealed through a mode of illusory presence (*scheinen*) that at once simulates and occludes her inward essence. One thinks in this connection of the Architect's paintings of angelic faces that resemble her and of the apparently incorruptible beauty of her body when it is exhibited during her obsequies. These forms of simulated presentation exemplify the Idealist notion of *scheinen* as an oscillation between manifestation and illusion.

Thus, in attempting to understand Ottilie as a character, it seems necessary first of all to realize that she embodies a principle of selfhood strongly at variance with the norms of the social or worldly novel, and so also of the conception of character that derives from it. Her resistance to the canons of worldly society, which she expresses more than once, serves to put into question the type of character presentation typical for the form of the novel. This is consistent with Goethe's own hesitation to probe too far into the makeup of the individual soul, an attitude he expressed in a letter to Lavater in 1780 in the following terms: "Hab ich dir das Wort *Individuum est ineffabile* woraus ich eine Welt ableite, schon geschrieben?"[41]

The case of Ottilie has been intended to illustrate a principle of character presentation that stands at the opposite pole from the kind of self-articulation and dramatization we found in Marianne or Wilhelm Meister. In fact, the conflict between the claims of a worldly circle and an inner-directed, inarticulate individual in *Die Wahlverwandtschaften* represents an unusually striking interplay of both principles. But the two principles—character as persona or social role, on the one hand, and character as person or soul, on the other—were not intended to be understood as absolutely separate types of character formation but rather as interdependent tendencies that may be distinguished for historical and theoretical purposes, as I have done, but that will typically both be at work in a given instance.

My discussion has addressed itself to an issue that, from a certain point of view, represents a preeminent theme of modern literature and

40. Ibid., p. 405. In English: "How strange it must seem to him that you, whom he has always seen in ordinary circumstances, should now appear under a mask." *Elective Affinities*, p. 405.

41. Cited in the article "Individuum, Individualität," in *Historisches Wörterbuch der Philosophie*, vol. 4, col. 312. In English: "Have I yet written you the phrase *Individuum est ineffabile*, from which I derive a whole world?"

particularly of the post-eighteenth-century novel, namely, the development of self-consciousness as it becomes manifest at both an individual and a social level. It is a theme that has, of course, been discussed frequently and from a variety of perspectives, for example, in terms of a typology of the hero or of fictional character in general. But my treatment was intended not primarily as a contribution to the thematics of the novel but more as an exploration, based on phenomenological assumptions, of the conception of the self as it developed in the eighteenth-century novel. Further, I have not had in view a definition of human nature or of man in general; rather, I have tried to explore ways in which the interplay between the individual and the social environment could disclose certain modalities of self-understanding and self-presentation available at a given period. Closely related to this issue is the question of why the novel became a preeminent vehicle for the articulation of individual self-consciousness.

One answer, it seems to me, is that the eighteenth-century novel drew on the codes of a highly structured, worldly society for models of character presentation but at the same time acknowledged the insufficiency of such models to account for the sense of a self-validating, unique identity that was becoming an urgent ethical concern during this period.[42] I have tried to illustrate how this situation could be variously articulated: in the way that Marianne's social ambition is made to serve as a cognitive instrument, in the way that Wilhelm Meister's drive for personal self-realization is forced to pass through the delusive spheres of the theater and the aristocracy, and finally in the way that Ottilie's inner-directed spirituality becomes the means of

---

42. A number of studies can be cited in this connection. W. J. Harvey in *Character and the Novel* (Ithaca, N.Y., 1965) proceeds from a fundamental distinction between "intrinsic" and "contextual" knowledge of personality. By intrinsic self-knowledge Harvey means a person's own sense of a discrete identity, "a hard, stable core within the flux," which we think of "as unique, isolate, discrete" (p. 31). A volume of the group Poetik und Hermeneutik (*Identität*, ed. Odo Marquard and Karlheinz Stierle [Munich, 1979]) contains a number of contributions of great relevance to my topic. I cite only two: Wolfhart Pannenberg's "Person und Subjekt," pp. 407–22, traces the Christian sources for the sense of a unique, temporally constituted self that, as person, is present in virtual form throughout an individual's existence. Dieter Henrich, in a wide-ranging and systematic survey of the philosophic issues—" 'Identität': Begriffe, Probleme, Grenzen," pp. 133–86—discusses a category of particular relevance to my argument, one he calls "kriterienlose Selbstzuschreibung," criterion-free self-reference. He argues that it represents "a necessary condition of all self-reference" whose detailed analysis "must be viewed as a philosophic task of high priority" (p. 178). Finally, Martin Price's "The Other Self: Thoughts about Character in the Novel" (in *Imagined Worlds: Essays . . . in Honour of John Butt*, ed. Maynard Mack and Ian Gregor [London, 1968], pp. 279–99), opens with a helpful discussion of the interplay of innate identity, role-playing, and self-scrutiny in the formation of the concept of character.

judging the worldly circle in which she is placed. Thus, the interplay of *personne* and *personnage* (to use Gusdorf's terms) represents not simply an ideological vestige of the "classical" (or premodernist) novel, as some of the structuralists claim, but rather a constitutive feature of the form as it has evolved since the eighteenth century, one that needs to be accounted for as part of its historical determination.

4 Parasitic Talk: Reflections on the Pragmatics of the Novel and *The Confidence-Man*

die alltägliche Ausgelegtheit der Welt   HEIDEGGER

my nature is subdued
To what it works in, like the dyer's hand.   SHAKESPEARE

The singularity of the novel as it evolved after the Renaissance lay in its capacity to harbor and combine an enormous variety of linguistic practices. The dissemination of printed matter from the sixteenth to the eighteenth centuries laid the basis for a literary form that proved to be comprehensive, continuous, and endlessly assimilative, a form that supplanted the principle of a unique, immutable, and total book (such as the Bible). The novel provided the mold for this infinitely reproducible book of a secularized age, a book inspired not by the single voice of a divine revelation but by the multiple voices of the social body.[1]

What distinguished the post-Renaissance novel from other literary forms was its fusion of extraliterary language practices (legal, commercial, religious, courtly) with literary modes (pastoral, epic, didactic, confessional, satiric). This new literary genre, while not especially original in strictly formal terms, revealed an extraordinary flexibility, a capacity to adapt forms of expression derived from social practices in such a way that their specific functionality could be maintained while their modality was profoundly altered. The novel served to facilitate the systematic conversion of pragmatic, experiential im-

---

1. Michel de Certeau notes in this connection, "The question of the speaker and of his identity became pressing after the exhaustion of the world that was thought to be spoken and speaking: who speaks when there is no longer a divine Speaker who provides a foundation for every individual enunciation?" *L'invention du quotidien*, vol. 1, p. 267.

79

pulses into formal and semantic values. It thus represents a vast store-house of "de-realized" or suspended discourse forms. As Michel de Certeau writes, the novel "has been the principal zoo in which every-day practices have been kept since the beginnings of modern science."[2] This decontextualization of pragmatic language forms goes hand in hand with their conversion into secondary pragmatic modes. The resultant order—that of narrative—is not to be conceived in simple opposition to a reality understood as its subject matter, as mimetic theories of representation have assumed. By virtue of its discursive function, narrative intervenes directly in the order of reality and participates in its construction. It is at this point that an approach by way of narrative pragmatics can prove effective.

Whereas formalist criticism focused primarily on elements of content in the novel—action, character, and description—recent theoretical approaches have stressed that the narrating *process* is itself a modus of action within narrative forms, and perhaps the most basic and pervasive of all.[3] Far from placing it outside the work, as a source or cause, critics have begun to demonstrate systematically that the discursive level—the "discours du récit," as the French Structuralists call it—is integral to any possible model of narrative form.

In considering the modern realist tradition in such terms we find that much that has hitherto been understood denotatively, that is, as an effect of representation, may also be taken intertextually or citationally. This would apply not solely to passages of dialogue or explicit allusion, such as parody. The whole fabric of the novel may be conceived as a conglomerate of voiced segments, but a highly differentiated conglomerate that signifies, or "speaks" to the reader, precisely by means of the mutually interacting strains.[4]

What I am seeking is a kind of situational definition of narrative forms, not precisely at the level of a sociology of literary genres, though much may be won from such a sociological approach. More to my purpose is a literary pragmatics, the determination of literary forms on the basis of social practices that motivate language usage.[5]

2. Ibid., p. 151.

3. Jean-François Lyotard has concisely summarized contemporary views of narrative as a foundational or culture-forming process. See *La Condition postmoderne* (Paris, 1979), esp. "Pragmatique du savoir narratif," pp. 35–43.

4. Cf. Rolf Kloepfer, "Dynamic Structures in Narrative Literature: 'The Dialogic Principle,'" *Poetics Today* 1(1979–80): 115–34, and "Dialogic Structure in *Wilhelm Meisters Wanderjahre*" in this volume.

5. Cf. Karlheinz Stierle, "Geschichte als Exemplum, Exemplum als Geschichte: Zur Pragmatik und Poetik narrativer Texte," in *Text als Handlung* (Munich, 1975).

Taking account of the pragmatic dimension of a text means that we attempt to situate it in terms of its intended application within the literary system; and further, it requires that the literary forms be reassessed (as Tynianov has urged) in terms of the convergence of literary and extraliterary discourse practices.[6] Thus, a given text would be understood initially as a confluence of speech forms, each with its distinct motivation or pragmatic orientation. Next, one would work out a secondary level of functions resulting from the combination of the primary pragmatic forms and their insertion into a literary order.

A first step in demonstrating the centrality of discourse leads us to deemphasize the function of action or plot and that of a controlling narrator. Instead of asking "Who tells the story?" (which assumes the primary significance of the teller and the story), I would break up the narrating instance and study its permutations along a circuit of transmission, analogous in some respects to a channel of communication (thus putting the emphasis on the telling). Certain structuralist critics have studied the convergence of a cognitive action with a communicative function in narrative.[7] In such a model, the quest of the hero (for information, for self-knowledge, for truth) will be understood in the first instance as a means of channeling the reader's interest or curiosity. Jean-François Lyotard has elaborated this position, arguing that a basic function of traditional narrative is to facilitate the storage and transmission of customs, of cultural wisdom (*savoir*). The narrative structure would then be analyzed as a means of facilitating the transmission of a message through a series of agencies in a communicative circuit, one made up of sender, receptor, and referent. Lyotard writes:

> A generally acknowledged property of traditional knowledge is that the narrative positions or stances (sender, receptor, hero) are so distributed that the right to occupy that of the sender is based on the double condition of having occupied that of the receiver and of having been, by virtue of his name, already the object of a narrative, that is, placed in the position of a diegetic referent of other narrative occurrences. . . . The information [*savoir*] that is circulated by such narratives, far from being attached solely to the enunciatory functions, determines at once what

6. See J. Tynianov, "De l'évolution littéraire," in *Théorie de la littérature*, ed. T. Todorov (Paris, 1965).

7. Cf. A.-J. Greimas and J. Courtès, "The Cognitive Dimension of Narrative Discourse," *New Literary History* 7(1975–76): 433–47, and T. Todorov, "The Quest of Narrative," in *Poetics of Prose* (Ithaca, N.Y., 1977).

one must say in order to be understood, what one must hear in order to be capable of speaking, and what one must enact [*jouer*] (on the scene of diegetic reality) in order to become the object of a tale.[8]

From this perspective the path of the narrative message, and notably its transformations at different points of the circuit, would serve to mark the stations that constitute the narrative situation and thus to bring to the foreground the cognitive dimension as itself a primary subject matter of the narrative.

A related development involves the citational, intertextual, or dialogic dimension of texts (not that these terms are synonymous, but for the present I am concerned primarily with what is common to them). Let me quote from three recent theoretical works that deal with this issue:

> For though usually viewed as a marginal problem, quotations are a semiotic problem par excellence. In fact they are THE semiotic problem. SEMIOTIC ANALYSIS IS UNFEASIBLE WITHOUT QUOTATIONS, in theory, as well as in practice. . . . The quotation AS A TOKEN IS AN ICONIC SIGN OF THE ORIGINAL EXPRESSION AS A TOKEN OR AS A TYPE. The quotation is an iconic sign of its extratextual, which, thanks to its exceptional, textual character, is one of the very few extratextuals language is able to REPRESENT ICONICALLY.[9]

> If language seems always to assume language, if one is unable to determine any point of departure that is non-linguistic, this is because language is not to be located between something seen (or felt) and something spoken, but moves always from a speaking to a speaking. Thus we do not believe that narrative consists in communicating what one has seen but rather in transmitting what one has heard, what someone else has told you. Overhearing [*Ouï-dire*] . . . [t]he "first" language, or rather the initial determination of what constitutes language, is neither tropology nor metaphor, it is *indirect discourse*. . . . There are many passions in a passion, and all sorts of voices in a voice, an immense rumor, glossolalia: that is why every discourse is indirect, and the form of translation proper to language is that of indirect discourse.[10]

> For, finally, is not what Austin excludes as anomalous, exceptional, "non-serious," that is, *citation* (on the stage, in a poem, or in a soliloquy), the determined modification of a general citationality—or rather, a general iterability—without which there would not even be a "suc-

8. *La Condition postmoderne*, p. 40.
9. Ivo Osolsobe, "Fifty Keys to Semiotics," *Semiotica* 7(1973): 276.
10. Gilles Deleuze-Felix Guattari, *Mille plateaux* (Paris, 1980), p. 97.

cessful" performative? . . . Thus one must less oppose citation or iteration to the noniteration of an event, than construct a differential typology of forms of iteration, supposing that this is a tenable project that
can give rise to an exhaustive program, a question I am holding off
here.[11]

As we have become well aware in recent years, the techniques of
literature are designed to mask, but cannot annul, the orphanage of
texts, their disconnection from source, from any "natural" authorizing agency.[12] The modern system of literary genres is in great part
fashioned to minimize this deficiency. Implicit in post-Renaissance
forms of narrative, for example, is a "science de la fable" (the term
derives from the eighteenth-century) whose function has been to develop accredited procedures for *writing the voice*. It has served to
collect, sift, and systematize the dispersed, fragmentary enunciations
of those who have no ready access to the institutions of writing—the
illiterate, the "folk," mystics, fanatics, infants (*infans* and *unmündig*
reflect this condition in their etymologies).[13]

Clearly, any approach to literary forms in terms of their citational, iconic (in Osolsobe's sense), or dialogic functions will not at
this juncture be used to support an unproblematic concept of voice or
phonic presence. In the theoretical field, we are witnessing a convergence of approaches that try to account for the effective force of the
language of literature, though they are perfectly aware of literature's
derivative staus. In narrative studies, notably, we are coming to realize
that the operative elements of the narrative process are to be sought
not in those fixed units that are derived from a cultural repertoire
(plot, character, and so on) but in mechanisms of suspension and
recall, in the combinatory practices capable of generating new permutations. This level of practice, far from being reducible to some
"aesthetic sense" or faculty of "as if," draws upon a wide range of
pragmatic language skills.

But are we not speaking simply of the analysis of literature in
terms of a cultural sociology, a systematic tracing of the sources of
literature to social practices? In discussing his book *S/Z*, Roland
Barthes formulated the problem in the following terms:

11. Jacques Derrida, "Signature Event Context," in *Margins of Philosophy*, trans.
Alan Bass (Chicago, 1982), p. 325f.
12. Cf. Geoffrey Hartman, "Words and Wounds," in *Saving the Text* (Baltimore,
1981), see esp. pp. 119ff.
13. I draw here on de Certeau's discussion of the "science de la fable," *L'Invention du
quotidien*, vol. 1, pp. 270ff.

Can semiology allow, through the intermediary of the notion of connotation, a return to a kind of sociology of literature? . . . there is indeed in S/Z, by virtue of the description of the codes . . . a possibility of sociological exploitation. . . . Thus, for example, it would be possible to conceive of re-reading Balzac in order to examine the cultural intertextuality that furnishes the somewhat dense and heavy, not to say overbearing and a little nauseous, layer of the Balzacian text. . . . Thus literary semiotics could provide a point of departure for a kind of cultural semiology, but once again, even there, one would have to conceive of a rather new kind of sociology of literature which could and should benefit from what I would call intertextual sensibility, sensibility with respect to the intertext. . . . The first rule of this intertextual analysis would be to understand that the intertext is not a problem of sources, for the source is a named origin while the intertext is without locatable origin.[14]

In a traditional sociological approach, Barthes suggests, a mere sensitivity to cultural codes cannot guard the interpreter from an exercise in reduplication, a collecting and classification of data that in the last analysis leads to a monumentalization of the very practices he treats. Any excessive concern with origins—whether social, economic, biographical, or literary—will lead him to reduce the issue of signification to a question of mere content (what Barthes sometimes calls the level of denotation). By contrast, the system of codes as he conceives it in S/Z is not merely a classifying mechanism but also a dialectical, self-reflexive, interpretive procedure. "We have to encode ourselves: in order to be able to outplay the codes it is necessary to enter into the play of codification," he writes. And, in answer to an interviewer's remark that he seems to be fascinated by the very codes that he attempts to "outplay," Barthes replies, "Absolutely. So much so that I am fascinated by extremely aggressive forms of codes, like, precisely, stupidity (la bêtise)."[15]

In S/Z, the "referential" or "cultural" code is the one most directly concerned with the intrusion of commonplace wisdom and commonsense know-how in the literary text. Barthes is interested in exposing the highly developed but covert practices whereby a culture propagates its political-ethical tenets. Since these practices derive from the most pervasive and unexamined customs and attitudes in a

14. Stephen Heath, "A Conversation with Roland Barthes," in Signs of the Times, ed. S. Heath (n.p., n.d.), p. 46.
15. "A Conversation with Roland Barthes," p. 49.

culture, they cannot be contradicted or denounced. They may, however, be exposed or laid bare ("mettre chaque code *ventre en l'air*").[16] They may be thematized by means of an anatomizing deformation that makes explicit the underlying authority principle. For example, Barthes argues, it is the stylistic appeal of proverbial expressions that accounts in great measure for their moral authority; or, the credit or popular science in an epoch derives from the prestige of the didactic genres that purvey it: "one might say that it is the major voice of minor science that is departing in this fashion. In fact, these citations are extracted from a body of knowledge, from an anonymous Book whose best model is doubtless the School Manual." Thus, Barthes's overall treatment of the endoxal sphere—the sphere of stale information and habituated social attitudes—is guided by a tactical adoption of the *doxa* (*la bêtise*) as a means of "outplaying" the codes. The Flaubertian strain is, of course, quite intentional.[17]

Barthes's fascination with degraded modes of discourse, his adherence to tactics of complicity, can be better understood, I think, if we set it beside Heidegger's discussion of logos (discourse, *Rede*) and (mere) talk (*Gerede*) in the early parts of *Sein und Zeit*. (I am not looking for a source for Barthes but am attempting to elaborate certain aspects of his argument.)

For Heidegger, discourse in its primordial, a priori sense is characterized through its disclosing and articulating potential:

Die Rede spricht sich zumeist aus und hat sich schon immer ausgesprochen. Sie ist Sprache. Im Ausgesprochenen liegt aber dann je schon Verständnis und Auslegung. Die Sprache als die Ausgesprochenheit birgt eine Ausgelegtheit des Daseinsverständnisses in sich. Diese Ausgelegtheit ist so wenig wie die Sprache nur noch vorhanden, sondern ihr Sein ist selbst daseinsmäßiges. Ihr ist das Dasein zunächst und in gewissen Grenzen ständig überantwortet.[18]

16. *S/Z: An Essay*, p. 100. The following passage is on p. 205.

17. Cf. Jonathan Culler's chapter on Flaubert's notion of stupidity in *Flaubert: The Uses of Uncertainty* (London, 1974), pp. 157–85.

18. Martin Heidegger, *Sein und Zeit* (Tübingen, 1949), p. 167. In English: "For the most part, discourse is expressed by being spoken out, and has always been so expressed; it is language. But in that case understanding and interpretation already lie in what has thus been expressed. In language, as a way things have been expressed or spoken out, there is hidden a way in which the understanding of Dasein has been interpreted. This way of interpreting it is no more just present-at-hand than language is; on the contrary, its Being is itself of the character of Dasein. Proximally, and with certain limits, Dasein is constantly delivered over to this interpretedness." *Being and Time*, trans. John Macquarrie and Edward Robinson (New York, 1962), p. 211.

This interpretedness (*Ausgelegtheit*) to which Dasein is given over is necessarily subject to the "lapsed" status (*Verfallen*) of all worldly commerce, and this Heidegger calls, in a powerfully suggestive but untranslatable formulation, *Gerede*. Idiomatically, of course, the word is familiar enough, signifying gossip, chatter, idle talk. But Heidegger's usage gives special prominence to the perfective sense (through the prefix *ge-*), the "already spoken." *Gerede* thus suggests the porosity of (mere) talk, its circular and medial nature, its incapacity to provide any definitive explication of reality in view of a constitutive self-entanglement:

> Das Hören und Verstehen hat sich vorgängig an das Geredete als solches geklammert. Die Mitteilung "teilt" nicht den primären Seinsbezug zum beredeten Seienden, sondern das Miteinandersein bewegt sich im Miteinanderreden und Besorgen des Geredeten. Ihm liegt daran, daß geredet wird. . . . Das Geredete als solches zieht weitere Kreise und übernimmt autoritativen Charakter. Die Sache ist so, weil man es sagt. In solchem Nach- und Weiterreden . . . konstituiert sich das Gerede.[19]

Seldom has the "phatic" function in the communicative process (in Jakobson's sense) been revealed in a more ominous light.

Now there is a temptation in interpreting this concept to take it as a failure of human discourse, a "bad" way of talking which might be redeemed by a more appropriate, authentic mode. But within the argument of *Sein und Zeit, Gerede* represents the concretization of discourse, of logos; it is the totality of words, the what-has-been-spoken, put in the service of Dasein's dealing with the world. At this level language takes on the features of all tool or "equipmental" structures available to man. Characteristic of Dasein's "thrownness" (*Geworfenheit*) is that it has to deal with what it has, in terms not of its own choosing. Language, as an aspect of its communicative-expressive apparatus, also partakes of this structure. Insofar as Dasein is enmeshed in the context of worldly occupations it utilizes *Gerede,* the what-has-been-spoken, inescapably, unthinkingly.

The degraded status of *Gerede* is thus a consequence of the lapsed

---

19. Ibid., p. 168. In English: "Hearing and understanding have attached themselves beforehand to what is said-in-the-talk as such. The primary relationship-of-Being towards the entity talked about is not 'imparted' by communication; but Being-with-one-another takes place in talking with one another and in concern with what is said-in-the-talk. To this Being-with-one-another, the fact that talking is going on is a matter of consequence. . . . What is said-in-the-talk as such, spreads in wider circles and takes on an authoritative character. Things are so because one says so. Idle talk is constituted by just such gossiping and passing the word along." *Being and Time,* p. 212.

condition (*Verfallen*) of Dasein. As Jan Alper puts it, "Man's Being-in [the world] as a Being-with [the things of the world] is inclined toward Being away from."[20] This well expresses the constitutive alienation of Dasein, but as an ontological alienation, not an existential and ethical one. It follows from this that the "lapse" of *Gerede* consists precisely in its need of support, its incapacity to speak of itself, since it can only speak of the things-in-the-world. Such a condition is not to be made good by some kind of purified, "authentic" form of discourse. That would be to substitute one form of *Gerede* for another. Put differently, speech as a manifestation of Dasein's Being-in-the-world cannot realize a condition of logos.

Gerede, as we have seen, is "interpretable," and necessarily so by virtue of its derivation from language in general. More specifically, Heidegger maintains that Dasein realizes an ongoing process of understanding and explicitation by means of *Gerede:* "Der Ausdruck 'Gerede' soll hier nicht in 'herabziehenden' Bedeutung gebraucht werden. Er bedeutet terminologisch ein positives Phänomen, das die Seinsart des Verstehens und Auslegens des alltäglichen Daseins konstituiert."[21] But of course this level of understanding is not conceived as conclusive by Heidegger. It constitutes the first part of the program of *Sein und Zeit,* the "interpretation of Dasein in its everydayness," which is to be recognized at a later stage as having been partial and distorted. I am not concerned here to trace this development in Heidegger's work. Rather, I have limited myself to the "anthropological" level of the work, what Foucault calls "the analytic of finitude,"[22] since it is preeminently here, as we see it, that Heidegger points the way to the kind of analysis which critics like Barthes have pursued and which is most pertinent for a reevaluation of the realist novel and its modernist progeny.

If, now, we seek to specify what *Gerede* refers to within the system of literature, we might initially define it as a means of exhibiting *la bêtise* and thus making it available for parody and ridicule.

---

20. "Heidegger's Conception of Language in *Being and Time,*" in *On Heidegger and Language,* ed. Joseph J. Kockelmans (Evanston, Ill., 1972), pp. 33–62. This quotation is on p. 55.

21. *Sein und Zeit,* p. 167. In English: "The expression 'idle talk' is not to be used here in a 'disparaging' signification. Terminologically, it signifies a positive phenomenon which constitutes the kind of Being of everyday Dasein's understanding and interpreting." *Being and Time,* p. 211.

22. Cited in Hubert L. Dreyfus and Paul Rabinow, *Michel Foucault: Beyond Structuralism and Hermeneutics* (Chicago, 1982), pp. 38ff. I draw on this work regarding Heidegger's program in *Sein und Zeit.*

"How can stupidity be pinned down without declaring oneself intelligent?" asks Barthes.[23] But I am fascinated by another feature in the notion of *Gerede*, a cognitive and disclosing function, consistent with Heidegger's "alltägliche Ausgelegtheit der Welt." At this level *Gerede* would be a scene of parasitism that saps the instrumental, purely communicative function of everyday talk and brings about an effect of displacement and supplementarity.

For *Gerede* knows no master. If it can be termed a code, it is a singularly unstructured one. But it has the characteristic of any *koine* or common tongue, that its baseness (commonness) underwrites its universality (being common to all), and vice versa. If it is to be isolated, to be made available for examination and analysis, it will be by means of a logic of cunning, perhaps something like Michel Serres's principle of the parasite[24] or de Certeau's tactical *coups,* or strikes.[25]

In Melville's *Confidence-Man* the Missourian ponders the deception played on him, "He revolves the crafty process of sociable chat, by which, as he fancies, the man with the brass-plate wormed into him" (p. 113).[26] Melville's master of proxies, his chameleon interlocutor, who has, of course, tricked the Missourian, among many others, thrives within a murmur of voices that he is able to discriminate and articulate by means of "the crafty process." At one point he himself identifies the medium that has bred and that sustains him: "For the voice of the people is the voice of truth. Don't you think so?" "Of course I do [replies Charlie Noble]. If Truth don't speak through the people, it never speaks at all; so I heard one say" (p. 142).

* * *

Vox Populi—Melville evokes here another variant of the debased logos, the ready currency of social intercourse ("sociable chat"). *The Confidence-Man* may be placed in a line of modern novels—including *Don Quixote, Tristram Shandy, The Pickwick Papers, L'Éducation sentimentale, Bouvard et Pécuchet, Der Stechlin,* and *Ulysses*—that could be termed novels of idle talk, of *Gerede.* They are works whose sustaining principle, their red thread, is neither the action nor a central protagonist but rather a principle of discourse, a principle that cannot be reduced to a formula, a turn, or a trick, although it can be

23. *S/Z: An Essay,* p. 206.
24. See *The Parasite,* trans. Lawrence R. Schehr (Baltimore, 1982).
25. See *L'Invention du quotidien,* chaps. 3 and 6.
26. Herman Melville, *The Confidence-Man,* ed. Hershel Parker (New York, 1971). Page references are given parenthetically in the text.

shown, in each case, to manifest a continuous, cumulative pattern. Many readers of *The Confidence-Man* seek a unity of character beyond the masks, the successive metamorphoses. Their tendency has been to allegorize the protagonist, to see in his various permutations a constant type, whether it be divine or demonic.[27] Alternatively, some critics who have recognized the novel's linguistic focus have generally been too quick to treat language in terms of an absence of meaning, of sincerity, of truth values. Such a reading remains bound to a dualistic view of language and neglects its medial nature, its capacity for indirection.[28]

In this novel Melville undertakes to foreground the dialogic situation itself while underspecifying the narrative posts or agencies. In terms of the communicative circuit outlined above we may note a radical instability in all three narrative posts, that of sender, receptor, and referent. The referent or subject matter is a reiterated appeal for "confidence" (or one of its analogues like "charity" or "trust"). But this notion is no more than a lure, a concept emptied from the start so as to serve as a means of manipulation.[29] The receptor is inconsequential in terms of personality or individuality but interesting only insofar as he is more or less of a dupe (or, to put it another way, the receptor is no more than a function of the sender, his "personality" wholly constituted by his reaction to the blandishments of the confidence man). The sender, finally, the confidence-man figure, is by no means a stable, consistently successful master of the game. Although he succeeds in

27. John W. Shroeder, "Sources and Symbols for Melville's *Confidence-Man*" (reprinted in the Norton edition cited above, pp. 298–316), is typical of the widespread view of the confidence man as a devil figure. The editor of the Norton edition, Hershel Parker, also argues this position in his annotations. Warwick Wadlington, *The Confidence Game in American Literature* (Princeton, 1975), surveys a range of interpretations, p. 139n. His own warns us against falling prey to any reductive identification; see pp. 168ff.

28. Cf. Cecelia Tichi, "Melville's Craft and the Theme of Language Debased in *The Confidence-Man*," ELH 39(1972): 639–58. One can agree with Tichi's view of *The Confidence-Man* "as a manual of the epistemology of language" (p. 658) without subscribing to her sense of just how "craft and theme" combine in the novel. Her analysis assumes a simple, incontrovertible measure for the authenticity of language: "Since language is the symbolic cache of ethical commitment, the diction of ethics becomes a very cheap commodity whenever, as in *The Confidence-Man*, the commitment is lacking" (p. 648). But what is to reveal this supposed lack of commitment but language itself, and then where is the standard to be drawn for assessing *that* language? Melville is operating with a much more elusive issue than Tichi can get hold of through her thematic approach.

29. Cf. *The Confidence Game in American Literature*, p. 158f. "Most of the Confidence-Man's statements, the most outrageous optimistic lies, can be seen as a species of heuristic truth once we recognize the hero's motivations and the strategies of his confidence game."

besting his interlocutors in every encounter in the first part of the novel, the price he pays—his fluidity, the virtual dissipation of any personal substance—is exorbitant. In the middle of the work (chaps. 21–24) he encounters the Missourian Pitch, the first of his interlocutors to see through him. Thereafter, in the role the confidence man assumes as the Cosmopolitan, he is himself repeatedly blocked and brought low.[30] This relinquishment of mastery is consistent with the pattern I have been tracing. Since the several agencies that normally structure the narrative message suffer displacement and erosion, what remains as the primary subject matter is not a narrative substance, a story situated in a determinate channel of transmission, but the problematic nature of the channel itself.

But this conclusion only identifies the issue to be addressed; it does not resolve it. What model of action, what form of protagonist would need to be posited to account for a focus on the channel of transmission rather than on the basic narrative posts? Michel Serres's concept of the parasite can help us here. Serres's is a theory of communication and of power. Insofar as it is relevant to narrative structure, its concern is with the pragmatic dimension, that is, with the *effects* of storytelling—who gains, who loses, in what ways does the story content alter the relation of the sender and receptor?

What is a parasite? It is, of course, an organism that feeds on another, with the implication that it gains its sustenance invalidly, by theft or stealth rather than by work or exchange. This moral connotation would not apply in certain contexts where parasitism is an acknowledged phenomenon, notably, in biology and radio communication (for the French, *parasite* also means static, the noise or interference in an electronic transmission). Etymologically, parasite involves food (Gr. *sitos*), and more specifically, being next to, proximate to (*para-*) food (of another).[31] Clearly, this scientific-technical term involves an anthropomorphic element. Conversely, the language dealing with social and moral relations may be stretched and shaded by notions that are operative in a technical discourse. We cannot avoid such contamination, or rather, cross-fertilization between semantic registers. "I am using words in an unusual way," (p. 6) Serres writes in explaining why he is prepared to extend the terminology of para-

30. Henry Sussman's excellent study of the novel underlines this feature: "The Deconstructor as Politician: Melville's *Confidence-Man*," *Glyph 4: Johns Hopkins Textual Studies* (Baltimore, 1978), 32–56, see esp. p. 43f.

31. Cf. *The Parasite*, pp. 6f. and 144.

sitology beyond the domain of invertebrates, to which it properly applies.

> Here's the answer. The basic vocabulary of this science comes from such ancient and common customs and habits that the earliest monuments of our culture tell of them, and we still see them, at least in part: hospitality, conviviality, table manners, hostelry, general relations with strangers. Thus the vocabulary is imported to this pure science and bears several traces of anthropomorphism. The animal-host offers a meal from the larder or from his own flesh; as a hotel or a hostel, he provides a place to sleep, quite graciously, of course.
>
> These customs and manners can be the object of anthropological study; they were once the pleasures of idle reading, when literature still existed. Literature made clear, even for the blind, a kind of figural, instructive anthropology that was both accessible and profound. (p. 6)

Serres is fully cognizant that a theory of communication, with its inherent logical and technological constraints, implies relations of power, and that these relations in turn give rise to a variant logic. Thus it is that the "figural anthropology" referred to above comes into play.

The Parasite is a wide-ranging book that has relevance for a number of disciplines. I shall try to elicit from it those arguments that pertain to a narrative pragmatics as exemplified in *The Confidence-Man.* (Serres himself, it should be noted, makes no reference to this novel.) Let us posit two interlocutors—they are within the *doxa,* the accredited order of a traditional discourse. Such a dual or specular communicative model constitutes a closed system and assumes the possibility of maximal communication, of a nearly perfect transmission between two poles. But such an exchange would also be tautological, since the model ignores a basic factor in any communication, the channel of transmission. In order to complete the model we need to posit an agency capable of accounting for the resistance inherent in the medium of transmission.

Such an agency may be conceived as operating either through force, through a violent intervention in the system, or through a tactical maneuver that would arouse minimal resistance and yet still modify or transform it. The parasite is such a mobile agent, one that stands prepared to seize its chance, to turn a situation to its advantage, but one that is also ready to retreat, to disappear and revert to the status of a mere disturbance in the channel, to static or "noise." It represents the possibility of nonviolent transformation in every system. The parasite splices into an existent system or circuit and func-

tions as a "joker," a polyvalent hinge or connector capable of adapting to a situation so as to facilitate its transformation.[32] It is the
tactician of the quotidian. It saps, not combats, the system that serves
as its host. It is itself expendable, subject at every moment to being
displaced and eliminated, though its function does not thereby
disappear.

The parasite is in the position of an observer vis-à-vis the observed, of a subject vis-à-vis an object. That is to say, in what is
apparently a reciprocal relation, a communicative dyad, the parasite
holds secretly aloof. He has a special interest to guard. Serres writes:

> The observer is perhaps the inobservable. He must, at least, be last on
> the chain of observables. If he is supplanted, he becomes observed. Thus
> he is in a position of a parasite. Not only because he takes the observa-
> tion that he doesn't return, but also because he plays the last posi-
> tion. . . . Thus the parasite is the most silent of beings, and that is the
> paradox, since *parasite* also means noise. Small, protozoan, insect, it is
> invisible; it cannot be felt; it copies so as to disappear; it puts on a
> spotless white shirt; it keeps quiet; it listens. It observes. (p. 237)

For Serres the interesting point is to disclose what is at stake in
this apparently intrusive element, the asystemic factor that is nonetheless integral to a system and capable of transforming it. For the parasite is a constant rather than an anomaly in a system, but it will
disappear once it is noticed, once its share in the exchange, whether of
goods or of language, becomes evident.

> The system is cancelled when the parasited one makes noise in feedback.
> But this signal does not last. . . . At the first noise, the system is can-
> celled: if the noise stops, everything comes back to where it was. That
> shows at least that the parasites are always there, even in the absence of a
> signal. Only the noticeable signal cancels them. They are inevitable, like
> white noise. White noise [*bruit de fond*] is the heart [*fond*] of being;
> parasitism is the heart of relation. (p. 52)

What Serres terms the "signal" on the part of the host, the parasited
one, is a complex operation. It may serve to expose and to dissipate
the parasitic intervention. It may function as a kind of feedback that
insures the continued operation of a system, but it always threatens to
escape the control of the host by canceling the system altogether.
There is a predisposition on the part of the accredited interlocutors to

32. Cf. Ibid., pp. 162ff.
33. *The Confidence Game in American Literature*, pp. 140 and 142.

protect the channel that connects them, to cleanse it, to purge it of alien matter. This gives rise to the form of an "excluded third," a logical or rhetorical pattern that is often projected as a figure of demon or devil, what Serres terms a "prosopopeia of noise" (p. 56). "In order to succeed," he writes, "the dialogue needs an excluded third; our logic requires the same thing" (p. 57). The repeated emergence of the parasite testifies to the insufficiency of a logic based exclusively on a principle of inclusion and exclusion. Once the excluded third is spotted, it may disappear, but it does so either by usurping one of the authorized positions (and thus generating another parasite) or by retreating and adopting a new tactic.

We are now prepared to see that in *The Confidence-Man* the tactics of *Gerede*, the pervasive use of a hollowed-out form of speech, represents not merely a stylistic device, a surface feature, but also the very core of the action. One of the most acute critics of the novel, Warwick Wadlington, has written that the work gives the impression of "being stuffed with words. . . . It seems clear that the author, like his hero, seeks to escape the universal tyranny of words by indulging them in a certain fashion."[33] Certainly, it is a work in which the play of language seems not only extravagant but wasteful, disregardful of the accountability of language, of what is generally taken as its basic normative and referential obligation. In what ways, then, is the language of the novel to be held accountable? Wadlington makes an important point in speaking of a "lack of telos." Referring to the novel's conclusion he says that

> there is no "event" because nothing *finally* happens. Quite to the contrary. Something originally is undone in a quiet decreation. For the most remarkable truth about the novel is that it goes backward, not in history but in human process defined in traditional terms. . . . So the book is directly the reverse of what criticism has tended to call it: apocalyptic. It is anti-apocalyptic and counter-teleological. More exactly, in the root senses, it is apocryphal and archeological; it disappears into the *arche*, concealing itself there, in the primal darkness of a reverse creation.[34]

I would now like to demonstrate such a "decreation" at the level of the discourse. My use of *Gerede* as a clue is designed to push backward, as Wadlington suggests, "not in history but in human process defined in traditional terms." *The Confidence-Man* seems to me to be a phe-

---

34. Ibid., p. 165. Wadlington is alluding to the discussion between the Cosmopolitan and the old man regarding the biblical Apocrypha in chap. 45.

nomenological exploration of the ways that societal patterns and ethical norms emerge out of a more primordial activity, one in which the speech of interpersonal exchanges is not yet tamed, not yet under the full control of individual agents.

The setting of *The Confidence-Man* is a steamboat, the *Fidèle*, engaged in its circular journey up and down the Mississippi—a conveyance without origin, without terminus, populated by a crowd that is itself a miscellaneous aggregate. It is a pattern of apparently chaotic, criss-crossing motion, a maze of pathways suspended within a frame, like an immense circuit board, with multiple vectors but no apparent source or telos that defines any of them.

> Though her voyage of twelve hundred miles extends from apple to orange, from clime to clime, yet, like any small ferry-boat, to right and left, at every landing, the huge Fidèle still receives additional passengers in exchange for those that disembark; so that, though always full of strangers, she continually, in some degree, adds to, or replaces them with strangers still more strange; like Rio Janeiro fountain, fed from the Corcovado mountains, which is ever overflowing with strange waters, but never with the same strange particle in every part. (p. 5)

The confidence man in his first embodiment is characterized by a singular blankness, an absence of distinctive features: he is a deaf-mute, dressed in cream colors, "his cheek was fair, his chin downy, his hair flaxen, his hat a white fur one, with a long fleecy nap" (p. 1). His behavior betokens an inveterate latency, a status totally subject to the circumstances around him. At one point, as he lies sleeping on deck, he is characterized through a series of phrases spoken by members of the crowd milling about,

> "Odd fish!"
> "Poor fellow!"
> "Who can he be?"
> "Casper Hauser."
> "Bless my soul!"
> "Uncommon countenance."
> "Green prophet from Utah."
> "Humbug!" (p. 4)

The definition of this figure, his very substance, seems to arise only from the speech of others, from the conventional or proverbial epithets that are thrown out by nameless voices. Later, too, in some of his subsequent manifestations, the confidence man seems very much a creature of words, more specifically, of conversation, of sociable intercourse. Like Poe's "man of the crowd" the confidence man has a tendency to shrink and fade when not buoyed by society.[35]

His most evident action in his first impersonation is to manipulate a slate tablet on which he writes a series of slogans or biblical tags (drawn from I Corinthians), each beginning with the word *Charity*, thus: "Charity thinketh no evil," or "Charity suffereth long, and is kind." The initial term remains fixed while the rest of the phrase is repeatedly erased and revised. These messages, addressed to a jostling, unsympathetic crowd, are patently ineffectual. The whole spectacle is nugatory, self-canceling, which may be ascribed in equal measure to the familiarity of the tags, the flimsiness of the communicative medium, and the insignificance of the scribe. Furthermore, the form of inscription and display—a single term followed by a variety of predicates—may be taken as a syntactic version of the pattern behind the successive appearances of the confidence man himself. In each case we have a stable function, an invariant structural element, attached to a series of discrete, qualitative features.

In the first part of the novel the "masquerade" is still overt. The relays of the confidence man reflect a continuity of tactics among the multiple identities. Also, the partners with whom he deals are in every case clearly delineated types (e.g., Roberts, the merchant; the collegian). The confidence man is able in each encounter to come off with a prize of some sort—a contribution, a dole, some sapping of the wealth of the other. But in the second part, beginning with chapter 24, there is a change. The confidence man is now concentrated in a single figure, the Cosmopolitan, one who "federates, in heart as in costume, something of the various gallantries of men under various suns" (p. 115). This emphasis on the outward costume, on ornamental features, suggests yet a further attenuation of personality, of individual substance. There are fewer encounters in this later part than in the first, the later part having only six—the Missourian Pitch, Charlie Noble, Mark Winsome, his disciple Egbert (who then assumes the name of Charlie Noble), the barber, and the old man. And the two longest involve the Charlie Noble figures, whose functional similarity is underscored by the doubling of the name.

In the first part the exchanges involved a range of monetary transactions, from the throwing of coppers at the negro cripple (chap.

35. "Society his stimulus, loneliness was his lethargy. . . . In short, left to himself, with none to charm forth his latent lymphatic, he insensibly resumes his original air, a quiescent one, blended of sad humility and demureness" p. 37. Cf. also p. 124. Poe's tale "The Man of the Crowd" was published in 1840.

3) to the stock transactions of the Black Rapids Coal Company (chap. 10). But in the second part of the monetary factor is barely an issue—in one episode, in fact, it is reduced to a purely symbolic function, a prop in a mock ceremony whereby the Cosmopolitan disarms Charlie Noble's ire (chaps. 31–32). The seam between the two parts is neatly marked by Pitch's meditation on "the crafty process of sociable chat," which is interrupted by "a voice, sweet as a seraph's: 'A penny for your thoughts, my fine fellow'" (p. 113). This introduces the Cosmopolitan. His invocation of the stereotypical "penny" (a saying in this instance and not a monetary token) marks the shift to the new principle of exchange, one that will operate not so much in terms of specie but of tokens of sociability—courtesies, compliments, stories, mere talk.

The contestants now vie for a measure of social precedence. Proffered courtesies and narratives become maneuvers in a contest that is still intense, though more veiled than in the first part. The extended discussion of Polonius, the scrutiny of his advice to Laertes ("Crams him with maxims smacking of my Lord Chesterfield, with maxims of France, with maxims of Italy" [p. 148]), brings the issue of verbal manipulation more to the fore. Further, the confidence man's partners are no longer put in the position of straight men who serve primarily to display his superior cunning. The contestants in this later part are more like equals. It becomes evident, in fact, that the confidence man is less a figure than a function, one that may migrate among the several parties in the course of an encounter.

Much of the exchange between the Cosmopolitan and the stranger he first encounters, Charlie Noble, involves sharing a bottle of port (chaps. 28–35). This ritual of hospitality and conviviality serves as the basis for a mutual testing of the partners. Although it is Charlie Noble who suggests ordering the wine, he is decidedly hesitant to drink it. His first small draught is "followed by a slight involuntary wryness to the mouth" (p. 140). Through the whole exchange that follows, each repeatedly urges the other to drink, while at the same time himself maintaining considerable reserve regarding the wine. The episode concludes with Charlie Noble's departure with a headache. "This confounded elixir of logwood, little as I drank of it, has played the deuce with me," he exclaims in leaving (p. 161). The wine itself is successively characterized as poison, medicine, sacrament, intoxicant, agent of conviviality and geniality, source of knowledge.

What is the true object, the referent, of these metaphoric variants? Embedded in this episode we find a formal panegyric, "a poetical eulogy" of "the press" (chaps. 29–30). What is being praised? The "black press" or "the red" (printing or wine)? Again, the referent seems to elude the spoken exercise, the ritual of the panegyric in this case. Although this exercise may appear to be nothing but a verbal exhibition, "a kind of poetry, . . . A sort of free-and-easy chant with refrains to it" (p. 143), it retains a pragmatic orientation. Some practical consequence is at stake depending on what referent is stipulated, even if that consequence is as slight as having to drink a bottle of bad wine.

In both instances just discussed, that of the wine and of the press, the parasite serves as an index of the object in question, of the referent. The interest extracted by the parasite, far from being a dead loss, a diminution of property, may well be what confirms its worth. Even with so dubious an object as the bottle of port, the point is not to determine its quality in absolute terms but rather to stipulate its identity through an act of appropriation (making it one's own, turning it to some use). The referent or substance (noting the etymological sense, what stands *under* the object) cannot be discerned or identified directly. We follow the clue of what feeds on it, what saps it. The parasite marks the vector of substance in its use, in its expropriation (in the erosion of the *propre*).

The kinds of displacement I have sought to chart in the social exchanges are operative as well in the narrative practices, in the manipulation and conveyance of story material. Stories are generated in the course of the encounters, but responsibility for them is evaded, and their significance, their illustrative function, is repeatedly obscured. At the level of narrative voices an elaborate ventriloquism is at work. "Not my story, mind, or my thoughts, but another's" (p. 135), remarks Judge Hall, the narrator of the story of Colonel Moredock the Indian-hater, and Hall is himself, of course, being cited by the first Charlie Noble. This form of intricately nested narration is carried still further in the telling of the story of China Aster. Here it is Egbert, Mark Winsome's disciple (who also calls himself Charlie Noble), who is the narrator, and again, he claims to speak only as the mouthpiece of another (cf. p. 177). The pragmatic function of the tale as far as Egbert is concerned is clear—to justify his refusal of a loan to the Cosmopolitan. Its moral is made perfectly explicit: "the folly on both sides, of a friend's helping a friend" (p. 190). And yet, as the Cosmopolitan realizes, the consequence of the tale for him would be to relinquish his own control over the roles he assumes. Egbert's tale threatens to box him in, no less than China Aster had been disposed of (encrypted) in his grave at the end of the tale. The Cosmopolitan protests, "for neither am I China Aster, nor do I stand in his position" (p. 191). And though Egbert tries once more to force an identity upon him ("bow over to the ground, and supplicate an alms of me in the way of London streets" p. 192), the Cosmopolitan makes his escape, "leaving his companion at a loss to determine where exactly the fictitious character had been dropped, and the real one, if any, resumed" (p. 192).

Who wins? This remains unclear. The Cosmopolitan leaves in scorn, having failed to win a loan. Egbert has succeeded in avoiding any pecuniary obligation, though he cannot feel secure about having outmaneuvered his companion. The tale itself, exceeding its exemplary function, fails to provide sanction for either of the interlocutors.

Let us recall that the story of China Aster is about a modest candlemaker who is prevailed upon by a seeming friend, Orchis, to accept a loan for the purpose of expanding his enterprise. After a series of misfortunes and miscalculations China Aster is reduced to penury and eventually dies a ruined man. He leaves behind a wife, who also dies in misery, and children, who end up in the poorhouse, as their grandfather had done before them. All this is witnessed and commented on by two advisers, Old Plain Talk and Old Prudence, who had from the start counseled China Aster against assuming any financial obligation. The story, one might say, is an object lesson perfectly calculated to drive home Egbert's self-regarding philosophy. And yet, what appears to be a clear pattern of entropic decay proves otherwise. "The action bifurcates and the tautology starts to predicate; it slips; it jumps to something else" (*The Parasite*, p. 160).

What characterizes China Aster throughout the tale is his extraordinary pliancy and impotence. He is a toy of circumstance, or of anyone who wishes to impose on him. As John Carlos Rowe observes:

> Much of the story's irony depends upon the doubling of fertility and impotence, eros and thanatos. China Aster appears to supplement the infertility of his financial relation with Orchis by producing several children, who subsequently become such burdens to his indigent widow that she is hurried to her grave. The children are themselves condemned to the poorhouse. Although this relation between impotence and fertility merely repeats an old cliché ("the rich get richer; the poor get children"), it also suggests how every system of representation produces its

meanings only by repressing its own dissipation: the straying of the letter that is the fear of every author.[36]

For China Aster in his grave is not quite dead, or rather, his death provides the occasion for preserving his story, storing its meaning through a scriptive afterlife that has the effect of rescuing the message and of setting it loose, of severing it from its source.

An epitaph has been found in his "otherwise empty wallet," one written by China Aster himself. His two counselors, "thinking that, since a dead man was to be spoken about, it was but just to let him speak for himself" (p. 188), arrange to have it inscribed on his gravestone. The message of the epitaph only confirms the prevalent moral that the confidence man has heard throughout his encounters, namely, "No trust" (to cite the version from the barber's placard). But the form in which it surfaces in this tale represents the most extreme instance of that ventriloquism that has become more and more prominent as the book proceeds. China Aster, who throughout his life had had his voice usurped by another, whether by the seeming friend Orchis or by the reproachful counselors, now finally descends to the lowest position possible, one where he must apparently be altogether speechless. And here he is granted a voice, an "epitaphic" speech. What this voice expresses is not new; it can only repeat a moral already enunciated. But the form of its expression, the "figure" of its speech, is noteworthy. The principle of ventriloquism mentioned earlier, a principle of narrative displacement along a parasitic chain, finds an appropriate exemplar in this voice from the grave, the source of a commemorative inscription that marks the site of its own story. The story of China Aster displays the model of a Chinese box, a device of endless "boxing" or framing whose heart or center can never be shown but only figured by something like the hypothetical vocalization of an epitaph.[37]

I began this chapter with a discussion of the citational dimension of the novel and of the novel's dependence on a discursivity that is embedded in social practices, at the levels of *doxa* and of *koine*. What is paradoxical about this level of discourse is that it is both pervasive

36. "Ecliptic Voyaging: Orbits of the Sign in Melville's 'Bartleby the Scrivener,' " in *Through the Custom-House* (Baltimore, 1982), p. 117.

37. I have profited from Paul Fry's discussion of certain forms of Romantic epitaph as "the burial of voice, a concession to the tomblike bar between signifier and signified that leaves only the bar itself as theme and place of presentation." "The Absent Dead: Wordsworth, Byron, and the Epitaph," *Studies in Romanticism* 17(1978): p. 433.

and unnoticed. In one sense it has the status of "white noise," a screening effect designed to cover up other noise, to suppress content or referent. But it may, in unpredictable ways, itself assume a referential status, make a claim to meaning. It is this irruption of a blank or negative factor that, I think, Heidegger suggests through his treatment of the interpretability of everydayness. I have used his notion of *Gerede* to identify a stage at which quotidian talk (language nearly unnoticed) begins to emerge and to assume an operative force of its own. My aim has been to reveal a primary level of language use, one which, because of its apparent neutrality, its lack of affect and personal agency, might be least subject to conceptual appropriation.

The novel, as the most assimilative and leveling of genres, has proven itself singularly hospitable to this type of language use. In exploring the tactical deployment of a form of *Gerede* in a given instance I have tried to work out just what kind of energy (what exercise of power) may be put into play in this manner.

At the level of discursive practice we may say that the parasitic function involves the maintenance of a channel of communication without a betrayal of the tax or toll that is being extraced from it. The parasite facilitates intercourse by bringing the channels to the surface, making it evident. But it can never be altogether disinterested in regard to the channel, and this "interest" may become so prominent as to absorb the communicative function itself. At this point a pragmatic force, a performative dimension, emerges out of quotidian (idle) talk.

The task for the confidence man is to maintain his privileged position without revealing it, and this he attempts by maintaining a stream of talk, by continually adapting his speech to that of his interlocutor so that he will not betray his purpose. Speech of this type— *Gerede* or parasitic talk—is normally conceived simply as a facilitating medium of social intercourse but it may also turn into a systematic diversion of meaning. Such talk is never merely noise. It cannot help but betray a purpose. Serres writes, "People hardly ever talk about the noise attached like a string to the tongue, indispensable for speaking; people hardly ever talk about the signal attached to the sign. . . . Whom do these noises make flee?" (p. 236). The confidence man's tactic can only be maintained through unremitting vigilance. It involves a continual effort to neutralize his talk, shifting its direction whenever the point, his own (the subject's) *interest,* becomes too prominent. This interest (the underlying concern but also the anticipated gain, the tax) must be dissimulated, kept out of sight, while all the time it fuels the talk, keeps it "idling."

PART II

5 The Two Julies: Conversion and Imagination in *La Nouvelle Héloïse*

Rousseau's Julie, like Ottilie in *Die Wahlverwandtschaften,* may be understood in terms of the kind of hidden or recessive conception of character discussed in Chapter 3, as an attempt to veil a dimension of the self in order to preserve the integrity of the *person.* But in the case of Rousseau such a tendency would not be realized through an opposition to the worldly social sphere. His own sense of society was too eccentric (in both senses, singular and displaced or marginal) to allow him to question its worldly codes from the inside, as Goethe did. Also, the author of the *Confessions* could hardly be accused of reticence in exposing the deepest layers of personal motivation. Nonetheless, in the figure of Julie, Rousseau by no means provides the kind of exposure and analysis of inner self that will become a central feature of nineteenth-century fiction. One reason for this is to be sought in the status of imagination as a compensatory, a "supplementary," capacity (in the Derridean sense). What this signifies for *La Nouvelle Héloïse* can be explored by focusing on the apparent discrepancy between the two Julies. Let us glance first at the history of the work's composition.

We know that Rousseau considered concluding the novel with part 4; Julie and Saint-Preux were to die in the course of their outing on the Lake of Geneva as they were returning from Meillerie.[1] Had Rousseau adopted this plan, the pattern of the book—moving directly from the idyll of the early parts to a tragic denouement that unites the lovers in death—would undoubtedly have been less problematic than it is. But Rousseau did continue. In the last two parts he elaborates

1. See Bernard Guyon's introduction to the Pléiade edition of *La Nouvelle Héloïse,* in *Œuvres Complètes,* vol. 2 (Paris, 1964), pp. xliii–xliv and lxi–lxii, and Robert Osmont, "Remarques sur la genèse et la composition de *La Nouvelle Héloïse,*" *Annales J.J.R.* 33 (1953–55): 93–148.

Julie's transformation into Mme. de Wolmar, stressing her religious turning and her unifying role for the utopian community of Clarens. What is remarkable, however, is that in this development the force of passionate love, dominant in the first two parts, is not rejected or supplanted. At the end of part 4, on her deathbed, Julie looks forward to a union beyond death with Saint-Preux, admitting that she had never ceased to love him. Yet this admission, which her husband transmits to Saint-Preux, is made without transgressing the spirit of her marriage.

It would appear that there are discrepancies, even disturbing inconsistencies, in the place of the work. At the level of genre, it is difficult to reconcile the romantic idyll of the early parts with the didactic and theoretical tone of the later. At the level of character, it is difficult to identify the passionate and witty Julie d'Étange with the preachy, mystically inclined paragon who is the Mme. de Wolmar of the last half.[2]

My aim will be to deal with such indications of a divided structure in terms of a common source, although the problematic status of a "source" will itself emerge as an element of the structure. Such a source is not to be located in any real moment during or after the action; rather, it represents a virtual origin whose "truth" can only be recovered by dramatizing the self's awareness of its separation from an origin. When Julie, as a consequence of her mother's death, renounces her lover, Saint-Preux exclaims, "Cette éternité de bonheur ne fut qu'un instant de ma vie" (p. 296).[3] The oxymoron *éternité-instant* may be understood not only as a heightened expression of the lovers' despair but as a fundamental characterization of the nature of their love. It is a love conceived not so much in terms of real desire, of actual consummation or frustration, as of an activity of the imagination at once productive and self-negating.

In the early stages of the action, the growth and consummation of the love between Julie and Saint-Preux cover some two years (though the letters seem to telescope this period, giving the impression of a more rapid and uninterrupted progression). Marriage is out of the question because of the inveterate opposition of Julie's father, who has already decided on a husband for her. The lovers are forced to sepa-

2. I am aware that this issue has been treated on the level of biography and the genesis of the novel—e.g., by Guyon, in the *Œuvres Complètes* 2: lvi–lvii. But my discussion goes in a quite different direction.

3. Parenthetical citations refer to *Julie, ou La Nouvelle Héloïse,* ed. René Pomeau (Paris, 1960). In English: "That eternity of happiness was but an instant in my life."

rate when their liaison is in danger of being revealed. Julie's mother actually discovers the lovers' letters shortly thereafter. She falls ill and dies, possibly from chagrin related to this discovery. Julie's remorse leads her to renounce her lover forever, though she is not yet ready to accept the husband chosen by her father. Finally she assents even to this, surrendering herself totally to her father's wishes in a spirit of self-abnegation and despair. So far the plot (though not the manner of its treatment) seems to move within the conventions of the sentimental bourgeois fiction of the period. It is what follows in the action that is singular.

Julie does not merely accept her lot in a spirit of compliance and resignation. During the marriage ceremony she undergoes a radical transformation in consequence of which she may be viewed as choosing this act with full personal commitment. And this sudden but nonetheless total and unreserved choice includes the consequences of the act, namely, a definitive rejection of her former lover and, what is more, the condemnation of passionate love. She now zealously defends the institution of matrimony as a support for society and religion and as a necessary defense against irrational drives.

Thus Julie decides, and the decision is a condition for the continuance of the novel beyond part 4 to its ultimate conclusion. She justifies her decision to Saint-Preux in one of the longest letters of the collection, part 3, 18. In it she not only delineates in great detail the inner transformation that allows her to embrace her new position as Wolmar's wife but also inaugurates that self-examination of her religious feelings and beliefs that is to figure so prominently in the last two parts. Bernard Guyon, the editor of the Pléiade edition of the novel, states on the basis of an examination of the manuscripts that the form in which we now have this letter represents a substantial modification of what Rousseau had written at this point when the novel was still to have only four parts.[4] This detail regarding the composition of the work is, of course, not in itself an interpretation, but it confirms my sense that part 3, 18 may fruitfully be read from the perspective of the conclusion.

In her last communication to Saint-Preux, Julie writes, "Oui, j'eus beau vouloir étouffer le premier sentiment qui m'a fait vivre, il s'est concentré dans mon coeur. Il s'y réveille au moment qu'il n'est plus à craindre; il me soutient quand mes forces m'abandonnent; il me

---

4. See Œuvres Complètes 2: xl, lxi. But we possess no draft of this presumed earlier version of part 3, 18.

ranime quand je me meurs" (p. 728).[5] If we bear in mind her admission in this letter that she still loves, and has always loved, Saint-Preux, there is no question but that part 3, 18 is equivocal. Not that it represents conscious dissimulation, but it reveals an effort by Julie to reconcile opposed yet equally essential impulses, and to reconcile them in a manner that will allow neither to obliterate the other. Clearly, the way we understand this reconciliation is significant for any interpretation of this novel as a whole.

It is tempting to accept Julie's self-assessment in part 3, 18 as a basis for resolving this problem, to take such statements as the following as evidence of an authentic religious conversion: "Je connus dès ce moment que j'étais réellement changée. . . . Je crus me sentir renaître; je crus recommencer une autre vie" (p. 334).[6] Robert Mauzi, in an essay entitled "La Conversion de Julie dans La Nouvelle Héloïse," says unequivocally: "We are dealing . . . with both an authentic religious illumination and a profound psychological revolution. . . . Her conversion . . . has nothing to do with an act of will; on the contrary it is a sudden illumination which Rousseau shows us as an act of divine grace."[7] In order to evaluate such a position we must first examine the sense in which the notion of conversion may best be applied to Rousseau in general, and then look more closely at the context of the "conversion" of part 3, 18 in order to determine whether this category is really appropriate.

If one searched Rousseau's biography for some analogue to such a moment of divine illumination, one might be tempted first to think of the experience on the road to Vincennes that afternoon in 1779, when Rousseau read the announcement of the Dijon Academy that was to call forth his *First Discourse* and that he was to describe some thirteen years later in a letter to Malesherbes as "une inspiration subite, . . . l'esprit ébloui de mille lumières; . . . un étourdissement semblable à l'ivresse."[8]

What the Vincennes experience demonstrates is that Rousseau may well be one of those recipients "of the more instantaneous grace" whom William James discusses in *The Varieties of Religious Experi-*

5. In English: "Indeed, do what I could to stifle the first affection that gave me life, it found a refuge in my heart. It awakens there at the moment when it need no longer be feared; it sustains me as my strength abandons me; it revives me as I die."

6. In English: "From that instant I realized that I had really changed. . . . I seemed to be reborn; I seemed to begin another life."

7. *Annales J.J.R.* 35(1962): 29, 33.

8. *Œuvres Complètes* 1: 1135. In English: "a sudden inspiration, . . . the mind dazzled by countless lamps; . . . a dizziness akin to intoxication."

ence: "One of those Subjects who are in possession of a large region in which mental work can go on subliminally, and from which invasive experiences, abruptly upsetting the equilibrium of the primary consciousness, may come."[9] And yet, while this offers a certain parallelism to Julie's experience, we have to recognize that for Julie there is nothing of that inundation of insight regarding a specific subject that Rousseau experienced on the road to Vincennes. If one looks in James's treatise for those features that allow us best to classify Julie's experience among the types of conversion, what seems most applicable to Julie's case is a discussion of the sense of exhaustion, of not caring any longer, that often precedes the moment of illumination; the subject surrenders by *withdrawing from* the struggle before he can surrender to a new and transforming infusion of experience.[10] There is much of this in what Julie describes to Saint-Preux as her state of mind just prior to her marriage to Wolmar: "Enfin, je me lassai de combattre inutilement. Dans l'instant même où j'étais prête à jurer à un autre une éternelle fidélité, mon cœur vous jurait encore un amour éternel, et je fus menée au temple comme une victime impure qui souille le sacrifice où l'on va l'immoler" (p. 332).[11]

It may be, however, that the type of instantaneous transformation discussed in James is not the most appropriate model for Julie's case. More significant is the example of Saint Augustine, in whom the process of conversion was grounded in a meditation on memory and time. Memory is developed in book 10 of the *Confessions* in terms of that awesome and magnificent topography that recalls the Platonic myth of the cave. In Augustine the movement toward the interior, toward distant and deeper recesses of the mind, parallels Plato's ascent out of the cave toward the surface of the earth and up to the sky. What is particularly significant for our purposes, however, is not so much this imagery of interiorization but the "futurity" of memory as Augustine develops it in book 11, on time and eternity. For in Augustine's terms memory is not an inert repository of particles of experience or sensation. It is at once stratefied and dynamic, oriented toward the present through its labor of recovery and recollection and toward the future through its stance of expectation: "But perhaps it might prop-

9. *The Varieties of Religious Experience* (New York, 1929), p. 232.
10. cf. *Ibid.*, pp. 208ff.
11. In English: "Finally I grew tired of struggling uselessly. In the very instant when I was prepared to swear eternal fidelity to another, my heart still swore an eternal love to you, and I was led to the temple like an impure victim who defiles the rite in which she will be sacrificed."

erly be said that there are three times, the present of things past, the present of things present, and the present of things future. These three are in the soul, but elsewhere I do not see them: the present of things past is in memory, the present of things present is in intuition; the present of things future is in expectation."[12] Memory for Augustine, as Étienne Gilson has noted, is not essentially characterized by association with the past.[13] Augustine's "present of things past" suggests a conception of memory as a process of blending and transforming different modes of temporal experience for the sake of present consciousness.

With William James we viewed the question of conversion in terms of an abrupt, overwhelming instant, an assault that overcomes a passive consciousness and "transports" it into a new identity. Now, with Augustine, we are prepared to investigate the states of conversion in the narrower sense, the ways in which consciousness converts traces of past experiences ("like footsteps as they passed through the senses")[14] into present intuitions and aspirations, in short, into the foundations of a temporally structured identity. But although these instances move us closer to the case at hand, they do not yet offer any precise analogues. We need to account for a function of memory in *La Nouvelle Héloïse* that not only supports an emergent identity but also underlies the process whereby a consciousness assumes responsibility for its own mutations. Here we reach a limit for the concept of memory and require another, that of imagination.

The lovers in this novel have no past except the one they create. But this progressive creation and recreation of a past becomes for them the fiction of their love and the basis of their identity. Over and over in the first two books, one or another of the lovers looks back to the beginnings of their attachment and these backward glances, whether brief or extended, are not so much recapitulations of a well-known event as renewed and ever varied efforts to locate and define a virtual point of origin in light of the present stage of evolution. The experience of the bower where Julie grants Saint-Preux a first kiss is only the first of many occasions to elicit the reaction: "Je ne suis plus le même, et ne te vois plus la même" (p. 39).[15] After the first consummation of their love, it is Julie's turn to exclaim, "Il fut un temps, mon

12. *Confessions*, trans. John K. Ryan, bk. 11, chap. 44.
13. *The Christian Philosophy of Saint Augustine* (New York, 1960), p. 102.
14. *Confessions*, bk. 11, chap. 18.
15. In English: "I am no longer the same, and see you no longer the same."

aimable ami, . . . Cet heureux temps n'est plus: hélas! il ne peut revenir" (p. 75).[16] And we are still only in the middle of part 1.

From the start of their relationship the aim of the lovers was to endow their love with an absolute origin, an origin, that is, that would be elevated above the few, transient moments of communion and consummation they experience. And the means whereby this is to be achieved is the letter, that form of contact which transforms certain moments into something else, something that is both more and less than lived experience. The epistolary form of the novel is to be understood not, in the first instance, as a device whereby the author gains access to the characters' intimate thoughts and feelings. It serves that function too, of course, but, in contrast to *Clarissa* or *Les Liaisons dangéreuses*, that is not its primary function. For Julie and Saint-Preux the writing of letters serves as an essential stage in the distillation of experience into memory, and memory becomes the uncreated, quasi-mythic source that nourishes the identity of the couple as lovers.

The usual order of precedence between experience and recollection appears to be inverted in this novel. The lovers' experience when together is characterized by a kind of defective reality. It is rendered either as already past or as a future event exhausted in advance by anticipation. (An instance of the latter is letter 54 in part 1, where Saint-Preux describes Julie's bedchamber as he awaits her arrival for one of the rare consummations of their love.) In both cases the experience is rendered not in the plenitude of present experience but as an occasion to be memorialized. Its articulation seems designed above all to provide the basis for some appeal or point of reference in the lovers' continuing relationship. It is particularly after their separation in part 2 that this drama of a repeatedly sought renewal becomes most anxious and most intense. When Julie, writing to Saint-Preux in Paris, admonishes him to recall the spirit of their love, her invocation of their past does not simply awaken a dormant or submerged memory, but endows that past with a constitutive, sanctifying power:

> Songe surtout à nos premières amours: . . . Dis-moi, que serions-nous si nous n'aimions plus? Eh! ne vaudrait il pas mieux cesser d'être que d'exister sans rien sentir, et pourrais tu te résoudre à traîner sur la terre l'insipide vie d'un homme ordinaire, après avoir goûté tous les transports qui peuvent ravir une âme humaine? (p. 201f.)[17]

16. In English: "There was a time, my dear friend, . . . That happy time is no more, alas! it cannot return."

17. In English: "Think above all of our early love: . . . Tell me, what would we be if

Such appeals to the source of their being as lovers are less evocations of a real past than posterior fabrications necessary to justify a new condition. The lovers appeal to the memory of their past: it is not a memory, however, but a fictive creation that is involved, though part of that fiction is that the past is something given and not invented. What Julie offers as the evocation of a past reality is a response to a present, existential need. She is compelled both to assuage this need by fabricating a past and to believe in the unalterable priority of such a past. One may be tempted here to speak of a self-mystification whereby the self produces what, in the order of belief, can only come to it from another agency. But such an interpretation needs to be carefully qualified. We should not attribute to a psychological mechanism of the characters that which derives from the ontological structure of the novel.

Bernard Guyon, in an essay entitled "La Mémoire et l'oubli dans La Nouvelle Héloïse," has perceived the singularity of this conception insofar as it is reflected in the form of memory operative within the work. He cites Wolmar's remarks on Saint-Preux after the latter's return from his voyage: "Ce n'est pas de Julie de Wolmar qu'il est amoureux, c'est de Julie d'Étange. . . . Il l'aime dans le temps passé: voilà le vrai mot de l'énigme. Ôtez-lui la mémoire, il n'aura plus d'amour" (p. 492).[18] And then Guyon comments,

> The concrete, practical decisions of Wolmar represent the necessary, logical conclusion of these long analyses. The most powerful force against memory is life. It is necessary, then, that the lovers meet again and realize day after day that they are no longer the same. It is necessary that the present be superposed over the past; it is necessary that the present block out, efface, negate memory.[19]

The "superposition" of the present over the past suggests the type of projective memory that I have been discussing. But Guyon's interpretation, essentially psychological like that of most commentators of this novel, is too exclusively focused on the action—in this case, the manipulations whereby Wolmar brings the former lovers together in order to impress on them the radical change they have undergone. My

we no longer loved? Well! wouldn't it be better to cease to be than to exist without feeling anything, and could you decide to drag out on the earth the insipid life of an ordinary man after having tasted all the emotions that are capable of enrapturing a human soul?"

18. In English: "It is not with Julie de Wolmar that he is in love, it is with Julie d'Étange. . . . He loves her in time past: this is the true solution of the puzzle. Eliminate his memory and he would no longer love."

19. *Annales J.J.R.* 35(1962): 56.

point is different. I would not say that life absorbs memory, that the present triumphs over the past. Rather, I would see memory as the indispensable instrument for a certain kind of life project, namely, for the mode of experience manifested by means of these letters. The letters, as I have already indicated, are to be taken not only as a record of certain events and states of mind but more fundamentally as the enactment of a passionate and at the same time highly deliberate drama of self-justification and self-realization. From this perspective memory may, with only slight exaggeration, be termed an alibi for the exercise of the imagination.[20]

The letter already referred to of Julie to Saint-Preux (part 3, 18) offers one of the best examples of that creation of the self with which the lovers are occupied throughout the work. It is one of many re-enactments of a past in the light of a project for the future. And it is one that demonstrates how the very faculty that is engaged in uncovering a pure origin tends in the selfsame impulse to expose its own calculation and thus to put into doubt the spontaneity of its act. The following passage is typical:

> Je voulais vous rendre si doux votre état présent, que la crainte d'en changer augmentât votre retenue. Tout cela me réussit mal: on ne sort point de son naturel impunément. Insensée que j'étais! j'accélérai ma perte au lieu de la prévenir, j'employai du poison pour palliatif; et ce qui devait vous faire taire fut précisément ce qui vous fit parler. J'eus beau, par une froideur affectée, vous tenir éloigné dans le tête-à-tête; cette contrainte même me trahit: vous écrivîtes. Au lieu de jeter au feu votre première lettre ou de la porter à ma mère, j'osai l'ouvrir: ce fut là mon crime, et tout le reste fut forcé (p. 320).[21]

Here we see the compensatory strategy of an imagination, grounded in unfulfillment, seeking to rectify an imbalance but only displacing it to another level. Julie's projective fiction can only succeed mo-

---

20. On the filiation of memory and imagination in Rousseau, see the introduction to the *Confessions* by Bernard Gagnebin and Marcel Raymond in *Œuvres Complètes, vol. 1,* esp. pp. xxxvff. Their citation from C.-F. Ramuz is particularly apt, "On ne sépare pas mémoire et imagination; l'imagination est dans la mémoire comme un ferment" (p. xxxvii).

21. In English: "I tried to make your present condition so agreeable that the fear of changing it increased your discretion. I didn't succeed at all: one cannot alter one's natural disposition with impunity. Fool that I was! I hastened my fall instead of averting it, I employed poison as a remedy; and what should have made you keep silent was precisely what caused you to speak. Although I tried to keep you at a distance in our tête-à-tête through an affected coolness, this very constraint betrayed me: you wrote. Instead of throwing your first letter into the fire or giving it to my mother, I dared to open it: that was my crime, everything else followed of itself."

mentarily; its flights are short, though repeatedly renewed. It maintains itself in a spiral movement whose direction may be called a
transcendence toward death.

In attempting to attain a state of equilibrium Julie sets to work
the very faculty that cannot help but destroy her. This is the imagination in the sense in which Jacques Derrida has analyzed it in his study
of Rousseau's "Essai sur l'origine des langues." He calls imagination
the faculty whereby the self, in supplementing its present consciousness, supplants it by an image, a re-presentation, that will invariably lay claim to the status of an originating presence and thus cancel
out the source from which it derives. This play of substitution, whereby the self moves through alternative but unrecoverable versions of its
truth or essence, represents at once an activation of imagination and a
manifestation of the self's awareness of its own death. To quote
Derrida:

> Imagination is at bottom the relationship with death. . . . Imagination
> is the power that allows life to affect itself with its own re-presentation.
> The image cannot represent and add the representer to the represented,
> except in so far as the presence of the re-presented is already folded back
> upon itself in the world, in so far as life refers to itself as to its own lack,
> to its own wish for a supplement. The presence of the represented is
> constituted with the help of the addition to itself of that nothing which is
> the image, announcement of its dispossession within its own representer
> and within its death.[22]

In the sense that imagination and death fuse in a single impulse,
Julie's death in part 6 represents an absolutely consistent and logical,
in no way sentimental, resolution of her situation. We need not won-
der that Rousseau brings it about with such patent contrivance after
her final letter of self-justification to Saint-Preux, part 6, 8; for she has
led her imagination to its ultimate point; no new action in life, no
modification of her role, could supervene.

At one point Claire quite lucidly exposes the mechanism of this
drive in Julie: "On dirait que rien de terrestre ne pouvant suffire au
besoin d'aimer dont elle est dévorée, cet excès de sensibilité soit forcé
de remonter à sa source" (p. 576).[23] But this source, the God that Julie
speaks of in the last part, is more a function of her hunger, her depriva-

---

22. *Of Grammatology*, trans. Gayatri Chakravorty Spivak (Baltimore, 1976), p. 184.
23. In English: "One might say that since nothing earthly was capable of satisfying
the need to love that devoured her, this excess of sensibility was forced to turn back to its
source."

tion, than of an illumination, as is amply born out in Julie's own words, notably in part 6, 8: "Ne trouvant donc rien ici-bas qui lui suffise, mon âme avide cherche ailleurs de quoi la remplir: . . . Je ne dis pas que ce goût soit sage; je dis seulement qu'il est doux, qu'il supplée au sentiment du bonheur qui s'épuise, qu'il remplit le vide de l'âme, qu'il jette un nouvel intérêt sur la vie passée à le mériter" (p. 683).[24]

In this letter, the last that Julie writes before the accident that causes her death, Rousseau brings together the diverse, often contradictory impulses that have possessed Julie in the course of the novel, and, without subjecting any of the earlier positions to simplification or facile resolution, gives them voice once more in a document that is the outpouring of a passionate soul and, at the same time, an enthralling instance of argumentation and persuasion. I will only touch on one strand of this letter. Julie undertakes to defend herself against Saint-Preux's charge that she has become *dévote,*—pious, narrowly religious—and, in the course of her defense, she describes what she might have been like if she had had the support of a positive religiosity when she was tempted to succumb, and did in fact succumb, to her secret suitor. One might expect that she, having introduced this theme, would continue to extoll the principles of religious faith, steadfastness, and self-control, in effect, to pursue the argument of the last part of part 3, 18. But what she says now is that she recognizes that the path of refusal, of renunciation, is the better way, not because it adheres to religious principles but because resistance maintained, gratification refused, puts the soul into a condition of expectation, of permanent futurity, of "illusion," that is immeasurably more satisfying and lasting than the satisfaction of desire would be.[25] Here is the climax of this mediation:

> Tant qu'on désire on peut se passer d'être heureux; on s'attend à le devenir: si le bonheur ne vient point, l'espoir se prolonge, et le charme de l'illusion dure autant que la passion qui le cause. Ainsi cet état se suffit à lui-même, et l'inquiétude qu'il donne est une sorte de jouissance qui

24. In English: "Thus, finding nothing here below that would suffice, my eager soul looked elsewhere for nourishment: . . . I do not say that this inclination was wise; I say only that it was agreeable, that it proved a supplement for a sense of happiness about to expire, that it filled the void of the soul, that it gave a new interest to a life that had sought to be deserving of it."

25. On the general theme of the perpetual deferment of possession in love, see Jean-Louis Bellenot's perceptive analysis, "Les Formes de l'amour dans *La Nouvelle Héloïse,*" *Annales J.J.R.* 33(1953–55): 149–207, esp. pp. 180ff.

supplée à la realité, qui vaut mieux peut-être. . . . En effet, l'homme, avide et borné, fait pour tout vouloir et peu obtenir, a reçu du ciel une force consolante qui rapproche de lui tout ce qu'il désire, qui le soumet à son imagination, qui le lui rend présent et sensible, qui le lui livre en quelque sorte, et, pour lui rendre cette imaginaire propriété plus douce, le modifie au gré de sa passion. Mais tout ce prestige disparaît devant l'objet même; rien n'embellit plus cet objet aux yeux du possesseur; on ne se figure point ce qu'on voit; l'imagination ne pare plus rien de ce qu'on possède, l'illusion cesse où commence la jouissance. (p. 681).[26]

Strange words indeed if we still see in Julie the triumph of duty or devotion over passion, but not so surprising once we have recognized the law of supplementarity in Rousseau and discerned its operation in the force of desire and imagination in Julie. And from this perspective we shall hardly take the following sentence, which concludes the passage just quoted, as a conventional Christian devaluation of the earthly in favor of the divine, the actual in favor of the eternal:

Le pays des chimères est en ce monde le seul digne d'être habité, et tel est le néant des choses humaines, qu'hors l'Être existant par lui-même il n'y a rien de beau que ce qui n'est pas. (p. 682)[27]

Here Julie voices once again an impulse toward transcendence interwoven with a strain of self-negation, what I have called a transcendence toward death. "Le pays des chimères," the domain of imagination, is at the same time a void, "ce qui n'est pas." And this void is made the repository of Beauty insofar as it is accessible to consciousness. In reflecting on this sentence we may be tempted to endow the "pays des chimères" with a positive compensatory function, to view it as a sphere of ideal fulfillment or fictive plenitude. But the final clause, with its absolute, reiterated negative ("rien de beau que ce qui

26. In English: "As long as one desires one can do without happiness; one awaits it: if happiness does not come, hope is prolonged, and the charm of illusion lasts as long as the passion that caused it. Thus, this condition is sufficient unto itself, and whatever unrest it causes is a kind of pleasure that is a supplement for reality, worth even more, perhaps. . . . In effect, man in his greed and limitations, fashioned to want everything and obtain little, has been granted a consoling power by heaven, a power that brings everything he desires close to him, submits it to his imagination, renders it present and palpable, offers it up to him after a fashion, and, in order to make this imaginary property yet more agreeable, modifies it according to his feelings. But all of this prestige disappears before the object itself; before the eyes of the possessor the object is no longer embellished; one cannot have an image of what one sees; the imagination no longer enhances what one possesses, illusion ceases where pleasure begins."

27. In English: "The land of dreams is the only one in this world that is worth inhabiting, and such is the insignificance of human concerns that, except for the Being existing in himself, there is nothing of beauty except what is not."

n'est pas"), restricts any such interpretation and points instead to the negative path of the imagination as this novel exemplifies it.[28]

28. Paul de Man's comment on the passage just quoted is relevant to my own interpretation: "One entirely misunderstands this assertion of the priority of fiction over reality, of imagination over perception, if one considers it as the compensatory expression of a shortcoming, of a deficient sense of reality. It is attributed to a fictional character who knows all there is to know of human happiness and who is about to face death with Socratic equanimity. It transcends the notion of a nostalgia or a desire, since it discovers desire as a fundamental pattern of being that discards any possibility of satisfaction." "Criticism and Crisis," in *Blindness and Insight* (New York, 1971), p. 17.

6 Dialogic Structure in *Wilhelm Meisters Wanderjahre*

Mit solchem Büchlein aber [the Wanderjahre*] ist es wie mit dem Leben selbst: es findet sich in dem Komplex des Ganzen Notwendiges und Zufälliges, Vorgesetztes und Angeschlossenes, bald gelungen, bald vereitelt, wodurch es eine Art von Unendlichkeit erhält, die sich in verständige und vernünftige Worte nicht durchaus fassen noch einschliessen läßt.*[1]

I

More than once Goethe spoke of the symbolic method of his later work in terms of a multiperspectivism, "durch einander gegenübergestellte und sich gleichsam ineinander abspiegelnde Gebilde den geheimeren Sinn . . . zu offenbaren."[2] In statements like these, Goethe projects an ideally suited instance of reception, a readership capable of penetrating the complexities of this body of work. Of course, such remarks need not be taken too strictly in a theoretical sense. They were oriented to a specific correspondent or interlocutor, and may have expressed also a wish that Goethe knew was unlikely to be realized in the German public in the last twenty years of his life. Nonetheless, the formulations I have cited represent a useful heuristic model for the kind of reading of the *Wanderjahre* that I propose.

1. Letter from Goethe to Johann Friedrich Rochlitz, November 23, 1829. Cited in the edition of the *Wanderjahre* in *Goethes Werke,* ed. Erich Trunz (Hamburg, 1950), 8:578. In English: "Now books of this sort are like the very stuff of life: You will find in the intricate whole some things that are there by necessity, others by accident, some that have been put in by design, others that have only found their way in, some successful, others flawed, whereby the work is endowed with a kind of endlessness that cannot be altogether grasped or circumscribed by means of comprehensible, rational language."

2. Letter to Iken, September 23, 1827. Cited in Ibid. 3:448. In English: "to disclose a more hidden meaning through contrasting and mutually reflecting forms."

116

Many interpreters have sought to specify the kind of adequate reader that Goethe occasionally evoked (e.g., in such formulations as "der echte Leser," "[der] Aufmerkende," and "[der] einsichtige Leser"),[3] and to make this the basis of a determinate interpretation of the work, usually in terms of some thematic or philosophic thesis. But I would suggest that Goethe does not so much project a model of total comprehension, of crystallized meaning (at the level of the signified), as a process of signification (at the level of signifiers) that the work in itself cannot altogether anticipate or circumscribe. "Jede Lösung eines Problems ist ein neues Problem," he remarked to the Kanzler von Müller in connection with the *Wanderjahre*.[4] And in the passage already cited, where he ascribed to the work "eine Art von Unendlichkeit," I would interpret the phrase not as some kind of infinity but as a principle of seriality, of propagation and dispersal.

Goethe's work on the two Meister novels stretches over some fifty-two years of his life—only *Faust* occupied him for so long and in so varied and productive a way. There are two novels: the *Lehrjahre* (published in 1796) and the *Wanderjahre* (first version, 1821, second version, 1829). Are they to be considered as a single unified work, as successive yet separable stages of a single project, or as two wholly distinct creations? The second alternative is probably the most reasonable choice, but in adopting it we become involved in immensely complex issues relating to the whole span of Goethe's creative career. (Imagine the difficulties of interpreting *The Tempest* if Shakespeare had made Prospero a reincarnation of a figure from an earlier play.) Although as a practical matter we tend to proceed in terms of the third alternative—considering the two novels as distinct creations—we still cannot overlook the earlier work in dealing with the *Wanderjahre*, even if we view it as something that needed to be left behind and overcome. On the one hand, there is an obvious continuity between the two works in that Wilhelm in the *Wanderjahre* is still in search of his destiny—which is to say, his character. But the later work raises altogether new formal problems, since now we have a relatively weak, or at least discontinuous, frame story that is designed not only to trace Wilhelm's career but also to provide a context for no less than eight relatively substantial novellas, half of them with characters who spill over into the frame story. The *Lehrjahre* tolerated no such dispersal.

---

3. "Der echte Leser," Ibid. 8:575; "dem Aufmerkenden," Ibid. 3:448; "Dem einsichtigen Leser," Ibid. 8:578.

4. June 8, 1821. Cited in Ibid., p. 574. In English: "Every solution of a problem raises a new problem."

The one interpolated narrative there, the "Bekenntnisse einer schönen Seele," was carefully integrated into the larger plan. Everything there worked centripetally. In the *Wanderjahre* it is all centrifugal. Yet still this later work has a coherence that we do not find in Goethe's earlier collection of novellas tied together by a weak frame story, *Unterhaltungen deutscher Ausgewanderten*.

This, I trust, will help to situate my method in what follows. Instead of drawing on a type of interpretation based largely on themes or ideas, or even a kind of formal analysis based on accredited genre concepts (e.g., the novella), I have tried to adapt elements of a narrative pragmatics, utilizing principles of communications theory and of a reader-oriented aesthetics.

Near the beginning of the *Wanderjahre*, in Wilhelm's first letter to Natalie, he mentions the rules of his journeymanship as stipulated by the Society of the Tower, including the requirement that he change his locale every three days. It appears at this point that we may expect a continuation of the pattern of the *Lehrjahre*, that is, a period of searching and testing in which the chance experiences of the journey will serve as instruments of formation. But Wilhelm does not sustain the impulse to journey for very long. In his first encounter with a member of the Society, Montan-Jarno, he asks to be relieved of this obligation, since he wants to devote himself to learning a craft, and his request is eventually granted. In spite of its title, the *Wanderjahre* is not, like *Don Quixote* or *Tom Jones*, structured in terms of the hero's peregrination. The road, with its potential for incidents and encounters, does not serve as an integrating narrative device. As a recent interpreter of the novel puts it, "We find here a decided abandonment of the Romantic topos of journeying."[5]

Alternatively, a unifying principle for the novellas has been sought in Wilhelm's personal project of growth and self-realization. Thus H. M. Waidson argues, "the structural centre of the *Wanderjahre* lies in Wilhelm's decision to become a surgeon in order to place his new skill at the disposal of the community."[6] Certainly, this decision is enunciated early in the work, and two narrative segments mark stages of the project—the story of the drowning of the fisher boy, which Wilhelm gives as the earliest motivation for his choice of a profession; and the account of his anatomical studies in book 3. The

5. Heide Gidion, *Zur Darstellungsweise von Goethes 'Wilhelm Meisters Wanderjahre'* (Göttingen, 1969), Palaestra, Vol. 256, p. 27f.
6. "Death by Water: or, The Childhood of Wilhelm Meister," *Modern Language Review* 56(1961): 44–53, this passage is on p. 50.

concluding incident of the novel shows Wilhelm treating his son Felix after the youth had lost consciousness through an accidental fall, and this is undoubtedly meant to demonstrate what Wilhelm has learned since the tragic episode of the fisher boy, when he could only embrace the body of the drowned boy in impotent grief. But a link between these episodes does not yet give us a means of unifying the work as a whole. It is true that in reworking the *Wanderjahre* for the second and final version between 1821 and 1829 Goethe took pains to elaborate the frame story, thus significantly transforming what had been more a collection of tales, in the Boccaccian sense, than a novel.[7] The relations among Hersilie, Felix, and Wilhelm, on the one hand, and Wilhelm's choice and attainment of the surgeon's craft, on the other, represent the major elements in this elaboration of the frame action. But these two strands, separately or in combination, are still far from integrating the diverse segments and themes of the novel, whether the unity is sought at the level of the novellas and other interpolations or of the figure of Wilhelm. I will try to justify this view through a discussion of the fisher boy story.

The incident is recounted by Wilhelm himself in a long letter to Natalie (book 2, 11). It stands out in both of the Meister novels as Wilhelm's sole recollection of his early childhood. What is particularly striking is the passionate intensity of the recital itself. Wilhelm's tone, recalling certain features of Werther, is far removed from his typically deliberate and reflective style in this novel. The story itself, of course, has all that one could ask in terms of sensibility, pathos, and erotic coloring. In the course of an outing with his family to visit friends in the country, the young Wilhelm meets a boy slightly older than himself, the son of a local fisherman, who draws him away from the family gathering to a place along a river nearby. After lingering on the shore for a time, the fisher boy, irresistibly attracted by the water on the sunny day, undresses and jumps in. Wilhelm is soon prevailed on to join him. They swim together for a time and then, as they emerge naked from the water, Wilhelm has a revelation in which a sense of physical beauty, of friendship, and of sexual awakening all play a part:

> und als er sich heraushob, sich aufrichtete, im höheren Sonnenschein sich abzutrocknen, glaubt' ich meine Augen vor einer dreifachen Sonne geblendet: so schön war die menschliche Gestalt, von der ich nie einen Begriff gehabt. Er schien mich mit gleicher Aufmerksamkeit zu be-

---

7. Cf. Hans Reiss, "'Wilhelm Meisters Wanderjahre': Der Weg von der ersten zur zweiten Fassung," *D.V.L.G.* 39(1965): 34–57.

trachten. Schnell angekleidet standen wir uns noch immer unverhüllt gegeneinander, unsere Gemüter zogen sich an, und unter den feurigsten Küssen schwuren wir eine ewige Freundschaft.[8]

Soon after, the boys are forced to part, since Wilhelm must join his family for another visit, and they make plans to meet later in the day. But in the course of the afternoon the fisher boy, while diving for crabs in the river, drowns, together with four other children. In the evening, as Wilhelm and his family return to the village, they learn of the catastrophe, and Wilhelm, beside himself with grief, finds a way to get into the house where the bodies have been laid out. Desperately crying, he throws himself on the corpse of his friend.

In reflecting on this episode later in the same letter, Wilhelm writes, "Unerwartet, in demselbigen Augenblick ergriff mich das Vorgefühl von Freundschaft und Liebe." But he goes further and speaks of the experience as representing, "jenes erste Aufblühen der Außenwelt," which he identifies with "die eigentliche Originalnatur . . . , gegen die alles übrige, was uns nachher zu den Sinnen kommt, nur Kopien zu sein scheinen."[9] Later in the letter Wilhelm makes a link between this experience and the emotional and imaginative powers that will eventually find an outlet in his theatrical career (with which we are familiar from the *Lehrjahre*), "Das Bedürfnis nach Freundschaft und Liebe war aufgeregt, überall schaut' ich mich um, es zu befriedigen. Indessen ward Sinnlichkeit, Einbildungskraft und Geist durch das Theater übermäßig beschäftigt."[10]

The reenactment of an overpowering childhood experience, the fusion of the themes of friendship, eroticism, and death, the evocation of a paradisiacal, preternatural state of existence—all these endow the episode with a singular quality. Wilhelm has revealed a psyche still in close proximity to a primal natural state. But this revelation, for all its intensity, is exceptional for this novel. In the later part of the letter

8. *Goethes Werke*, 8:272. In English: "and as he emerged, standing straight in order to dry himself in the sunshine, it was as if my eyes were dazzled by a triple sun: how lovely was the human form, of which I had never yet had an idea. He seemed to examine me in a similar way. Quickly dressed, we faced each other still totally exposed. Our souls were drawn to each other and, kissing passionately, we swore eternal friendship."

9. Ibid., p. 273. In English: "Unexpectedly, in the same instant, I was overcome by an anticipation of friendship and love." "that first emergence of the outer world . . . nature in its veritable original form . . . , in comparison to which everything that subsequently affects us seems only like copies."

10. Ibid., p. 279. In English: "The need for friendship and love was awakened; I looked all about me in order to satisfy it. Soon after, my imagination, my senses, my spirit were aroused beyond measure by the theater."

Wilhelm draws a lesson from the episode that seems wholly to ignore its spiritual and affective dimensions. He stresses the merely relative value of any single motive in shaping an individual's future. He seems intent on distancing himself from the more emotional and impenetrable aspects of the experience and seeks to assimilate it to a rational life plan. Thus, he interprets his grief and helplessness over the drowning of his friend as the motivating impulse in his quest for practical medical skills and for his abandonment of the journeymanship in favor of the study of surgery. The letter, then—though it at one point contrasts "nature in its veritable original form" to a lapsed, derivative state in which everything seems to affect us as "copies"—itself testifies to such a loss of immediacy and participation.

Karl Schlechta, in a controversial book, has argued that after the attachment to Mariane early in the *Lehrjahre*, Wilhelm falls increasingly under the sway of a petrifying, authoritarian spirit, a spirit typified by members of the Society of the Tower. The effect of the Society's influence is to deaden and suppress Wilhelm's affective and imaginative impulses.[11] While I cannot altogether subscribe to this position, Schlechta's study represents a serious challenge to any overly positive or unproblematic view of Wilhelm's career. As my discussion of the one letter has tried to show, there are striking shifts in tone and in narrative form that make it difficult to view the action in terms of a linear, teleological pattern.[12]

The evolving, cumulative form of self-consciousness that is characteristic for the *Bildungsroman*, and that is to some degree present in the *Lehrjahre*, is markedly absent in the *Wanderjahre*. Let us briefly sketch the *Bildung* pattern by way of contrast. What is typical for the protagonist of a story of growth and formation is that his most significant acts involve not what he does in direct commerce with individuals and circumstances but what he comes to know through a retrospective interpretation of his acts. Greimas and Courtès have put

11. *Goethes Wilhelm Meister* (Frankfurt am Main, 1953). Cf. Arthur Henkel's review, *G.R.M.* N.F. 5 (1955): 85–89.
12. The overwhelming tendency of modern interpreters to understand the Wilhelm Meister novels in this progressive manner can be traced back at least to Max Wundt's *Goethes Wilhelm Meister und die Entwicklung des modernen Lebensideals* (Berlin, 1913). But recent studies like those by Gidion (see n. 5 above), Karnick (see n. 35 below), Heinz Schlaffer ("Exoterik und Esoterik in Goethes Romanen," *Goethe Jahrbuch* 95[1978]: 212–226), and Hans Vaget ("Goethe the Novelist. On the Coherence of His Fiction," in *Goethe's Narrative Fiction: The Irvine Goethe Symposium*, ed. William J. Lillyman [Berlin, 1983]) have moved in an opposite direction. Schlechta, in spite of the extreme thesis he maintains, can be viewed as their predecessor.

forward a structural narrative model that tries to establish a common ground for action and for the attainment of knowledge by narrative agents, an approach that is pertinent to our topic. They posit first an elementary level, a "simple narrative," where "there is no distance between the events and the knowledge about the events," and then proceed to develop various forms of "cognitive action" that constitute a second degree of narrative.[13] This level may take the form of an interpretive investment on the part of the protagonist, an investment that adds the new function of being a recipient (of knowledge) to that already operative of being the agent of action ("the subject of doing," in their terminology). The protagonist realizes that actions undertaken for apparently self-evident motives must be revised in the light of his new stage of self-understanding. But the earlier, unreflective agent of action is not thereby simply eliminated and supplanted. Rather, the split in the subject is itself now thematized, and this brings about a transformation of the narrative form. The shift is from a first level of narrative where the pivots are acts of a unified protagonist, a single "subject of doing," to a second level where the pivots (e.g., dissimulation, self-deception, recognition, peripeteia) are not so much acts as conditions or states of mind of the "cognitive subject."

In drawing on this model I wish to identify the principal elements of a *Bildung* narrative in structural rather than historical terms. The model proves to be perfectly congruent with an analysis that Goethe offered regarding the *Lehrjahre*. In it he speaks of the errors and false turnings that seem to pursue his protagonist during his life, and concludes, "und doch ist es möglich, daß alle die falschen Schritte zu einem unschätzbaren Guten hinführen: eine Ahnung, die sich im 'Wilhelm Meister' immer mehr entfaltet, aufklärt und bestätigt, ja sich zuletzt mit klaren Worten ausspricht: 'Du kommst mir vor wie Saul, der Sohn Kis, der ausging seines Vaters Eselinnen zu suchen, und ein Königreich fand.'"[14]

But in the *Wanderjahre,* Wilhelm, though involved throughout the frame action and privy to all of the interpolated texts, rarely

---

13. A. J. Greimas and J. Courtès, "The Cognitive Dimension of Narrative Discourse," *New Literary History* 7(1975–76): 433–447.

14. From *Tag- und Jahreshefte*. Cited in *Goethes Werke*, 8:519. In English: "And it may well be that all the false steps lead to a priceless achievement: an intimation that is unfolded, clarified, and confirmed in the course of *Wilhelm Meister* and that is finally articulated in the clearest terms: 'You seem to me like Saul, the son of Kish, who set out to seek his father's she-asses and found a kingdom.' "

assumes the function of a cognitive subject in the sense just discussed. In the letter to Natalie that includes the fisher boy story, Wilhelm, of course, serves as narrator. More often his part in the action is rendered by a third-person narrator, but this does not bring a greater focus on stages of growth and self-awareness. Thus, the diverse forms of aesthetic experience evoked in the episodes of Saint Joseph the Second, the trip of Lago Maggiore, and the visit to the Artists' Province do not seem to affect Wilhelm in a cumulative manner. He takes in the system of instruction in the Artists' Province without giving the slightest indication that only a little earlier, when he was in the company of the painter on Lago Maggiore, he had been exposed to a conception of art that represents its very antithesis.[15] One could almost speak of a kind of amnesia on Wilhelm's part, or at least of a disinterestedness that makes him eminently adaptable to the various situations in which he finds himself but, correspondingly, leaves him relatively immune to being strongly affected by them.

We do not find in the *Wanderjahre* anything like the passionate self-scrutiny and projection of purpose of that long letter to Werner in the *Lehrjahre*, where Wilhelm had stated, "Daß ich dir's mit *einem* Worte sage: mich selbst, ganz wie ich da bin, auszubilden, das war dunkel von Jugend auf mein Wunsch und meine Absicht."[16] What best corresponds to this in the *Wanderjahre* is the parable of the *Ruderpflock* (book 2, 11), though it projects a far more tenuous and indeterminate path. In spite of the fact that he is the nominal hero of the *Wanderjahre,* Wilhelm does not provide the kind of unifying thread that we might expect from a general account of the frame story or from the antecedent pattern of the *Lehrjahre*. Although the dispersal of personal identity is not so extreme in the *Wanderjahre* as in the second part of *Faust,* there is a marked loosening of structure in the second part of both works. Goethe's well-known characterization of Wilhelm as "armer Hund" was made in 1821 when he was just putting out the first version of the *Wanderjahre,* and it seems more applicable to the Wilhelm of that work than of the *Lehrjahre*: "Wilhelm ist freilich ein armer Hund, aber nur an solchen lassen sich das Wechselspiel des Lebens und die tausend verschiedenen Lebensaufgaben recht deutlich zeigen, nicht an schon abgeschlossenen festen

---

15. Cf. *Zur Darstellungsweise von Goethes 'Wilhelm Meisters Wanderjahre,'* p. 30.

16. *Goethes Werke,* 7:290. In English: "To speak it in a word: the cultivation of my individual self, wholly as I am, has from my youth upwards been constantly though dimly my wish and purpose." Cf. Chap. 3, pp. 69ff. above.

Charakteren."[17] But while this remark supports us in not looking for a structuring principle for this novel at the level of character or psychology, it does not provide a specific indication of what to look for. We still need to find a way of converting "das Wechselspiel des Lebens und die tausend verschiedenen Lebensaufgaben," into a principle of narrative sequence and linkage, and for this we will do well to turn to a consideration of the narrative structure in its own right.

II

It is not easy to characterize the novellas in the *Wanderjahre* as a group. Most interpretations underline certain consolidating themes that tie them to one another and to the frame story.[18] But I would stress their open-ended, discontinuous features, their tendency toward dispersal and fragmentation. Some break off unexpectedly. Some introduce new narrative strands that displace the original focus. Some cross over into the frame action in ways that leave one uncertain as regards the link between novella and frame. There are abrupt transformations in figures who appear in both a novella and in the frame action (e.g., Wilhelm, Odoard).

Telling a story about oneself rarely serves as a means of self-revelation (as in the fisher boy episode) but is more often a kind of strategy, a modus of behavior adapted to the given situation (e.g., the burlesque romance that the Foolish Pilgrim sings as payment for her reception; the Barber's storytelling for the amusement of the company). We are not generally given finished life stories but images or episodes of a life in progress (e.g., Lenardo, Makarie), and often the recital of such an episode itself contributes to the furtherance of a more general process whose outcome remains unarticulated. Lenardo's words at the beginning of "Das nußbraune Mädchen" have a more general application: "Ich darf ihnen wohl vertrauen und erzählen, was eigentlich keine Geschichte ist."[19] What he recounts is indeed not a unified narrative but the inaugural episode of a circuitous search involving mistaken identity, diversionary materials, and breaks in the manuscript.

17. In conversation to Kanzler von Müller, January 22, 1821. Cited Ibid. 8:519. In English: "Wilhelm is, of course, a sorry mutt, but it is only with such that one may clearly reveal life's intricate spectacle, its thousand diverse tasks, and not with fully realized, fixed characters."

18. One of the most discerning studies in this vein is Arthur Henkel, *Entsagung: Eine Studie zu Goethes Altersroman*, Hermaea, vol. 3 (Tübingen, 1964).

19. *Goethes Werke*, 8:129. In English: "I'm sure I may confide in you and recount what is actually not a story."

The search is for a woman who herself undergoes a series of transformations, from the intense, passionately pleading child who first arrests Lenardo's attention, to the shadowy, recessive figure dubbed "die Gute-Schöne." (This kind of fading from a proper name to an epithet says much about the conception of character in this novel.) Her eventual union with Lenardo is evoked but never resolved, and she is left in the end in the role of Makarie's assistant. Everything about her—the multiple names and epithets, the indeterminate fate—confirms Lenardo's impression of her as "die Ersehnte" (p. 416), the wished-for but never altogether palpable goal of his quest.

The *Wanderjahre* is composed of an assemblage of text forms that represent a great variety of language uses, and these uses or pragmatic functions cannot be readily reconciled to one another or made to depend on a single, authoritative narrative principle. To be attentive to the pragmatic dimension of a text means that we attempt to situate it in terms of its intended application, that we discern in its very form a directive or mode of transformation that implicates all the instances of a communicative process. Of course, the question of the application of a text, of its pragmatic dimension, is one that may be posed for all types of texts, fictive or nonfictive, narrative or non-narrative. And we cannot overlook that the structure of the *Wanderjahre* is perplexing in part because it includes a great heterogeneity of textual forms—novellas, letters, monologues, collections of maxims, scientific discussions, aesthetic speculations, accounts of dreams, data regarding techniques and crafts, and pedagogic theory.[20] All these forms are to some extent modalized by their inclusion in the novel, and yet they may still be analyzed by means of pragmatic models appropriate to each of them.

Walter Benjamin sought to define the pragmatic dimension of storytelling, "die Kunst des Erzählens," by underscoring its usefulness, "ihren Nutzen," its tendency to convey what we would call

---

20. Hans Reiss's comparison of the style of the two versions of the *Wanderjahre* is illuminating. In contrast to the relative homogeneity of the first, he lists some of the new stylistic registers of the second: "In der zweiten Fassung aber gibt es jene intensivierte Dichte der Makarie-Kapiel, wo wissenschaftliche Sprache und Darstellung in einer wohl höchsten Steigerung der Goetheschen Erzähler-Prosa verbunden sind. Es gibt außerdem noch eine an Sturm und Drang erinnernde Sprache, in der Flavios leidenschaftliche Erregung geschildert wird; . . . Außerdem gibt es noch den lakonisch abrupt konzentrierten Stil des zusammenfassenden Berichts, welcher, ähnlich wie in Goethes *Annalen* viele Ereignisse zusammenrafft und knapp angibt. Schließlich noch die prägnante Form der Sprüche und die symbolische Ausdrucksform der beiden weltanschaulichen Gedichte." "'Wilhelm Meisters Wanderjahre': Der Weg von der ersten zur zweiten Fassung," p. 56f.

home truths, words of wisdom—"Rat," "Weisheit." What is basic to
the traditional story in his sense is that it draws on a stock of communal experience, "Erfahrung," and is thus capable of fashioning exemplary cases, that is, such as replenish and extend a communally accredited image of man. Benjamin's argument is designed to set off the
traditional, orally based story from one of its modern derivatives,
namely, the novel, which is deprived of an exemplifying function
through the solitude, the infertile inwardness of its protagonist. "Die
Geburtskammer des Romans," he writes, "ist das Individuum in
seiner Einsamkeit, das sich über seine wichtigsten Anliegen nicht
mehr exemplarisch auszusprechen vermag, selbst unberaten ist und
keinen Rat geben kann."[21] The exemplary function that Benjamin
assigns to the story, and which differentiates it from the novel in the
modern sense, can help us to identify the *Wanderjahre* as a hybrid
form occupying an intermediate place between *Novellenkranz* and
novel.

The storyteller, Benjamin writes, "weiß Rat—nicht wie das
Sprichwort: für manche Fälle, sondern wie der Weise: für viele."[22]
When Benjamin speaks of "Rat" as one of the effects of storytelling, he
allows for a transformation of the exemplary function of narrative (in
the traditional sense, the story as an illustration of proverb or maxim)
into a more fluid principle of form. The level of proverbs, the explicit
condensation of wisdom and good counsel, is obviously very important in the *Wanderjahre,* but we cannot always assume that the
"truths" enunciated in this form are intended as propositional statements. There are in fact so many "truths" strewn through the multiple, interrelated stories that they contravene any fixed application.
The overdetermination of the level of wisdom and good counsel becomes veritably dizzying if we include the extra-narrative collections
of aphorisms and notations, "Betrachtungen im Sinne der Wanderer"
and "Aus Makariens Archiv," which Goethe published as part of the
Wanderjahre. Within the narrative proper a saying often stands in an
oblique relation to the action and may be enunciated primarily in
order to be tested.

21. "Der Erzähler," in *Gesammelte Schriften,* ed. R. Tiedemann and H. Schweppen-
häuser (Frankfurt am Main, 1977) Vol. 2, no.2, p. 443. In English: "The birthplace of the
novel is the solitary individual, who is no longer able to express himself by giving examples
of his most important concerns, is himself uncounseled, and cannot counsel others." "The
Storyteller," in *Illuminations,* ed. Hannah Arendt, trans. Harry Zohn (New York, 1969), p.
87.
22. Ibid., p. 464. In English: "has counsel—not for a few situations, as the proverb
does, but for many, like the sage." "The Storyteller," p. 108.

The clearest case involves the Uncle, whose estate Wilhelm and Felix visit early in the book. This typical Enlightenment figure is in the habit of affixing maxims on the gates and entryways of his estate, a penchant that is wittily subverted by his niece, Hersilie. During a conversation between Wilhelm and the two sisters, Hersilie and Juliette, Wilhelm notices one of the maxims that the Uncle has had posted in the garden, "Vom Nützlichen durchs Wahre zum Schönen." ("From the useful through the true to the beautiful.") And although we are told that Wilhelm undertakes to interpret it "in his manner" (which must be appropriately moralistic, since it gains the approbation of the gentle Juliette), Goethe does not actually give us this interpretation but a much less orthodox one offered by Hersilie, an explicitly feminine exegesis:

> Wir Frauen sind in einem besondern Zustande. Die Maximen der Männer hören wir immerfort wiederholen, ja wir müssen sie in goldnen Buchstaben über unsern Häupten sehen, und doch wüßten wir Mädchen im stillen das Umgekehrte zu sagen, das auch gölte, wie es gerade hier der Fall ist. Die *Schöne* findet Verehrer, auch Freier, und endlich wohl gar einen Mann; dann gelangt sie zum *Wahren*, das nicht immer höchst erfreulich sein mag, und wenn sie klug ist, widmet sie sich dem *Nützlichen*, sorgt für Haus und Kinder und verharrt dabei.[23]

A feminine exegesis, as I have said, and at a number of levels: first, in that Hersilie takes a general rule, supposedly operative at a universal level, and demonstrates its specific applicability for a subclass of the social body not usually taken account of in the principles of the Enlightenment. Second, it is feminine in the rhetorical sense—in the supple, ingratiating, yet basically subversive manner in which the language of authority is turned against itself.

Benjamin's study suggests that the "moral" of a story, its pragmatic point, may be understood not only as an effect of summation and closure but also as a kind of propagating energy that connects the single tale with a larger narrative current. This may take two forms. One involves the principle of linkage among stories, the network of what he calls narrative remembrance (*Gedächtnis*) or "das Netz, wel-

---

23. *Goethes Werke*, 8:66. In English: "We women are in a singular situation. We constantly hear the maxims of men recited, indeed, we are forced to view them inscribed in golden letters above our heads, and yet we for our part know just the opposite, which might also have some validity, as in this instance. *Beauty* finds suitors and finally even a husband; then she attains to the *truth*, which is not always especially pleasing, and if she is smart, she devotes herself to the *useful*, cares for house and children, and sticks to that."

ches alle Geschichten miteinander am Ende bilden." And he goes on, "Eine schließt an die andere an, wie es die großen Erzähler immer und vor allem die orientalischen gern gezeigt haben. In jedem derselben lebt eine Scheherazade, der zu jeder Stelle ihrer Geschichten eine neue Geschichte einfällt."[24] The other form this energy takes involves the formation of a body of auditors, "die Gemeinschaft der Lauschenden" ("the community of listeners"), a community specifically constituted by its receptivity to the story. Here, too, Benjamin utilizes an image from textile manufacture. The art of repeating stories, he writes, "verliert sich, weil nicht mehr gewebt und gesponnen wird, während man ihnen lauscht. Je selbstvergessener der Lauschende, desto tiefer prägt sich ihm das Gehörte ein. Wo ihn der Rhythmus der Arbeit ergriffen hat, da lauscht er den Geschichten auf solche Weise, daß ihm die Gabe, sie zu erzählen, von selber zufällt. So also ist das Netz beschafen, in das die Gabe zu erzählen gebettet ist."[25]

The association of spinning and weaving with the formation of stories is, of course, an ancient one—its mythological prototype is the three Fates. In the *Wanderjahre* we find more than one variant of this theme. In the case of the Beautiful Widow (in "Der Mann von funfzig Jahren") it is adapted to the luxurious world of an eighteenth-century salon. The Widow, in connection with an elaborately embroidered portfolio she has made, speaks of her handiwork in these terms: "Als junge Mädchen werden wir gewöhnt, mit den Fingern zu tifteln und mit den Gedanken umherzuschweifen; beides bleibt uns, indem wir nach und nach die schwersten und zierlichsten Arbeiten verfertigen lernen."[26] The musing, uncommitted play of fancy expressed here suggests a Penelope function, the endless weaving and undoing of a tapestry, emblematic for a protonarrative source from which every story is derived and to which it refers

24. "Der Erzähler," p. 453. In English: "the web which all stories form in the end." "One ties on to the next, as the great storytellers, particularly the Oriental ones, have always readily shown. In each of them there is a Scheherazade who thinks of a fresh story whenever her tale comes to a stop." "The Storyteller," p. 98.

25. Ibid., p. 447. In English: "is lost because there is no more weaving and spinning to go on while they are being listened to. The more self-forgetful the listener is, the more deeply is what he listens to impressed upon his memory. When the rhythm of work has seized him, he listens to the tales in such a way that the gift of retelling them comes to him all by itself. This, then, is the nature of the web in which the gift of storytelling is cradled." "The Storyteller," p. 91.

26. *Goethes Werke*, 8:189. In English: "As young girls we became accustomed to be busy with our fingers and to let our thoughts stray afield; both habits have remained with us as we gradually learned to master the most exacting and delicate tasks."

through some loose ends, some trace of its connection to other stories, to all stories.

By drawing on Benjamin's analysis I have sought to relate certain formal elements of narrative to a communal practice that brings into play the circuit of narrative transmission. "So haftet an der Erzählung," Benjamin writes, "die Spur des Erzählenden wie die Spur der Töpferhand an der Tonschale."[27] Now this foreign element in the tale, the trace of its origin, of who made it and for what purpose, should be projected forward as well, toward the recipient. When this is done we have all of the constituents of narrative structure in a pragmatic sense—the telling, the listening, the passing on.

III

We saw in "Parasitic Talk" that the path of narrative transmission may be analyzed as a primary structuring factor in certain novels. By tracing the permutation of narrative posts or stances (in Lyotard's sense) we are able to assess the nature of the "message," the narrative *savoir*.[28] Since, in the *Wanderjahre*, the narrating instance is distributed among many figures, the circuit of transmission is exceptionally complex. The novel includes, as I have already indicated, a great multiplicity of text forms, each one having its distinct mode of enunciation, transmission, and reception. Their presence together within the same narrative further complicates the communicative circuit. This is why I have been led to focus on the pragmatic dimension of the text—on the modes of transmission rather than on some definitive message.

Mikhail Bakhtin's work allows us to extend the notion of a narrative pragmatics through a model of dialogic discourse designed to account for the heterogeneous materials that enter into the structure of the novel. Of the various terms that Bakhtin uses, "heteroglossia" is perhaps the most suggestive for characterizing the medley of styles and attitudes that make up the fabric of prose fiction. In Bakhtin's view the multiplicity of discursive modes in a text are not simply citations or remnants of antecedent speech forms, as Barthes interprets them in the context of his referential or endoxal code;[29] rather, Bakhtin underscores a dynamic interplay, a collision of singular, though not necessarily personal, "voices." It is through their

27. "Der Erzähler," p. 447. In English: "Thus traces of the storyteller cling to the story the way the handprints of the potter cling to the clay vessel." "The Storyteller," p. 92.
28. See above, p. 81f.
29. Cf. Roland Barthes, *S/Z: An Essay*, p. 205f.

conjunction that the novel is able to generate a new form of meaning. The dialogic novel, as he conceives it, can assimilate these heterogeneous elements without altogether normalizing them. To some degree they retain the force of their various origins. Furthermore, Bakhtin makes us particularly attentive to the specific stance, the intentional vector, encoded in every statement, the very quality that makes it a voice in an active dialogue. But to call it a voice does not mean to make it dependent on a character. The polyphony of voices derives from a pre-personal discourse level that frequently, but not invariably, uses anthropomorphic agents as instances of enunciation. The speech of characters in a novel represents a secondary operation, and it presupposes a repertoire of registers, what has been called "normative genres of discourse,"[30] whose ultimate basis is social and cultural.

What is especially relevant for us in Bakhtin's notion of dialogue is that every word, or speech segment, is to be taken not as an invariant unit of meaning but as an enunciatory act, an act that betrays the pressure of other speech acts. "The word is not a thing," he writes, "but rather the eternally mobile, eternally changing medium of dialogical intercourse. It never coincides with a single consciousness or a single voice. The life of the word is in its transferral from one mouth to another, one context to another, one social collective to another, and one generation to another. In the process the word does not forget where it has been and can never wholly free itself from the dominion of the contexts of which it has been a part."[31]

Bakhtin's categories refer to different levels of the narrative process in ways that he himself did not fully indicate, thus any effort to apply his ideas to a work involves certain interpretive choices regarding the theory. I would suggest three ways in which the *Wanderjahre* exemplifies a dialogic practice: first, in destabilizing genre forms; then, in orienting representational devices toward the instance of reception; and finally, in thematizing the channels of communication as such.

At the level of genre, heteroglossia would signify a loosening of normative genre forms. In many of the novellas of the *Wanderjahre* we find a marked displacement of the expected narrative structure through the introduction of contrastive devices characteristic of other

30. John Frow, "Voice and Register in *Little Dorrit,*" *Comparative Literature,* 33(1981): 263.
31. Mikhail Bakhtin, *Problems of Dostoevsky's Poetics* (Ann Arbor, 1973), p. 167.

literary forms, such as legend, comic drama, or fairy tale. In constructing the stories for the novel, the basic pattern that Goethe
started with was that of the Renaissance novella, a form in which
exemplarity and entertainment, moral point and witty *pointe,* are
subtly interwoven. As a background to this form, we may take, as
Karlheinz Stierle has argued, the medieval fable, where the narrative
sequence is unequivocally oriented toward an apothegm, a *sententia.*
Conversely, this moral point may be viewed as the kernel that gives
rise to a narrative expansion. Now in various Renaissance forms the
expansion went well beyond the limits implicit in the didactic or
moralistic kernel, without, however, altogether obliterating the initial
pragmatic orientation. What is noteworthy about the Boccaccian novella, Stierle argues, is the way that the exemplum, the illustrative
narrative, wins a certain autonomy, establishing an oblique relation to
the pragmatic context on which it is based. The exemplum is over-
determined; its applicability in moral or social terms is no longer self-
evident, though the field of that applicability remains as a point of
reference. The problematization of the exemplum in the novella may
be viewed in terms of the narrative form as such (at the level of the
sender) and in terms of the intended audience (or receptor). In fact,
this element will often lead to a more complex interplay of frame and
embedded narratives. "The new mode of representation of the novella," Stierle writes with respect to Boccaccio, "is thematized as a function of the self-understanding of the kind of society that is delineated
in the frame."[32]

One could find numerous instances in the *Wanderjahre* where the
exemplifying function typical of the novella form is put into question,
instances both in the interpolated stories (as in "Die Gefährliche Wet-
te," where a farce takes an unexpected tragic turn) and in the frame (as
in various episodes where there is a disequilibrium between what we
know of the speaker and what he recounts about himself, e.g., the case
of Wilhelm already discussed, or Odoard's recounting of "Nicht zu
Weit"). In a pioneering study, Ernst Friedrich von Monroy showed
that many of the novellas displace the basic narrative pattern by introducing contrastive devices characteristic of other literary forms, such
as legend, comic drama, or fairy tale.[33]

A second way of approaching the dialogic mode in the *Wander-*

---

32. "Geschichte als Exemplum, Exemplum als Geschichte: Zur Pragmatik und Poetik narrativer Texte," in *Text als Handlung,* pp. 14–48, esp. p. 36.

33. Cf. Ernst Friedrich von Monroy, "Zur Form der Novelle in 'Wilhelm Meisters
Wanderjahre,' " *G.R.M.* 31(1943): 1–19.

jahre is to note the frequency of speech forms, whether in monologue or dialogue, that are markedly oriented toward their recipient. In one sense this device may be seen as a distancing factor in the representation of an action, since the focus on the speaking voice subordinates the subject matter of the story in favor of the frame in which it is set. But in another sense it serves to modify the modality of the action itself, placing the emphasis neither on the speaker as an individuated figure nor on the substance of his story, but on the impact that the speech has on an auditor. We may view this as a thematization of the dialogic by means of dramatic or theatrical devices. In such utterances the intention to move or influence the auditor may be clearly exhibited by way of manner and gesture. But there is also in the substance of the enunciation a strategy aimed at forestalling and modifying the anticipated response. Bakhtin speaks of the "alien word," which inhabits all our utterances and which we, consciously or not, take account of in all acts of communication. This alien word, he writes, is "in the consciousness of the listener, of his apperceptive background, pregnant with responses and objections. And every utterance is oriented toward this apperceptive background of understanding, which is not a linguistic background but rather one composed of specific objects and emotional expressions."[34]

A number of episodes in the *Wanderjahre* hinge not on what is directly stated in a speech or dialogue but rather on this type of orientation toward the reception. This is patent in instances where a speaker directly manipulates an interlocutor, as in the Foolish Pilgrim's intimations to Herr von Revanne and to his son that she has become pregnant by the other. But it is operative, too, in less overt instances where we become attentive less to the motives of the speaker than to the effects of the speaking—thus, in the Foolish Pilgrim's ballad, in Nachodine's plea to Lenardo not to cancel the lease on her father's farm, in Lucidor's passionate monologues in "Wer ist der Verräter?" (the plot here turns on their being overheard), in the echo effects of the poems that Flavio and Hilarie exchange, not to mention the *Wechselgedichte* that they read together and that serve to kindle their love. Of course, each of these instances, viewed in the context of

34. M. M. Bakhtin, *The Dialogic Imagination: Four Essays,* ed. Michael Holquist (Austin, 1981), p. 281. I have already spoken in connection with Benjamin and Lyotard of the ways that the context of reception is constitutive for the form of a narrative. For Bakhtin, too, a narrative event cannot be established in abstract terms as part of some self-contained logic of narrative. There is an "evaluative function" encoded in the telling without which there would be no story. (I cite this phrase from the stimulating article by Kloepfer, "Dynamic Structures in Narrative Literature" [see Chap. 4, n. 4], p. 118.)

its episode, fulfills a traditional pattern of dramatized representation. But, through its repeated, cumulative use in the novel, this kind of strategic address in monologue and dialogue may be accounted a basic structuring principle, subverting the authority of a narrative persona and shaping the reception of the work.

Finally, I see the dialogic principle operative in the *Wanderjahre* in a recurrent focus on the communicative channel as such, or rather on the interferences or blockages that impede the full circulation of narrative information. An important recent study of the novel is entitled *Wilhelm Meisters Wanderjahre oder die Kunst des Mittelbaren: Studien zum Problem der Verständigung in Goethes Altersepoche* ["*Wilhelm Meister's Journeymanship* or the Art of Communicative Practice: Studies on the Problem of Comprehension in Goethe's Late Period"].[35] In it Manfred Karnick deals with what may be called Goethe's communicative reticence, and he offers some excellent analyses of its implications for the mode of indirect and symbolic presentation characteristic of the *Wanderjahre*. What for him, however, are privative categories at a biographical, existential level—such as secrecy and hiddenness (*Verschlossenheit*)—I would take more as strategic choices that open up new possibilities of the form. I will illustrate this point through two characters—the Beautiful Widow and Hersilie.

The Beautiful Widow moves through the action of the novel at a diagonal. She is introduced in one of the novellas, "Der Mann von funfzig Jahren," and then reappears in the frame story when, in company with Hilarie, also from that tale, she meets Wilhelm and the artist on Lago Maggiore and takes part in the waiting game that characterizes the "Entsagenden," the renunciants. Characters like the Widow represent a disturbing factor in the linearity of a plot. The roles they assume are never altogether congruent with what others expect of them, and they seem to exist on the borders of more than one of the stories, their identity made unstable by such crossings. Nachodine (the Nutbrown Maiden) and the Foolish Pilgrim also fall into this category. Two other feminine figures realize it in contrasting ways: the New Melusine's fragmented existence is predicated on the supernatural or fairy tale context in which she appears; Hersilie, at the other extreme, is apparently stuck on the verge of a romantic tale, but, to her regret, unable to move into it, doomed to an incipient condition.

35. (Munich, 1968).

What is common to all of these feminine figures is that they produce a network that is both erotic and topographic, that is, marked by roads, pathways, and stations of a journey, the journey being made either by one of them for the sake of a man (the Foolish Pilgrim, the New Melusine) or by a man *for* one of them (Lenardo's search for the Nutbrown Maiden, Felix's pursuit of Hersilie, who herself, by means of letters, tries to attract Wilhelm). The Widow falls into both categories—she is sought by Flavio and his father, the Major. She is the cause of Flavio's melodramatic flight back to his father's estate. In the end, though, she recoils at what she has done and leaves her home to journey in the Italian lake district, where she encounters Wilhelm.

I have already called attention to the Widow's pastime of embroidering and its association with Penelope, with the endless weaving and undoing of a narrative fabric. But we may extend her function and recognize a conjunction of Penelope and Hermes.[36] When we superimpose the figure of the god of boundaries and crossings, the guide of travelers, the divine messenger, onto that of the tireless weaver, we become aware that the formation of a narrative strand (a *discours*) is isomorphic to the tracing of an itinerary, the passage (*parcours*) that connects discrete points or junctions in order to produce a manageable, unitary space.[37] What I mean to suggest by these mythological parallels is a deep structure at a discourse level for the narrative action. The Widow is one of the preeminent agents in the construction of such a discursive space. As an alluring woman of the world, an accomplished hostess, she situates, stimulates, connects all the guests in her salon. Later, as a member of the foursome on the Lago Maggiore, she is again notable for her composure in the midst of a tricky, unstable environment. Her function in the novel is to establish a provisional order amidst shifting, discrete elements. She possesses the capacity to facilitate a viable social discourse, though only within a highly restricted context. In this novel, with its medley of discursive and narrative forms, the function that might otherwise belong to hero or heroine—tracing an itinerary and creating an oriented space—devolves on figures like the Widow.

Hersilie represents another instance of what I have called communicative reticence in the structure of the novel. She provides her

36. Cf. Michel Serres, *Hermes: Literature, Science, Philosophy,* ed. Josué V. Harari and David F. Bell (Baltimore, 1982), p. xxxiii.
37. Cf. above, p. 31.

own characterization, and that of her household, in a consciously parodistic listing of the cast of characters that Wilhelm meets on the Uncle's estate: "ein wunderlicher Oheim, eine sanfte und eine muntere Nichte, eine kluge Tante, Hausgenossen nach bekannter Art."[38] She, of course, is the "muntere Nichte." Her first letter to her aunt, Makarie, opens with a complaint that strikes us as singular when we consider the highly disciplined, well-nigh ritualistic pattern of intercourse practiced in Makarie's house. "Ich will und muß sehr kurz sein, liebe Tante," Hersilie writes, "denn der Bote zeigt sich unartig ungeduldig." How could a messenger from Makarie's household behave in such an impertinent manner? Later in the letter she writes, "Der Bote! der Bote! Ziehen Sie Ihre alten Leute besser, oder schicken sie junge. Diesem ist weder mit Schmeichelei noch mit Wein beizukommen." We never hear again about this annoying courier. Now if we attempt to assign him a function in the action we hardly know what to do with him. He is a kind of noise, an intrusive, unassimilable element in the communicative circuit. But the insistent, thrice-reiterated reference to the messenger—"Der Bote! der verwünschte Bote!"[39]—foregrounds a metanarrative function that we cannot altogether ignore.

Later in the novel a *young* courier does in fact appear. This one bears a message (*eine Botschaft*) from Felix, who at this point is in school in the Pedagogic Province. The whole episode is recounted by Hersilie in a letter to Wilhelm. (It is worth noting that her sole entry into the novel after her initial appearance at the Uncle's estate is by way of a series of letters which she addresses to Wilhelm, though we never learn that he replies to any of them.) What is it that the courier brings from Felix? A slate school tablet with the rudimentary inscription,

> Felix
> liebt
> Hersilien.
> Der Stallmeister
> kommt bald.[40]

---

38. *Goethes Werke*, 8:68. In English: "a strange uncle, a gentle niece and a lively one, a wise aunt, the other usual members of the household."

39. Ibid., pp. 75–77. In English: "I must be very brief, dear aunt, for the courier is being most impatient." "The courier! the courier! Train your old servants better or send young ones. This one cannot be gotten around either by flattery or with wine." "The courier! the accursed courier!"

40. Ibid., p. 265. In English: "Felix loves Hersilie. The groom is coming soon."

Hersilie is perturbed, baffled, and uncertain how to reply. In the end the young itinerant pedlar gives her a similar tablet on which she writes her response, a slightly askew mirroring of Felix's words designed both to satisfy him and to show her good-humored reception of his message,

Hersiliens
Gruß
an Felix.
Der Stallmeister
halte sich gut.[41]

Goethe here undoubtedly alludes to far more exalted instances of a courtship carried on through an exchange of verse where each partner echoes the other—there is his own cycle, the *West-östlicher Divan,* and in this novel there is the exchange of poems between Flavio and Hilarie already mentioned. The exchange of messages on slate tablets between Hersilie and Felix appears to be a kind of parody of such a courtship.[42]

It serves, though, to introduce this second courier figure, the itinerant pedlar, who is perhaps gypsy or Jew. "Etwas Orientalisches," is how Hersilie characterizes him. Typically, he is gone before she can get a clear image of him, and she muses, "Allerdings etwas Geheimnisvolles war in der Figur; dergleichen sind jetzt im Roman nicht zu entbehren, sollten sie uns denn auch im Leben begegnen? Angenehm, doch verdächtig, fremdartig, doch Vertrauen erregend; warum schied er auch vor aufgelöster Verwirrung? warum hatt' ich nicht Gegenwart des Geistes genug, um ihn schicklicherweise festzuhalten?"[43]

Hersilie and the elusive courier—here is a motif that does not fill out into a story. It is a narrative kernel of indefinite mass. Hersilie, of course, is a figure who tries to resist typification. She knows the stereotypes of fiction all too well. Her own story, her attachment to

---

41. Ibid., p. 266. In English: "Hersilie's greetings to Felix. Regards to the groom."

42. I note two recent essays focusing on the figure of Hersilie, though neither parallels my discussion: Marianne Jabs-Kriegsmann, "Felix und Hersilie," in *Studien zu Goethes Alterswerken,* ed. Erich Trunz (Frankfurt am Main, 1971); Françoise Derré, "Die Beziehung zwischen Felix, Hersilie und Wilhelm in 'Wilhelm Meisters Wanderjahre,' " *Goethe Jahrbuch* 94(1977): 38–48.

43. Ibid., p. 267. In English: "Yet there was something mysterious in that figure; one cannot do without such things in the novel these days, might they not also come to us in reality? Pleasant yet suspicious, singular yet able to inspire confidence; why did he depart before the confusion could be resolved? Why did I not have sufficient presence of mind to hold him back in a proper manner?"

Felix or to his father, never quite gets off the ground. She is the guardian of the mysterious little box that Felix had found, but she never gets to see what is in it, even when the key is finally restored to her. Her plea to Wilhelm regarding this box— "Daß es ein Ende werde, wenigsten daß eine Deutung vorgehe, was damit gemeint sei, mit diesem wunderbaren Finden, Wiederfinden, Trennen und Vereinigen"[44]—remains unanswered. The plea, of course, refers not only to the box but also to her own stranded, inconclusive situation. Hersilie does not enjoy the resources of the Widow, who, unsuccessful in one setting, is able to shift to another and exercise her combinatory talents once more. If Makarie is the repository of everyone's secrets, the wise counselor, the secular mystic, what is Hersilie, who cannot decide between father and son, whose letters go unanswered, who remains in possession of a mysterious box that she cannot or will not open?

There seems to be a function in the communicative channel that facilitates narrative without being altogether part of it. It may be allied to the parasite. Its agents have no great dignity in the roster of narrative roles. Hermes may be invoked but will not always appear or be recognized. Perhaps we touch here on an emergent stage of the narrative impulse, one not yet fully conscious of itself, not yet informed by a narrative subject. If so, Hersilie names it, since she is akin to it— "Der Bote! der verwünschte Bote!"

44. Ibid., p. 378. In English: "Let us be done with this, at least let there be some solution, what all this means, this marvelous finding, recovery, separation, and reunion."

7 Flaubert's Quotidian Tale: The Reality Effect in "Un Coeur simple"

In a well-known study Erich Auerbach characterizes Flaubert as a kind of saintly quester of the Grail of language:

> We hear the writer speak; but he expresses no opinion and makes no comment. His role is limited to selecting the events and translating them into language; and this is done in the conviction that every event, if one is able to express it purely and completely, interprets itself and the persons involved in it far better and more completely than any opinion or judgment appended to it could do. . . . In this fashion subjects completely fill the writer; he forgets himself, his heart no longer serves him save to feel the hearts of others, and when, by fanatical patience, this condition is achieved, the perfect expression, which at once entirely comprehends the momentary subject and impartially judges it, comes of itself; subjects are seen as God sees them, in their true essence.[1]

This heroism of the writer in the name of style represents, of course, an ideal that Flaubert himself articulated more than once in his correspondence (e.g., "le style étant à lui tout seul une manière absolue de voir les choses"),[2] but it represents a position that, from our present vantage point, can hardly be accepted in a straightforward, univocal manner. For such an approach is too much allied with myths of the creative personality, with an aesthetics of genius, and in consequence it blocks any serious consideration of what the labor of style can bring about.

There is another aspect of Auerbach's analysis, however, that deserves to be reassessed, and this is the sharp split that he perceived

---

1. *Mimesis*, trans. Willard Trask (Garden City, N.Y., 1957), p. 429.

2. *Extraits de la correspondance ou Préface à la vie d'écrivain*, ed. G. Bollème (Paris, 1963), p. 63. Henceforth cited as *Préface*. In English: "style in itself being an absolute manner of seeing things."

between a character's experiences and feelings, on the one hand, and his or her power of expression, of linguistic articulation, on the other. In interpreting that famous scene at the dinner table between Emma and Charles, Auerbach showed with great subtlety how the whole sensuous and affective aura of the experience derives from Emma's personality, from the specific potentialities of her modes of experiencing and feeling. But through all this she is cut off from a decisive element of this reality, namely, its verbal, articulated dimension:

> Here it is not Emma who speaks, but the writer. . . . To be sure, there is nothing of Flaubert's life in these words, but only Emma's; Flaubert does nothing but bestow the power of mature expression upon the material which she affords, in its complete subjectivity. If Emma could do this herself, she would no longer be what she is, she would have outgrown herself and thereby saved herself.[3]

Yet if the language passes Emma by, if it reveals in her a kind of alienation from her experience, or rather an inchoate, oppressive immersion *in* that experience, does this mean that the writer is to be credited with a perfect control of language? To do this would be only to shift the source of the language impulse, to alter the authorizing subject; it would in no way question the myth of a translucent, naturally grounded force of language.

The dominant critical orientations today, of course, view Flaubert very differently. Barthes's position is characteristic: "Flaubert . . . working with an irony impregnated with uncertainty, achieves a salutary discomfort of writing: he does not stop the play of codes (or stops it only partially), so that (and this is indubitably the *proof* of writing) *one never knows if he is responsible for what he writes* (if there is a subject *behind* his language)."[4] But one does not only have to appeal to present-day opinion. The myth of a plenitude of language is sufficiently undermined in Flaubert's own pronouncements and practice. Any reader of the correspondence knows that there are many passages that testify to the writer's sense of frustration in regard to his means of expression. It is not only that he despairs over his own efficacy. The doubts regarding the nature of language are far more fundamental.

Auerbach's sense of a radical gap between experiential reality and linguistic expression in Flaubert is certainly pertinent, but the conclusion he draws from this needs to be inverted. It is not the glory or the

---

3. *Mimesis*, p. 427.
4. *S/Z: An Essay*, p. 140.

autonomy of language that is revealed thereby but, on the contrary, the impoverishment, the voiding of its denotative force, of its capacity to designate a reality beyond itself. The search for referential correspondence, for an equivalence between the semantic and the experiential orders, represents as fundamental a drive in Flaubert as in his heroine: "Et Emma cherchait à savoir ce que l'on entendait au juste dans la vie par les mots de *félicité,* de *passion* et d'*ivresse,* qui lui avaient paru si beaux dans les livres."[5] And though the "deux bonhommes" of his final work do not possess the intensity, the obsessive drive that casts a hue of grand pathos, even of tragedy, over Emma's career, their effort is similarly oriented to trying to force the world to conform to a certain order of language. As with Emma, so with Bouvard and Pécuchet, what appears initially as a delusive ambition in the protagonists, an object of mockery and exposure, assumes in the course of each of the works the status of a positive, if inaccessible, value, one that figures Flaubert's most deep-seated artistic ambition. The narrator's contemptuous judgment of Rodolphe—"Il ne distinguait pas, cet homme si plein de pratique, la dissemblance des sentiments sous la parité des expressions."—leads to that astonishingly direct and anguished plaint over the insufficiency of language: "que la parole humaine est comme un chaudron fêlé où nous battons des mélodies à faire danser les ours, quand on voudrait attendrir les étoiles."[6]

My interest in this issue, however, is not so much oriented to its consequences for the writer in existential terms as to its effects on a system of representation and nomination within which Flaubert represents a decisive, but not isolated, instance. Françoise Gaillard has put the matter in terms of a radical disfunctioning of the linguistic sign:

> The failure of words reveals that the signifying relation has been distorted, flawed. . . . With Flaubert it is not only certain rebellious elements of the vocabulary which have become problematic; the system of signs in its entirety has begun to vacillate: the exhibition of the irreality

5. *Madame Bovary: Moeurs de province,* ed. E. Maynial (Paris, 1961), p. 32. In English: "And Emma tried to find out what one meant exactly in life by the words *bliss, passion, ecstasy,* that had seemed to her so beautiful in books." *Madame Bovary,* trans. Paul de Man (see Chap. 1, n. 27), p. 24.

6. *Madame Bovary,* p. 178f. In English: "He was unable to see, this man so full of experience, the variety of feelings hidden within the same expressions." "the human tongue is like a cracked cauldron on which we beat out tunes to set a bear dancing when we would make the stars weep with our melodies." *Madame Bovary,* p. 138.

of its autofunctioning destroys its pretense of being the mode of production of meaning.[7]

One way to deal with this crisis at the level of meaning is to assign a meaning to the sign's very depletion. Thus Gaillard continues:

> And then, given Flaubert's own ideological enclosure, what other language is possible if not a diversion directed to the signification of *insignificance itself*. . . . One avoids stupidity, then, by reproducing it as *subject*.[8]

To reify "la bêtise," to endow it with the status of an object and thereby constitute its "meaning," is unquestionably a fundamental project in Flaubert. One could pursue it in any number of directions. There is the *Dictionnaire des idées reçues,* begun in the early 1850s and then incorporated into the work on *Bouvard et Pécuchet,* still unfinished at Flaubert's death. There is, in Flaubert's youth, the figure of the *Garçon,* which comes up frequently in the exchanges with his intimates, the role of a loutish creature assumed in order to mock some target in their milieu. This figure was designed to operate in terms of a subversive mimicry, objectifying bourgeois attitudes in such a way as to discredit them in the eyes of the initiates without revealing their game to outsiders. There is, most notably, Flaubert's self-lacerating engagement with a banal subject matter in the writing of *Madame Bovary*: "Ce à quoi je me heurte, c'est à des situations communes et un dialogue trivial. Bien écrire *le médiocre* et faire qu'il garde en même temps son aspect, sa coupe, ses mots même, cela est vraiment diabolique."[9] What is common to all these cases is that the writer must insinuate himself into the debased medium that constitutes his subject matter. The intent, of course, is corrosive, critical; he must demolish what he simulates. But in the process he cannot escape a taint, a moment of identity with the despised element.

I have already discussed Barthes's view of *bêtise* as a tactic for "outplaying" the level of unconsidered *doxa,* of quotidian language.[10] I want now to make a link between the treatment of the stereotype and the treatment of the object in Flaubert, between the

7. "L'En-signement du réel (ou la nécessaire écriture de la répétition)," in *La production du sens chez Flaubert,* ed. C. Gothot-Mersch (Paris, 1975), pp. 197–220; this quote is on p. 212.

8. Ibid., p. 214.

9. *Préface,* p. 147. In English: "What I am struggling with are commonplace situations and trivial dialogue. To write well about *mediocrity* and make it retain at the same time its true aspect, its cut, its very words, this is truly diabolical."

10. See above, pp. 84ff.

exhibition of ordinary speech by way of citation and the delineation of material reality by way of description. Here, too, Barthes's reflections are pertinent. He begins his essay "The Reality Effect" with a consideration of a fundamental opposition between the aims of narrative and those of description. Narrative is "essentially predictive," its whole structure being determined by a finality toward which it is oriented. Description, by contrast, is "purely additive" ("purement sommatoire"). Though it may, and typically is, put in the service of a narrative meaning (that is, assimilated to a narrative function), its own mode of signification is alien to the integrative structure of narrative. Thus Barthes may claim, "Insignificant *notation* (taking 'insignificant' in the strong sense—apparently detached from the semiotic structure of narrative) is related to description," and he elaborates this point thus:

> The singularity of the description (or of the 'useless detail') in the narrative fabric, its isolatedness, brings up a question of primary importance for the structural analysis of narrative. This question is the following: is everything in the narrative meaningful, significant? And if not, if there exist insignificant stretches, what is, so to speak, the ultimate significance of this insignificance?[11]

Barthes's answer, his resolution of the "significance of this insignificance" is that the normal, the proper function of the descriptive mode—namely, of denotation—has, in a certain type of fiction, been subverted in favor of a secondary function, one of connotation. The subject matter of description, the type of "concrete detail" that had been justified in neo-classical aesthetics by a principle of verisimilitude (*le vraisemblable*) is, in modern realism, subject to no other constraint than the (possible) existence of a referent:

> Semiotically, the 'concrete detail' is constituted by the *direct* collusion of a referent and a signifier; the signified is expelled from the sign. . . . This is what might be called the *referential illusion*. The truth behind this illusion is this: eliminated from the realist utterance as a signified of denotation, the 'real' slips back in as a signified of connotation; for at the very moment when these details are supposed to denote reality directly, all that they do, tacitly, is signify it. Flaubert's barometer [in "Un Coeur simple"], Michelet's little door, say, in the last analysis, only this: *we are the real*. It is the category of the 'real,' and not its various contents, which is being signified; in other words, the very absence of the signified,

11. *French Literary Theory Today*, p. 12.

to the advantage of the referent, standing alone, becomes the true signifier of realism.[12]

What is at issue here, as Barthes well realizes, is the very foundation of
a representational system. The referent at issue can, of course, only be
a *possible* referent in this case, a fictive or imaginary entity. Its accreditation, its right to be named in a text, has traditionally derived
from an institutional or ideological system, such as the neo-classical
system of literary genres. Nineteenth-century realism will still use the
earlier genres, but their function as determinants of content, of subject
matter, becomes markedly attenuated.

The example that Barthes takes from Flaubert—the barometer
that figures in the furnishings of Mme. Aubain's house—is, of course,
in itself hardly conclusive. One could easily enough find a justification
for this detail in terms of narrative functionality (as typical of a class,
as symbolic of certain values). But the point at issue is that every
naming of an object in realist narrative, specific as it is, and just on
account of that specificity, exposes a contingent, an arbitrary principle
of selection.

According to the structuralist analysis,[13] realist narrative is
obliged to manufacture something like a "represener function"
(what Philippe Hamon calls "thématique vide") in order to motivate
the represented objectivities of a work of fiction. But such motivation, it should be remembered, exists for the sake of a principle of
verisimilitude. Its purpose is to naturalize what is, in truth, a circumstantial, culturally determined situation. Thus, the realist text will
seek to realize a balance between the represener and the represented, it will try to match an intensity of interest in the former with
a vividness of presentation in the latter; or, if there be a discrepancy
between the two, this itself will be thematized, possibly by means of
supplementary represeners. In short, the norms of realism require
that the represener function, however constituted, must be capable
of bearing the weight of what is represented.

One consequence of this structure is that a support must be
assumed at the level of the diegesis (within the represented world) for
what the text stipulates at an extradiegetic level (the level of reception).
Philippe Bonnefis puts it in the following terms:

12. Ibid., p. 16.
13. See above, pp. 10ff.

Arts based on imitation, in their diversity, all have recourse to the same artifice. It is always a question of covering with a relation of signification what is, in fact, a relation of designation. In the latter case, one copies an original whose exteriority poses no problem, in the former, the exterior is perceived (if not defined) as that which problematizes the inside of a practice.[14]

Thus, in what Bonnefis calls a relation of signification, the meaning may be constructed by means of some motivation within the diegesis. But with the other, the relation of designation, the issue is altogether different. *Its* justification can not be based on any direct form of mimesis but must be sought at the level of representational practices that underlie the *kind* of text in question (that is, at the level of genre, of fiction, of "literature"). The diegesis cannot authenticate its own contents. And yet the tactic of realist representation is to camouflage this incapacity, to make the relation of signification (the motivated, representer function) into a stand-in for the designating function.[15]

The singularity of Flaubert's fiction is that while it participates in the tendency just discussed by ascribing great weight to the personal vision of a character in validating descriptive data, it does not fulfill the second part of what may be called the "realist contract"—it does not make such psychological or mental experience commensurate with the reality that it filters. In Flaubert the fictive subject for whom, and in terms of whom, a context is rendered will be hollowed out and emptied as a world structure emerges. And we may not, I think, follow Auerbach's explanation that the task of validation is then assumed by language itself as manipulated by a quasi-omniscient writer.

This is not to say that a distinction between "Who speaks?" and "Who sees?" is inapplicable in this instance. Félicité in "Un Coeur simple," like Emma in *Madame Bovary,* serves as an indispensable agent of attribution. Emma's singularity resides in her capacity to elicit objects at the periphery of her focal field, at a level distinct from what she consciously understands and perceives, and these objects become meaningful for the reader precisely in consequence of her

---

14. "Le descripteur mélancolique," in *La description* (Lille, 1974), pp. 103–51; this quote is on p. 103.

15. Cf. Roland Barthes, "The Reality Effect," *French Literary Theory Today*, p. 14. "Nevertheless, the aesthetic intention of Flaubertian description is totally interwoven with the imperatives of 'realism,' as if exactitude of reference, superior or indifferent to all other functions, of itself commanded and justified description of the referent, or, in the case of a description reduced to a single word, its denotation. Here aesthetic constraints are impregnated—at least as an alibi—with referential constraints."

inchoate yearning. In Félicité we have a character with a radically impoverished field of awareness. Flaubert's objectivity (perhaps only another name for his irony) consists in making the reader constantly aware of the gap that exists between the forms of cognition available to his characters and a reality that in some manner derives from their sensibility, their impressionability. But the text does not valorize this reality, or set it up as the objective pole to the characters' variously deficient modes of vision. This level of reality is itself radically delimited, the product of an occultation parallel to that of the characters in the fiction, though less evident to the reader since it lies at the heart of his own manner of reading, his own construction of reality on the basis of fiction.

Félicité provides an exceptionally revealing instance of a type of figure which, in sponsoring a certain context, undergoes a process of shrinking and fading as its world emerges. What interests me especially is the way that this diminution of the subject is inscribed in the represented world of the tale.[16] In Bonnefis's terms we may say that the signifying relation, far from confirming the designating function, approaches it only asymptotically.

Chapter 1 of "Un Coeur simple" does not begin with the chronicle of Félicité's life, which will occupy the succeeding four chapters. Rather, it offers a synoptic view of the half-century of her existence as Mme. Aubain's servant. In this section Félicité is viewed altogether from the outside ("external focalization," in Genette's terminology), the perspective being that of the bourgeois world of Pont-l'Évêque. And the focus is not even so much on Félicité herself as on her mistress and the house in which they live. Félicité is portrayed only in her dependence on her mistress, and Mme. Aubain herself is subordinated to her possessions. The description of the house and its furnishings constitutes the centerpiece of this chapter, and it is organized in orderly fashion, following the path of an imaginary tour—first the outside, then the vestibule, and, passing by the kitchen, into the main downstairs living room, up to the first floor and "madame's" bedroom, and so on. The circuit closes with a mention of the dormer window into Félicité's room on the second floor, but this room itself is not further described.

I shall dwell on one stylistic feature of this chapter: the several topics dealt with are all at one point identified by the pronoun *elle*—

16. Cf. John R. O'Connor, "Flaubert: *Trois Contes* and the Figure of the Double Cone," *P.M.L.A.* 95(1980): 812–26. See esp. p. 817.

Félicité, Mme. Aubain, the house, a room in the house, and then, at the end of the chapter, Félicité again. And the syntax is managed so that with every occurrence of the pronoun, the antecedent is not immediately clear. Thus, instead of serving as a means of anaphoric integration, the pronoun introduces a disequilibrium into the linearity of the narrative. Each of the successive segments introduced by *elle* induces a slight shock from which the reader must recover before proceeding. This feature proves to be characteristic for the tale as a whole and deserves some consideration. As Raymonde Debray-Genette writes,

> From the genre of the tale Flaubert derives a typical device: the repetition of acts that are nearly identical in augmenting or diminishing gradation . . . and that have an unexpected conclusion that reverses the perspective according to which we have read the series of tests. But, with Flaubert, this device is transformed: the link between the episodes is erased, the meaning escapes not only the hero but also the reader; time seems not to produce anything, makes nothing "advance" (neither the hero nor the plot), but rather tosses the character from one chance occurrence to another.[17]

This pattern of discontinuous segmentation will prove to be fundamental to the tale's representational method.

The second chapter opens with the sentence, "Elle avait eu, comme une autre, son histoire d'amour" (p. 6).[18] What follows then, however, is not the story of her relationship with Théodore but a paragraph summarizing her parentage and early years. I would suggest that "son histoire d'amour" is to be taken not only in the narrow sense, as referring to that early, disastrous involvement with Théodore, but to the whole sequence of substitutive attachments that follow and that, in fact, constitute the story. Let us list the various objects of attachment: first, Théodore, followed much later in Félicité's life by a Polish veteran and by *le père Comiche,* both of them degraded versions of the first lover; then, the surrogate children, Paul and Virginie, and the nephew Victor; her mistress, Mme. Aubain; and finally, climactically, the parrot Loulou, both the living bird and the stuffed carcass that becomes transfigured in Félicité's imagination into the Holy Ghost.

17. "Les figures du récit dans 'Un Coeur simple,' " *Poétique* 1 (1970): 348–64. This passage is on p. 353.

18. "Un Coeur simple," in *Trois contes,* ed. E. Maynial (Paris, 1961). Parenthetical references are to this edition. In English: "Like everyone else, she had had her love-story." "A Simple Heart," in *Three Tales,* trans. Robert Baldick (Baltimore, 1961), p. 19.

Each of these figures enters Félicité's life for a time, arouses a degree of attachment, and is then removed or disappears. In most cases the love object displays little response to Félicité's devotion. What remains from each of these experiences sinks to some inarticulate level of Félicité's mind. But that something has been sedimented, we are told clearly enough, first, in the episode on the road to Honfleur, "Alors une faiblesse l'arrêta; et la misère de son enfance, la déception du premier amour, le départ de son neveu, la mort de Virginie, comme les flots d'une marée, revinrent à la fois, et, lui montant à la gorge, l'étouffaient" (p. 60);[19] and then in a later scene, when she sits in her room contemplating the stuffed parrot, "elle . . . se rappelait alors les jours disparus, et d'insignifiantes actions jusqu'en leurs moindres détails, sans douleur, pleine de tranquillité" (p. 62).[20]

The pattern, then, is the following: a love object enters the field of Félicité's experience, it disappears and leaves a void; Félicité is momentarily crushed, but then the void is somehow filled, and she accommodates herself to this new attachment. What is noteworthy here is not the nature of any of the objects in themselves but their dispensability, their susceptibility to substitution. The Théodore episode provides the model for this pattern:

> elle courut vers l'amoureux.
> À sa place, elle trouva un de ses amis. (p. 10)[21]

Most of the characters in the tale serve primarily as functions of such a substitutive process—Virginie and Victor, for example (note the alliteration of the names). When Virginie goes to the cloister school, Félicité is granted permission to receive Victor's visits "pour 'se dissiper' " (p. 30), as a distraction. After the news of Victor's death there follows the account of Virginie's illness and death. Since Victor died at sea, Félicité had no way of assimilating the loss, no mementos, no image of his end, no body to care for or to mourn. But she can compensate for this through Virginie's death. In mourning the girl she can think of Victor, "N'ayant pu lui rendre ces honneurs, [elle] avait un surcroît de tristesse, comme si on l'eût enterré avec l'autre" (p.

---

19. In English: "Then a sudden feeling of faintness made her stop; and the misery of her childhood, the disappointment of her first love, the departure of her nephew, and the death of Virginie all came back to her at once like the waves of a rising tide, and, welling up in her throat, choked her." Ibid., p. 48.

20. In English: "and then she remembered the old days, and the smallest details of insignificant actions, not in sorrow but in absolute tranquillity." Ibid., p. 50.

21. In English: "she hurried to meet her sweetheart. In his place she found one of his friends." Ibid., p. 21 (translation modified).

44).[22] This fantasized union of the two children in the grave is for Félicité a consolation, and more than that, a kind of restoration of their presence.

But to return to the status of the various love objects that I have listed: let us recognize here the form of an *actant,* or role function in Greimas's sense. The figure in its specific embodiment is less significant than in its function as the object of quest, love, desire. The content of that quest is variable, it is subject to repeated depletion and subsequent restoration. Twice the text provides a kind of scriptive, even an iconic, instantiation of this process, namely, of the evanescence of the referent to a point, a dot on the paper as well as a deictic pointing: first, as Victor's ship pulls out, Félicité sees "une tache noire," a black spot, on the horizon (p. 34); and again when M. Bourais points out on a map the place in America that Victor has now reached: "Enfin, avec son porte-crayon, il indiqua dans les découpures d'une tache ovale un point noir, imperceptible, en ajoutant: 'Voici'." (p. 37).[23]

There is no significant causal linkage among the series of episodes that chart Félicité's life. The connection between Virginie and Victor or that between the deceased M. Aubain ("le souvenir de 'Monsieur,' planant sur tout" [p. 11]) and Loulou ("planant au-dessus de sa tête" [p. 73])[24] is, at a surface level, the level of versimilitude or "realist" motivation, weak or non-existent. We recall the principle of discontinuous segmentation with which we characterized the form of the tale earlier. Obviously it is only Félicité that makes these connections meaningful, but in order to understand just what kind of meaning she provides without simply ascribing it to her own mental processes or feelings, we have to have recourse to another kind of structuring, one that is oriented to the narrative form as a whole. The *actant* model that I alluded to gives us a start on such a narrative deep-structure. We may develop it by considering the series of love objects in her life as metonymic displacements of an absent, irrecoverable object of desire. The metonymic structure makes clear that connections among these objects cannot be established in terms of any qualities in them (their

22. In English: "And since she had been unable to pay him these last honours, she felt an added grief, just as if they were burying him with the other." Ibid., p. 40 (translation modified).

23. In English: "Finally he pointed with his pencil at a minute black dot inside a ragged oval patch, saying: 'There it is.'" Ibid., p. 36.

24. In English: "the memory of 'Monsieur' hovering over everything." "hovering above her head." Ibid., p. 21, 56.

similarity or paradigmatic structure) but only by reference to some
alien, absent principle. We can chart the path of the series, its topography or temporal sequence, but cannot chart an underlying common
term, its "truth." On the connection between metonymic displacement and desire in Flaubert, Bonnefis writes,

> A description by Flaubert often says nothing of the real beyond what
> such and such a character projects upon it at any given moment of the
> narrative; it therefore inscribes the trajectory of a desire. But desire is not
> reducible to any given object. Economically, desire does not attain its
> object. For a simple but terrible reason, which is that *its* object, whatever
> it is, is never really "its." Desire can only satisfy itself from partial object
> to partial object, in an interminable metonymy. This delay in the ap-
> peasement of desire, this cleavage or separation, as if of a totality which
> from fragment to fragment could never succeed in rejoining itself, com-
> prises, in Flaubert's writing, what is called a description.[25]

Let us now survey the pattern of description in "Un Coeur simple" in the light of our conclusions thus far. In the description of the
house and furnishings in chapter 1 the representation works in terms
of the basic premise of external focalization in the realist system. The
data is presented in terms of overlapping protocols, in part rhetorical,
in part taxonomic. The rhetorical protocol, the order of presentation,
may choose any of a number of familiar models, notably, a pictorial
model, a process of action, the path of a viewer or visitor. The last is
the one used in our passage. The taxonomic protocol, the selection of
items to be named, is derived from a repertoire established in the
cultural code (in Barthes's sense). The reader attuned to the realist
manner takes a description of this type as "natural" not because it
imitates some preexistent model but because, by virtue of the code, he
already possesses a select vocabulary and, equally important, certain
schemas of combination and patterning.

From chapter 2 on, the descriptions are governed by a different
principle. Félicité serves as the authorizing agent for what is named
and shown, she "sees" even if she has no appropriate language to
express what reaches her awareness. But the reader "perceives" the
represented world in terms of her consciousness. And this too is, in the
system of realism, a way of authorizing the "naturalness" of a representation, though at this level another code is brought into play, name-

25. "The Melancholic Describer," *Yale French Studies*, no. 61, 1981, pp. 145–75; this passage is on p. 157f. (This is an abridged translation of the article cited earlier, cf. n. 14 above.)

ly, the code of character, of personality. It is not necessary for the narrative to evoke this code directly, that is, to provide an inventory of psychological traits, a direct form of characterization. The code of character can operate perfectly well through the detour of represented objects or events.[26] A fusion of the psychological and the descriptive is, of course, so deeply ingrained in realism that readers seldom stop to examine it, unless to question the bias of a given character, the psychological deviancy that might account for a representational deviancy. Thus, a literalist reading will be content to stop at this second level of naturalization.

In a sense, Flaubert encourages us to do so. He is sufficiently allied to the realist ideology to adhere to some extent to its practices. Let us not forget his own remark in connection with this story,

> L'Histoire d'un coeur simple est tout bonnement le récit d'une vie obscure, celle d'une pauvre fille de campagne, dévote mais mystique, dévouée sans exaltation et tendre comme du pain frais. Elle aime successivement un homme, les enfants de sa maîtresse, un neveu, un vieillard qu'elle soigne, puis son perroquet; quand le perroquet est mort, elle le fait empailler et, en mourant à son tour, elle confond le perroquet avec le Saint-Esprit. Cela n'est nullement ironique comme vous le supposez, mais au contraire très sérieux et très triste. Je veux apitoyer, faire pleurer les âmes sensibles, en étant une moi-même.[27]

A passage like this might lead us to take Félicité's life as an instance of an obscure, perfectly virtuous existence—a saintly life hidden in the midst of the quotidian, middle-class world—the kind of instance celebrated by Thomas Gray ("Elegy Written in a Country Churchyard"), by George Eliot, or by Flaubert himself (the figure of Catherine Leroux, awarded a silver medal for fifty-four years of faithful service, in Madame Bovary, part 2, 8). But the fact that Flaubert could discuss the story of Félicité in a spirit of direct, affective empathy does not signify that this marks the limit of his conception. Nor need we reject his remarks in the letter as a momentary lapse or an effort to please his correspondent.

26. See above, p. 23f.
27. Letter of June 19, 1876, in Préface, p. 272f. In English: " 'A Simple Heart' is, to be plain, the story of an obscure life, of a poor country girl, devout with a touch of the mystical, devoted without exaltation, and tender like fresh bread. She loves successively a man, the children of her mistress, a nephew, an old man whom she cares for, and her parrot. When the parrot dies, she has it stuffed and, when she dies herself, confuses it with the Holy Ghost. All this is not at all ironical, as you may imagine, but on the contrary very serious and very sad. I want to arouse pity, to make sensitive souls weep, since I am one myself."

Rainer Warning has, I think, given us the most just approach to
the strain of complicity, of *embourgeoisement,* in Flaubert's treatment
of the milieu from which he derives and which he subjects to such
merciless exposure:

> Certainly there can be no doubt as to his membership in the bourgeoisie.
> Ideologically, however, Flaubert distances himself from this class to the
> degree that he discovers the cliché in his own discourse and that of his
> peers. It seems to me that Sartre fails to recognize that such a discovery
> can be accomplished only in and through the phases of one's own discur-
> sive socialization. Only the discovery that the nature of one's being has
> been shaped by the cliché can lead to a self-conscious search. If the
> repetition in the citation is an act of liberation, it remains nonetheless a
> form of reassociation of the ironic subject with that part of his biography
> without which he could not have found his own ironic identity, in-
> asmuch as the latter is articulated in the negation of the former.[28]

Flaubert's "nullement ironique" in the letter to Mme. Genette is by no
means inconsistent with Warning's point that the achievement of an
"ironic identity" on the part of Flaubert could only derive from a
prior immersion in a discursive field dominated by the cliché. What is
particularly instructive in the story under consideration is that the
figure of Félicité functions both as a means of adherence to that field
("Je veux apitoyer, faire pleurer les âmes sensibles, en étant une moi-
même") and as an agent of distanciation.

Ross Chambers's recent study of "Un Coeur simple" develops the
latter alternative, arguing that Félicité should be taken not so much as
the model for a certain type of life but for a certain type of reader,
namely, the literalist reader for whom signs are too quickly transformed into experience, into reality:

> Félicité's . . . illiteracy translates into a kind of generalized semiotic in-
> capacity, a form of *literalism* that appears to be very much her own. . . .
> But semiotic naïveté can also be a model of competence for a type of
> reading that does not look beyond the signifier for an intended meaning,
> a signified, but is content to read the *meaning of the signifier* itself.
> Félicité, who cannot make sense of signs, is capable of giving meaning to
> the objects of reality; or, as Françoise Gaillard would perhaps say, she
> has the gift of "en-signement," of making reality into sign. This gift
> actually derives from the inability to distinguish the signifier and the
> signified in signs, for it is this that makes it possible to treat objects as

28. "Irony and the 'Order of Discourse' in Flaubert," in *New Literary History*
13(Winter, 1982): 253–86; this passage is on p. 272.

signs (and signs as objects). And it is this gift that qualifies Félicité as a model for the "textual" or "writerly" reading of a text, whose meaning can be grasped only if it is not decomposed into a signifier (say, "story" or *narré*) and signified (say, "discourse" or *narration*).[29]

Félicité's reading of objects, her "en-signement du réel" or direct conversion of objecthood into meaning or spiritual substance, is, as Chambers argues, perfectly consistent with the realist project, this being understood as the effort to elide the signifier in favor of the referent, of a pure signified. Put in terms of an *actant* model, the protagonist functions as *subject*—as a questor of some *object*—and also as a *donor* of value or meaning, with the readership put in the role of *receptor*.

Félicité literalizes the signifiers, takes the supplements as the real, and capitalizes these successively until she reaches the greatest value object that the culture affords her—the Holy Ghost. Having perceived this preeminent object in her deathbed fantasy, she has reached the limit of her scriptive capacity and, appropriately, she dies. The story too, appropriately, ends—appropriately, that is, for the reading that can endorse the climactic gradation of the series and see in the final image, "un perroquet gigantesque, planant au-dessus de sa tête" (p. 73),[30] its resolution, the master signified.

But not every reading mimics the linearity of a lived experience, of a life. In a sense, we read "Un Coeur simple" as Félicité reads the signs of her life, but in another sense, we encode these signs very differently. This brings me to a third level of Flaubertian representation, one that will necessarily short-circuit the code of character dealt with above and its naturalization as the real.

I spoke earlier of an occultation at the heart of the reading process, an occultation inseparable from the reader's construction of reality out of (through) fiction. I think we may find a figure of that occultation in the story. Félicité serves, as I have said, as a sender or donor of meaning for the reader. The reality she is able to mediate is disclosed in its most intense, purified aspect in a scene already referred to, when she sits in her room contemplating its contents, and notably the stuffed body of Loulou. This scene constitutes a continuation of the externally focused, "objective" description of the house of chapter

29. "An Invitation to Love: Simplicity of Heart and Textual Duplicity in 'Un Coeur simple,'" in *Story and Situation: Narrative Seduction and the Power of Fiction* (Minneapolis, 1984), p. 144f. For Françoise Gaillard's phrase see n. 7 above.

30. In English: "A gigantic parrot hovering above her head." *Three Tales*, p. 56.

1. What is distinctive about the items listed in the description now is their reliquary, their residual quality:

> On voyait contre les murs: des chapelets, des médailles, plusieurs bonnes Vierges, un bénitier en noix de coco; sur la commode, couverte d'un drap comme un autel, la boîte en coquillages que lui avait donnée Victor; puis un arrosoir et un ballon, des cahiers d'écriture, la géographie en estampes, une paire de bottines; et au clou du miroir, accroché par ses rubans, le petit chapeau de peluche! (p. 61)[31]

We are, of course, meant to identify these objects on the basis of earlier episodes, but their anterior existence, the meaning they had acquired through experiences in Félicité's life, is at this moment in the narrative to a great measure drained out of them. The effect is not of objects that bear the imprint of an individual's nature and feelings but of desiccated mementos whose link to a living past is only dimly discernible and rapidly fading.

I want to cite a passage from the correspondence, which, though it antedates our story by many years, offers an insight into the representational effect that I have sought to isolate in this essay: "Sonde-toi bien: y a-t-il un sentiment que tu aies eu qui soit disparu? Non, tout reste, n'est-ce pas? tout. Les momies que l'on a dans le cœur ne tombent jamais en poussière et, quand on penche la tête par le soupirail, on les voit en bas, qui vous regardent avec leurs yeux ouverts, immobiles."[32] It would take another essay to trace the thematic of these mummies in Flaubert's work and thought. But I use this passage to indicate that quality of reliquary presence that is central to the representational method of "Un Coeur simple," as it is of much of Flaubert's more realist fiction. Of course, one may attempt to reduce this, too, to a character code—one could speak of Félicité's fetishism, her necrophilic fascination with the effects, the leavings, of her departed loved ones.[33] And this kind of explanation is, in a sense, ines-

31. In English: "On the walls there were rosaries, medals, several pictures of the Virgin, and a holy-water stoup made out of a coconut. On the chest of drawers, which was draped with a cloth just like an altar, was the shell box Victor had given her, and also a watering-can and a ball, some copy-books, the illustrated geography book, and a pair of ankle-boots. And on the nail supporting the looking-glass, fastened by its ribbons, hung the little plush hat." Ibid., p. 49.

32. To Louise Colet, January 16, 1852, *Correspondance II*, ed. Jean Bruneau (Paris: Pléiade, 1980), p. 32. In English: "Examine yourself well: has any feeling that you have ever had disappeared? No, everything remains, does it not? Everything. The mummies that exist in your heart never crumble into dust and, when you bend your head over the railing, you see them below, looking at you with their eyes open, immobile."

33. Cf. *Story and Situation*, p. 141f.

capable and necessary. We are driven, as readers of fiction, to naturalize the inaccessibility, the withdrawal of what is represented. But in
Flaubert's mummified objects, husks of an anterior reality, we are
confronted by the real as an irreversible fading—apt figure of realist
representation.[34]

34. The significance of a thematic of death, interiorization, storage, and crypt in
Flaubert has been brilliantly analyzed by Eugenio Donato. Although his essays on this issue
came to my attention only after completion of this study, I wish to indicate them as a
supplement to my analysis: "The Crypt of Flaubert," in *Flaubert and Postmodernism*, ed.
Naomi Schor and Henry F. Majewski, (Lincoln and London, 1984), pp. 30–45, and "Who
Signs 'Flaubert,'" *MLN* 99(1984): 711–26.

8 Sighting the Scene: Representation and the Specular Model in Hawthorne's "Wakefield"

Here is the conclusion of Hawthorne's brief tale "Wakefield":

> He has left us much food for thought, a portion of which shall lend its wisdom to a moral; and be shaped into a figure. Amid the seeming confusion of our mysterious world, individuals are so nicely adjusted to a system, and systems to one another, and to a whole, that, by stepping aside for a moment, a man exposes himself to a fearful risk of losing his place forever. Like Wakefield, he may become, as it were, the Outcast of the Universe. (p. 298)[1]

If the errancy that the narrator hints at—"stepping aside . . . risk of losing his place forever"—is to be represented, it will be, we are told, by way of the "figure." And here, Hawthorne's use of the term may be glossed by the kind of explication that Jean-François Lyotard provides for what is a central concept in his *Discours, figure:*

> The position of art indicates a function of the figure that is not signified but that surrounds and penetrates discourse. It indicates that the transcendence of the symbol is the figure, that is to say, a spatial manifestation which the space of language cannot incorporate without being crushed. . . . The true symbol gives food for thought, but first of all it offers itself to be "seen." And what is astonishing is not that it gives food for thought, granted that with the existence of language every object is capable of signifying, . . . the enigma is that it remains to be "seen."[2]

What I wish to explore is the "visibility" of a narrative text in accordance with a conception of "figure" in the sense that Lyotard has

---

1. "Wakefield" was published first in 1835 and then, in *Twice-Told Tales*, in 1837. Parenthetical references are to *Tales and Sketches* (New York, 1982), The Library of America, pp. 290–98.
   2. (Paris, 1971), p. 13.

developed it, that is, as a mediating concept between a signifying function grounded in language and a visualizing or specular function realized through the imagination. My access to narrative structure will be made in terms of the *scene,* a category in which narrative and perceptual elements come together. The story "Wakefield" offers a particularly rewarding instance for this type of study since it fore-grounds—both in its structure and its theme—the interplay of the scenic and the specular. At the same time it allows us to draw on the specular dimension for an exploration of the narrative subject, under-stood in a double sense: the subject in the narrative, here, the figure of Wakefield, and the subject addressed by the narrative, a hypostasis of the reader. Thus, my analysis of the scene of the action leads to a scene of reading.

* * *

In some old magazine or newspaper, I recollect a story, told as truth, of a man—let us call him Wakefield—who absented himself for a long time, from his wife. (p. 290)

This first sentence of the story represents something like a James-ian germ, the inaugural, most condensed narrative substance, whose interest lies in its very sparseness, its small mass in relation to the finished product. It is followed by a fuller version, a true synopsis:

The wedded couple lived in London. The man, under pretence of going on a journey, took lodgings in the next street to his own house, and there, unheard of by his wife or friends, and without the shadow of a reason for such self-banishment, dwelt upwards of twenty years. During that period, he beheld his home every day, and frequently the forlorn Mrs. Wakefield. And after so great a gap in his matrimonial felicity—when his death was reckoned certain, his estate settled, his name dis-missed from memory, and his wife, long, long ago, resigned to her autumnal widowhood—he entered the door one evening, quietly, as from a day's absence, and became a loving spouse till death. (p. 290)

These introductory segments present two versions of what is appar-ently the same story in a sequence that moves from the barest summa-ry to fuller specification. What follows then is the third, and most extended, version—the story proper, one might say, where certain episodes are rendered in full scenic presentation.

How are such degrees of narrative articulation to be differenti-ated? Do they in fact constitute three variants of a single narrative message? To what extent do the familiar concepts of exposition, description, or scene help us to understand the modes of presentation involved?

Such questions deal with fundamental issues of narrative structure and, in the present-day context, touch also on more general questions regarding the coherence and reception of literary texts. The Jamesian tradition, as elaborated by Percy Lubbock and others, has taught us to understand the scene as the preeminent representational mode of narrative art: it governs the internal organization of the narrative segments (selection of key incidents, dramatic concentration of the action) and is most powerfully and directly oriented toward the act of reception.[3] In this tradition the scene denotes the highest degree of mimetic representation; it is designed to bring the reader into the most unobstructed proximity to the subject matter of the narrative.

Now terms like "proximity" and "mimetic" implicate a representational system that present-day theory, both in its deconstructive or Derridean side and in its semiotic and narratological variants, has consistently challenged. It is hardly surprising that current approaches to narrative tend either to avoid the issue of scenic presentation or to treat it in a way that is designed to neutralize its ostensive and visual elements. Thus Gérard Genette, in what is intended as a general "essay in method" (though it is predicated essentially on Proust's work), argues that mimesis is hardly ever operative in fictive narrative—the notable exception being direct dialogue—and that all narrative effects are therefore to be reclassified as species of diegesis, that is, in terms of the narrating or telling function.[4] Scene, accord-

---

3. The complementary concepts of pictorial (or panoramic) and scenic (or dramatic) are developed throughout Lubbock's *The Craft of Fiction* (New York, 1926; reprint, New York, 1957). Lubbock understands these not as opposed categories but as ways of marking degrees of mimetic presence. The panoramic allows for a greater involvement of the narrative persona and thus for a greater "distance" from the represented objects. In the scenic, "The motion of life is before us, the recording, registering mind of the author is eliminated" (*The Craft of Fiction*, p. 111). But even in the panoramic method as practiced by its greatest master, Thackeray, Lubbock stresses the immediacy and power of the impressions: "though the fullness of memory is directed into a consecutive tale, it is not the narrative, not its order and movement, that chiefly holds either Thackeray's attention or ours who read; the narrative is steeped in the suffusion of the general tone, the sensation of the place and the life that he is recalling" (p. 97). Behind Lubbock's position we discern Henry James's idea of "the discriminated occasion–that aspect of the subject which we have our noted choice of treating either as picture or scenically, but which is apt, I think, to show its fullest worth in the Scene. Beautiful exceedingly, for that matter, those occasions or parts of an occasion when the boundary line between picture and scene bears a little the weight of the double pressure." *The Art of the Novel: Critical Prefaces*, ed. R. P. Blackmur (New York, 1934), p. 300, from the preface to *The Wings of the Dove*.

4. *Narrative Discourse: An Essay in Method*, pp. 161ff. The argument was first put forward in "Frontières du récit," in *Figures II* (Paris, 1969).

ing to Genette—as opposed, for example, to summary, description, or ellipsis—comes about when "narrative time" (the duration of the telling) most nearly approaches "diegetic time" (the duration of the action told). Thus, for Genette, the scenic element is determined in terms of a quasi-temporal principle that is itself wholly defined in terms of textual organization. Genette and other structuralist critics have in effect so much reduced the notion of scene that it is not possible to problematize mimesis and representation in narrative if one accepts their formulation of the question.

It seems to me, however, that a theory of the scene in fiction could be used to test certain assumptions of a mimetic and representational model of narrative, assumptions like that of the "proximity" of the reader to what is represented. It could help us to account for the interplay of the staged or the "spectacle" (cf. the theatrical sense of the root term in Greek, *skēnē* with the *seen*, the specular investment appropriate to a given form of narrative. For the reader enters the narrative as an unsituated, variable subject, not as an absolute instance of vision, superior to what it views. The scene brings into play a type of specular investment that reveals the reader as both an agent of disclosure and an object of fixation.[5] What I am suggesting is a kind of phenomenological reduction of the narrative scene, a way of aligning an appearance with its most appropriate mode of givenness.

* * *

> After the door has closed behind him, she perceives it thrust partly open, and a vision of her husband's face, through the aperture, smiling on her, and gone in a moment. For the time, this little incident is dismissed without a thought. But, long afterwards, when she has been more years a widow than a wife, that smile recurs, and flickers across all her reminiscences of Wakefield's visage. (p. 292)

We have come to the moment of Wakefield's departure from his home and his unsuspecting wife. The glimpse of Wakefield's enigmatic smile

---

5. In a recent essay, Louis Marin deals with the perspectival system of high Renaissance painting in terms of a "specular image" predicated on an "equivalence between the eye of the spectator and the vision of the painter" in Lacan's sense. ("Toward a Theory of Reading in the Visual Arts: Poussin's *The Arcadian Shepherds*," in *The Reader in the Text*, ed. Susan R. Suleiman and Inge Crosman [Princeton, 1980], pp. 293–324, this passage is on p. 308f.) I find Marin's general aims exemplary for my own undertaking here. Like him, I attempt to locate a specular effect within a given representational system. And, like him, I see this endeavor as a contribution to current reader-response studies, although in contrast to the tendency of much of this work, my conception of the reader is neither empirical nor normative.

introduces a motif that will be richly varied in the course of the tale. In this case it is the wife who perceives and Wakefield who is framed in the aperture of the partly opened door. But on two other occasions Wakefield himself is placed in the position of viewer, directing a glance through a window at his wife:

> Before leaving the spot, he catches a far and momentary glimpse of his wife, passing athwart the front window, with her face turned towards the head of the street. The crafty nincompoop takes to his heels, scared with the idea, that, among a thousand such atoms of mortality, her eye must have detected him. (p. 294)

> Pausing near the house, Wakefield discerns, through the parlor-windows of the second floor, the red glow, and the glimmer and fitful flash, of a comfortable fire. On the ceiling, appears a grotesque shadow of good Mrs. Wakefield. (p. 297)

In episodes of this type the effect is that of an arrested scene, nearly a tableau, since what they consist of is nothing but the ostensive presentation of a figure or setting. The action of such scenes is not an action within the scene but the presenting or disclosing of the scene. The structure is that of a *mise en abîme* since the agent of disclosure, the viewer of the scene, is himself part of another scene that includes the first. Now what I have been describing is precisely what recent psychoanalytic theory has investigated in the structure of phantasy (or phantasm) as a scene of desire.[6]

Clearly, *scene* represents a richly ambiguous concept for narrative technique. On the one hand, it is related to tempo of narration and is thereby associated with categories like exposition, diegesis, ellipsis. On the other, it refers to a mode of focalization, to the status of the instance of narration in relation to the contents of a narrative. This aspect of the concept played an important role in Freud's theory of psychic defense mechanisms. We know how important for Freud's work in the period after the *Studies on Hysteria* (1895) was the notion

6. As the English version of Laplanche and Pontalis's *The Language of Psycho-Analysis* (New York, 1973), p. 314f, indicates, "phantasy" translates both the German *Phantasie* and the French *fantasme*, though these terms are not altogether congruent. "In French, the term '*fantasme*' was revived by psychoanalysis, with the result that it has more philosophical overtones than its German equivalent; nor does it correspond exactly to the German, in that it has a more restricted extension: '*fantasme*' refers to a specific imaginary production, not to the world of phantasy and imaginative activity in general." I follow this dictionary (and the Standard Edition of Freud) in using the English form "phantasy," though a good argument could be made for adopting "phantasm" in analogy to the French term.

of "primal scene" (*Urszene*), a term that designated a traumatic experience in the genetic development of the infant. The content of the experience might be variable—for example, viewing of parental coitus, seduction by an adult, threat of castration. But what is characteristic in every instance is the unstable position of the subject, both (or alternately) inside and outside the scene, as actor and viewer, as victim of a terrifying act and producer of the scene. It is through the analysis of this double structure of the scene that Freud developed his theory of phantasy. The phantasy is the product of an ongoing transformation of infantile traumatic experience, a process that makes this repressed psychic data available to consciousness in various figured or staged forms, e.g., as dreams, hallucinations, parapraxes, and so on.

Laplanche and Pontalis give this definition of phantasy in Freudian theory: "Imaginary scene in which the subject is a protagonist, representing the fulfillment of a wish (in the last analysis, an unconscious wish) in a manner that is distorted to a greater or lesser extent by defensive processes."[7] And this may be supplemented by the remarks they make on the relationship between phantasy and desire: "Even where they can be summed up in a single sentence, phantasies are still scripts (scenarios) of organized scenes which are capable of dramatisation—usually in a visual form. The subject is invariably present in these scenes. . . . It is not an *object* that the subject imagines and aims at, so to speak, but rather a *sequence* in which the subject has his own part to play and in which permutations of roles and attributions are possible."[8] What is particularly suggestive in this analysis is that it provides a topography in which the subject enacts his fascination or desire. The subject finds himself determined through an unstable identification with figures or objects in a scene in which he can never fix or survey his own placement. "In phantasy, in effect," write Laplanche and Pontalis, "the subject does not visualize the object or its sign; he is himself caught in the sequence of images. . . . The consequence is that while always being present in the phantasy, the subject may appear in desubjectivized form, that is, as part of the very syntax of the sequence in question."[9]

This "syntax" of the subject is articulated, for one thing, in the forms of access incorporated in the scene—apertures, frames, and borders—all of which serve both to limit the scene and to situate the

7. Ibid., p. 314.
8. Ibid., p. 318.
9. "Fantasme originaire, fantasmes des origines, origine du fantasme," *Temps modernes*, no. 215 (April, 1964): 1868.

viewer at its perimeter. In phantasy the framing effect, whether explicit or not, is projected onto the scene as a whole. The frame testifies
to the viewer's compromised status and to the consequent warping of
his act of vision.

Freud's studies of the primal scene have shown, as C.-B. Clément
puts it, that, "it is through a window that the primal spectacle views
itself: a window whose significance lies not on the side of the viewed
spectacle, but on the side of the viewing itself."[10] Drawing on Lacan's
notion of the gaze (*regard*) Clément then develops the idea of phantasy
as "a structure through which the gaze must pass, a frame, a passage
for vision, a narrow opening wherein the subject must manipulate its
objects. . . . *[The] gaze, directed onto the spectacle, is itself the object
of a phantasy.*"[11] The frame thus serves to situate a subject who
cannot escape the warping reflexivity of vision. Furthermore, the
méconnaissance—the constitutively deviant cognition that Lacan has
analyzed in the phantasy scene—applies not only to the fictive object,
the content of a representation, but to the mode of representation
itself:

> Scenario, *mise en scène, sequence of images*—the phantasy is at the limit
> of representation and of its cause; at the limit of the text and of its
> production; at the limit of structured subjectivity and of the time—
> anterior and future—that determines it.[12]

In executing his plan, Wakefield attempts to stage the scene of his
own exclusion. In the years of his self-exile he exists anonymous and
disguised in the midst of the city crowd. But, all the time, he is fascinated and possessed by what he views—his home, his wife as widow,
in effect, his absent self. But far from ever being able to survey and
master this spectacle, Wakefield's gaze gives rise to those permutations
of the viewing instance that have been discussed thus far. Himself
haunted by what he haunts, the figure of Wakefield disintegrates into a
"desubjectivized" articulation of the gaze—at once viewer, viewed,
and the unstable act of vision.

* * *

> But, our business is with the husband. We must hurry after him, along
> the street, ere he lose his individuality, and melt into the great mass of

10. "De la méconnaissance: fantasme, texte, scène," in *Sémiotiques textuelles*, ed.
M. Arrivé and J. C. Coquet, a special issue of *Langages* 31 (Sept., 1973): 36–52; this passage
is on p. 41.
    11. Ibid., p. 43.
    12. Ibid., p. 37.

London life. It would be vain searching for him there. Let us follow close
at his heels, therefore. (p. 292)

Who is this *we/us* with whom the reader is thus assimilated? Older
narrative theory would speak here of the narrative persona, a device
whose function in a major tradition of fiction has been to simulate a
type of interpersonal relation with the reader. This approach, however, with its assumption of a psychological entity, a quasi-character
behind the narrative voice, opens the way for fruitless speculations on
the presumed motives and prejudices of such a speaker. I am concerned rather with the force of certain "empty" indicators, notably the
deictics of the first person pronouns, whose meaning can only be
analyzed by the way they shape a pattern of discourse. For Lyotard,
such indicators are a preeminent instance of a negativity in language
that parallels and supports a negativity in vision. It is Émile Benveniste's notion of *indicateurs* that provides the point of departure for
this analysis.[13] These "indicators," or indexicals, are deictic elements
in language such as the personal pronouns, notably of the first and
second person, and adverbs of location and time that cannot be understood (that have no determinate meaning) except in terms of an implicit point of reference, a locus that situates objects in relation to the
discourse and thus grounds their referential status. We have here a
type of meaning or signification (*Sinn* in Frege's terminology) that is
inseparable from its designation (*Bedeutung*) or, as Lyotard puts it, "*I*
has no meaning, it is nothing but an 'indicator' which derives its
meaning from its insertion in a present discourse, where it designates
the subject in the act of speaking. It *designates* it but does not *signify*
it, as has been stated, or rather, its meaning [*signification*] lies in its
designation."[14] Such indicators cannot be assigned a semantic value
within the closed, differential system of language. They serve, "to
open language onto an experience that language itself cannot stock in
its inventory because it is that of a *hic et nunc*, of an *ego*, that is to say,
precisely of the certitude of the sensible. . . . By means of these 'indicators' language seems to be shot through with holes through which
sight can pass, the eye look out and fix itself there."[15]

In pragmatic communicative situations, deictics cause little diffi-

13. Émile Benveniste, *Problèmes de linguistique générale* (Paris, 1966). The most
relevant chapters are "De la subjectivité dans le langage," pp. 258–66, and "La nature des
pronoms," pp. 251–57.

14. *Discours, figure*, p. 119.

15. Ibid., p. 39.

culty. We usually convert a "you" or a "here" or a "soon" automatically on the basis of spatial and temporal referents that we dispose of in the given case. But texts, and notably literary texts, exhibit a constitutive mobility of the ego in consequence of the variable force of the first person pronoun. This mobility can never be contained within a system of the text, since it involves precisely the transgression of any such system brought about by the process of reception. It thus blocks the kinds of conversion operative in pragmatic communication and serves to unsettle or displace any "message" of the text. (We touch here on a decisive limitation to any communications theory model for fictive texts.) Thus, "we" and "us," as used in our citation from "Wakefield," involve a breach between meaning and reference, *Sinn* and *Bedeutung,* that would not obtain in a pragmatic discourse. This kind of systematic limitation on commutation, or the substitutability of viewpoints and voices operative in fiction, constitutes for Lyotard one of the key demonstrations of the negativity in language that he calls the figural.[16]

In a series of convergent analyses in *Discours, figure,* Lyotard demonstrates that this negativity in language (for which the status of deictics is only one instance) parallels and supports a negativity in vision. In developing his argument on this issue Lyotard builds on Freud's analysis of the way that the function of negation in language reflects a decisive stage in the development of the sense of reality and, correlatively, of the operation of desire. In a well-known passage from *Beyond the Pleasure Principle,* Freud illustrated the transformation of the elementary pleasure instinct into a reality principle by way of the child's game of *fort/da* (away/here), in which the child appears to gain a measure of control over the withdrawal of a beloved object (the mother, a toy) by assigning a name (or uttering a command) relative to the event. What is significant in this, Lyotard maintains, is not only the demonstration of a new level of autonomy on the child's part, but the fact that this volitional act is achieved through a language utterance. It involves, Lyotard remarks, "what the speech act [*la parole*] adds to (or subtracts from) the pleasure principle, the pulsation of the instinct." And Freud's achievement is to have shown that negation is "the mutation of drive or instinct [*la pulsion*] into desire by way of a passage through language."[17]

Desire, as Lyotard conceives it, represents a point of intersection

16. See ibid., p. 120. On the "limits of commutation," see pp. 110ff.
17. Ibid., p. 127.

between the instinctual level of the pleasure principle and the thetic or constitutive power of the mind, its capacity to envision a reality not immediately given to the senses. But this capacity, in order to become operative, has had to pass through the detour of negation, and it is this passage that Lyotard's concept of the figural seeks to chart. As Mikel Dufrenne remarks, "The figure is at once, according to its diverse senses, what ballasts discourse, loads it with meaning [*sens*] and what overthrows it, interjects a factor of non-sense. And this is the fundamental level, what Lyotard terms the princeps: no longer the sensible, but that mixture 'where one both reads and sees,' as in the dream or the phantasy."[18]

Historically, Lyotard's undertaking may be understood as both assuming and transcending a phenomenological notion of experience where, as he puts it, "the sensation and the sensing agent ["le senti et le sentant"] constitute each other in a common rhythm, like the fringes of the same wake, and where the constituent elements of the sensible world form an organic and diachronic totality."[19] Lyotard's critique here is directed specifically against the earlier Merleau-Ponty, but it could apply to a wide range of phenomenological criticism of recent years, from Georges Poulet and Jean-Pierre Richard to J. Hillis Miller. The point at issue involves the illusion of a fulfilled mode of cognition through the body or the perceptive level, a cognition in which the artist's experience, his "vision," is conceived as coextensive with his artistic medium (language, the pictorial image), and the imagination is taken as a kind of ontological ground adequate to the forms of disclosure of the phenomenal world. It is against this kind of position that Lyotard argues, "It is not true that we are always in the world as in a bath of perceptions and sensations. One has not said everything regarding our spatio-temporal experience in characterizing it as a kind of enveloping depth, an immanent transcendence, a chiasmus. The world is also susceptible to happenings [*événements*]. There are lapses of world, the emergence of non-enveloping zones, crises of 'transcendence' without any responding presence; worldly space and time can dispossess us in the same way as language."[20] The

18. "Doutes sur la 'libidiné,' " in *L'Arc*, 64 (n.d.): 13–27, esp. p. 15.

19. *Discours, figure*, p. 20.

20. Ibid., p. 136. Yet, while distancing himself from phenomenology, Lyotard does not embrace the kind of linguistic or semiological focus that is widely offered as an alternative. In this connection he warns against "drawing that altogether faulty conclusion [*ce contresens*]: there is nothing but text. The world is a function of language, but language is invested with a world-function, so to speak; all speech constitutes what it designates as world, as the density of the object to be synthesized, as the symbol to be deciphered; but

kind of dispossession that Lyotard speaks of is not, however, to be taken as an insufficiency or circumstantial failure of the perceptual apparatus. It is at this level that Lyotard locates "the other eye," "the symbol of desire" that enables one to conceive "the identity of the will to know ["vouloir savoir"] and of desire."[21]

The intentionality of desire, its quasi-cognitive potential, may be actualized through the figure. By means of this notion, Lyotard seeks to account for both the transgressive and the formative force of artistic creation. The figure, he writes, "takes hold of our words in order to fashion forms and images with them. The field of desire serves as the bed of our thoughts, where they are laid to rest. By means of *Ent-zweiung*[22] the object is lost; by means of the phantasy it is re-presented. One needs to take up the analysis of that eye which is no longer at the edge but at the heart of discourse."[23] The figure, then, specifies the "visionary" or image-forming power of poetic language as it derives from the zone of negation and desire. "The eye is inside speech," Lyotard writes, "because there is no articulated language without the exteriorization of something 'visible,' but also because there is an at least gesticulatory, 'visible,' exteriority at the heart of discourse, that is its expression."[24] The "eye . . . inside speech" testifies to an impulse that accompanies the continual dispossession of perception operative in language.

* * *

He can scarcely trust his good fortune, in having got thither unper-ceived—recollecting that, at one time, he was delayed by the throng, in the very focus of a lighted lantern; and, again, there were footsteps, that seemed to thread behind his own, distinct from the multitudinous tramp around him; and, anon, he heard a voice shouting afar, and fancied that it called his name. Doubtless, a dozen busybodies had been watching him, and told his wife the whole affair. Poor Wakefield! Little knowest thou thine own insignificance in this great world! No mortal eye but mine has traced thee. (p. 292)

Before leaving the spot, he catches a far and momentary glimpse of

---

these objects, these symbols offer themselves in a space where one can point them out, and this space which surrounds discourse is not itself the space of language where meaning production takes place, but a space of a worldly type." p. 83.

21. Ibid., p. 128.

22. Division or schism, in both a Freudian and a Hegelian sense.

23. *Discours, figure*, p. 129.

24. Ibid., p. 13f. Rodolphe Gasché offers a helpful discussion of the aesthetic dimen-sion of the figural in "Deconstruction as Criticism," *Glyph 6: Johns Hopkins Textual Studies* (Baltimore, 1979), 177–215, see esp. p. 189.

his wife, passing athwart the front window, with her face turned towards the head of the street. The crafty nincompoop takes to his heels, scared with the idea, that, among a thousand such atoms of mortality, her eye must have detected him. (p. 294)

Wakefield's effort to establish himself as an unseen seer in the midst of the city crowd involuntarily incites a returning gaze—a gaze that is manifested at a psychological or characterological level by his terror at being perceived. But my discussion has shown that the gaze is to be understood as the structure of a "spectacle" in which the viewing subject is dispersed in the syntax of the frame, not as the volitional act of an autonomous subject. Thus, we may interpret Wakefield's response in these instances in terms of a specular structure, one that projects an intentionality onto what it views and thus implants a returning gaze in the scene.

Jacques Lacan's notion of the mirror stage elucidates this very type of situation: the individual's awareness of self and world derives from a specular act whereby control and dependence, self-identity and objectification are inextricably linked. The child, in Lacan's model, sees itself seeing (in the mirror). It has before it the image of its sovereign gaze and at the same time of the dependent object of that gaze.[25]

It is possible now to recognize in the structure of the gaze the sort of negativity at the level of perception that we saw operative for deictics at the level of discourse. References to vision and to the seen in the text may be compared to deictics in that they function not primarily in terms of a content or of semantic values but as agencies of representation. Just as the first person pronoun was shown to be an indicator of a mobile subject of enunciation, so instances of vision pertain to the structure of the gaze. It is this structure that characterizes the reader's manner of visualizing what the text designates.

* * *

After the door has closed behind him, she perceives it thrust partly open, and a vision of her husband's face, through the aperture, smiling on her, and gone in a moment. . . . In her many musings, she surrounds the original smile with a multitude of fantasies, which make it strange and awful; as, for instance, if she imagines him a coffin, that parting look is frozen on his pale features; or, if she dreams of him in Heaven, still his blessed spirit wears a quiet and crafty smile. (p. 292)

25. "Le stade du miroir comme formateur de la fonction du Je," in *Ecrits* (Paris, 1966), pp. 93–100. Cf. Chapter 1 above, p. 27.

> The door opens. As he passes in, we have a parting glimpse of his visage, and recognize the crafty smile, which was the precursor of the little joke, that he has ever since been playing off at his wife's expense. (p. 298)

The face, whether viewed as an objectified entity or inserted into an interpersonal situation, is the most strongly expressive feature of an individual. In a description or a characterization it is normally the locus of maximal revelation, a point in which the multiple features of personality become most evident and comprehensible. Alternatively, in interpersonal contact, the face serves as the preeminent agency of recognition and response. But these functions are significantly elided in our story. The "crafty smile" denotes not so much a character trait as the dissociation of face from body, like the smile of the Cheshire cat. It is an abbreviated "expression," that is, an isolate feature that both masks and reveals. Yet it retains a kind of residual force, both as signature (an identifying trace of the departed Wakefield) and as message (a haunting token of his presence).

Tropologically, this smile seems to function like an inverted prosopopeia. If we understand prosopopeia as a figure that constructs a face or bestows facial features and their related powers (e.g., voice, sight) onto what would normally not possess them, we have here an instance of diminution, and more specifically, of fixation or reification.[26]

The matter may also be viewed in the context of Barthes's discussion of representations of the human body in terms of the symbolic code. In S/Z this code is designed to mark one of the impasses of representation, and to do so in a manner that exhibits the transgressive forms of such a blockage of meaning. (In this respect it converges with Lyotard's concept of the figure.) Unlike those objects that are used for a connotative function, which Barthes classifies under the semic code, images of the body or of body parts are often deployed in a significantly "charged" manner—and not only in erotic terms. The various forms of seduction and threat, of incitation and fixation figured by means of the body, challenge the very existence of a system of representation. What Barthes terms the "topological transgression" of the body in Balzac's Sarrasine[27] refers to the ways that this text disarticulates traditional rhetorical practices designed to master and

---

26. My discussion of prosopopeia draws on Paul de Man, "The Epistemology of Metaphor," *Critical Inquiry* 5(1978): 13–30, esp. pp. 6ff., and "Autobiography as De-facement," *MLN* 94(1979): 919–30, esp. pp. 926ff.

27. *S/Z: An Essay*, p. 215. See also p. 113f. on blazon.

reconcile the body's expressive potential—including such devices as portraiture and characterization.

Wakefield's smile, far from being an index of character (a semic indicator in Barthes's sense) or the embodiment of a meaning (the assumption of bodily expressivity in the traditional sense of prosopopeia), is the agency of a kind of "de-facement" that problematizes the forms of self-revelation and self-presencing possible in a narrative. The explicit association in the passage cited of the smile with a frame (door, aperture), with fantasy, and with death, confirms its place in the phantasmic articulation of the subject discussed earlier. But to that analysis we may now add the reader as another dimension of the specular structure that constitutes the subject of the narrative.

* * *

> Now for a scene! Amid the throng of a London street, we distinguish a man, now waxing elderly, with few characteristics to attract careless observers, yet bearing, in his whole aspect, the hand-writing of no common fate, for such as have the skill to read it. . . . Next, leaving him to sidle along the foot-walk, cast your eyes in the opposite direction, where a portly female, considerably in the wane of life, with a prayer-book in her hand, is proceeding to yonder church. . . . Just as the lean man and well conditioned woman are passing, a slight obstruction occurs, and brings these two figures directly in contact. Their hands touch; the pressure of the crowd forces her bosom against his shoulder; they stand, face to face, staring into each other's eyes. After a ten years' separation, thus Wakefield meets his wife!
>
> The throng eddies away, and carries them asunder. (p. 295f.)

With the scene, the story turns its "face" to the reader. What was said earlier of the human face—that it is a locus of maximal revelation, of direct expressivity—may be applied to the scene in narrative. Here the story apparently shows itself as it happens (recall Genette's principle of a near equivalence between reading time and diegetic time) rather than in the schematic or allusive forms of exposition, summary, or reflection. Here the reader's attention is directed to the place of the action and to the acting or speaking subjects with minimal interposition on the part of the narrator. Yet even as we thus align the scene with forms of perception, with visibility, we cannot overlook the basic qualifications of such a model that have been raised in this chapter. The concept of scene will hardly be exempt from them.

"Now for a scene!" the introductory formula is first of all a boundary, the sign of a shift in the tempo of narration in relation to the preceding section of summary. But more important is the ostensive force of the phrase, the manner whereby pointing and designating are fused, or more appropriately, pointing is made into a constituent of designation. This suggests that the nature of the scene will be demonstrated in what follows, and that the demonstration is predicated on a kind of presence of the reader. Such presence is indicated by further deictics: "we distinguish," "cast your eyes." We recall that deictics function in a narrative as a systematic limitation on the principle of commutation, on the substitutability of viewpoints and voices in a text. That is to say, a situational determination of the reader in relation to the scene is both implied and blocked. Take the passage, "Amid the throng of a London street we distinguish a man." There is already ambiguity in the opening phrase—does the "amid" phrase modify "we" or "man"? It may be objected that to include the "we" in the London crowd involves a patent confusion between what a text says *about* its subject and what it says about *its stance toward* the subject. And yet this kind of "confusion" cannot be eliminated. The operation of deictics already implies it.

At the level of the action, too, the reader's effort to find a secure stance in relation to the scene, whether within or outside, will be systematically blocked. Thus, with respect to the significant action of this episode, the meeting of husband and wife: "they stand face to face, staring into each other's eyes." The reader's capacity to visualize this image, to fulfill the narrator's "cast your eyes," is paralleled in the extraordinary combination of recognition and occultation in the confrontation of the couple. At one level the contradiction is, of course, neutralized in terms of the differing reactions of the two characters—Wakefield recognizes, but dares not acknowledge, his wife, while she does not (quite?) recognize him. But at another level the baffled sighting, the uncomprehending stare, marks the place of the reader in and before the scene.

The scene, I have suggested, functions as a lure for the reader, and it is in the nature of a lure that it attracts without yielding and offers itself in order to entrap. Let us briefly pursue this strategy of entrapment in our story. Near the beginning, after the exposition already cited, the narrator states,

> Whenever any subject so forcibly affects the mind, time is well spent in thinking of it. If the reader choose, let him do his own meditation; or if he prefer to ramble with me through the twenty years of Wakefield's vagary, I bid him welcome. (p. 290)

The reward for such a "ramble" will be the ostensible message or truth of the narrative, and it is designated by such terms as "moral," "wisdom," and "figure." The concluding sentences, cited at the start of this essay, suggest that the "moral" of the story applies to Wakefield himself. Yet in the opening section the narrator had already cast doubt on finding "a pervading spirit and a moral . . . done up neatly, and condensed into the final sentence" (p. 290f). Now one kind of moral that the narrator can not condense or articulate involves his own stance and that of the reader. The alternative suggested to the reader—to "do his own meditation" or "ramble with me"—touches on this embarrassment of the narrative message. Insofar as the narrating voice frankly exhibits its control over the narrative through such relatively distanced forms of presentation as exposition, and reflection, the reader has considerable freedom to "do his own meditation." But such forms are typically preliminary to more direct modes of representation in which the narrating voice seems to lose prominence.

Another function of the narrative persona, its status as a witness, comes to the fore here. For part of the authority of the narrator derives from the fact that he has seen what he recounts, or else that he possesses the ability to visualize it. And the token of this ability will be something like a scene—an effect of narrative discourse in which the narrating voice, with its hesitations, its partiality, its inescapable perspectival limitations, gives way to an image that is offered as fully present and self-authenticating. With the scene, the narrator becomes silent and turns into the fascinated viewer of an action he himself has staged. But perhaps, like Wakefield, his viewing is only a "gaze"—a fixation on a scene in which he himself is caught, held in the system of representation.

The concluding sentences of the story speak of the "nicely adjusted" system of "our mysterious world," and that, "by stepping aside for a moment, a man exposes himself to a fearful risk of losing his place forever" (p. 298). What I have tried to suggest in my reading of this tale is that Wakefield's "stepping aside" is to be taken not as an idiosyncratic personal gesture, whether aberrant or heroic, but as a deflection that is consistent with the "system" of representation, one that the system not only tolerates but requires. I have drawn on Lyotard's notion of figure to reveal this deflection, to make it "visible."

I said earlier that the reader, in registering what is described in a text, cannot altogether avoid nor yet remain content with a perceptual model of the image or scene. In this reading I have tried to suggest what complicates such a model, but without leaving the "lure" of the perceptible out of play. The text-oriented critics are right to question the workings of an overly direct mimetic or perceptual model of representation, but in doing so they ignore the strain of fascination that draws the reader into a scene. For the scene represents an arrest in the recital of the narrative, the promise of a revelation wherein the story shows its true face. (Thus the convention of climactic scenes of confrontation, of scenes in which characters, linked through love or hatred and separated for a period, finally confront each other "face to face" and thus enact in dramatic form that which functions by way of prosopopeia for the reader.) The narrative scene becomes the occasion of a phantasmic investment on the part of the reader. But this is not to say that the reader "fantasizes" a text in the manner of a mobile image, like a movie. Rather, the reader's "sighting" involves the kinds of displacement of the subject that have been discussed in connection with the structure of phantasy. In relation to the narrative scene, the reader becomes an unstable subject, seeking to survey and master what is being shown, but continually thwarted by the frame or "spectacle" that provides his means of access.

Index

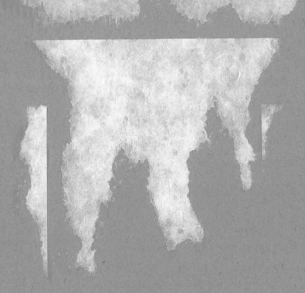